Trumped

Trumped

The 2016 Election That Broke All the Rules

WITHDRAWN

Edited by
Larry J. Sabato, Kyle Kondik,
and Geoffrey Skelley

ROWMAN & LITTLEFIELD
Lanham • Boulder • New York • London

FLIP

Published by Rowman & Littlefield
A wholly owned subsidiary of The Rowman & Littlefield Publishing Group, Inc.
4501 Forbes Boulevard, Suite 200, Lanham, Maryland 20706
www.rowman.com

Unit A, Whitacre Mews, 26–34 Stannary Street, London SE11 4AB

British Library Cataloguing in Publication Information Available

Library of Congress Cataloging-in-Publication Data

Names: Sabato, Larry, editor. | Kondik, Kyle, editor. | Skelley, Geoffrey, editor.
Title: Trumped : the 2016 election that broke all the rules / edited by Larry Sabato, Kyle Kondik, and Geoffrey Skelley.
Description: Lanham, Maryland : Rowman & Littlefield, 2017. | Includes bibliographical references and index.
Identifiers: LCCN 2017004184 (print) | LCCN 2017009798 (ebook) | ISBN 9781442279384 (cloth) | ISBN 9781442279391 (pbk.) | ISBN 9781442279407 (electronic) | ISBN 9781442279407 (ebook)
Subjects: LCSH: Presidents—United States—Election—2016. | United States. Congress—Elections, 2016. | Trump, Donald, 1946-
Classification: LCC JK526 2016 .T78 2017 (print) | LCC JK526 2016 (ebook) | DDC 324.973/0932—dc23
LC record available at https://lccn.loc.gov/2017004184

♾ ™ The paper used in this publication meets the minimum requirements of American National Standard for Information Sciences—Permanence of Paper for Printed Library Materials, ANSI/NISO Z39.48–1992.

Printed in the United States of America

Contents

Preface and Acknowledgments

Trumped will be one of the first, but not even close to the last, attempts to unpack what happened in the stunning 2016 presidential election. Donald Trump broke almost all of the rules of politics to first lead and then win the Republican presidential nomination. He followed that triumph with a victory that was even more improbable: edging out heavily favored Hillary Clinton in one of the great upsets in presidential campaign history.

Among the "rules" that Trump broke: winning a presidential election despite being considerably outspent in the general election; losing the national popular vote by over two percentage points but still winning the Electoral College, something that has happened rarely in American history; emitting a constant stream of controversial statements that would have sunk most previous candidacies; and capturing a presidential nomination despite having very little support from his own party's leadership.

Our book starts with the three of us breaking down what happened in the presidential race (chapter 1, Larry J. Sabato), the closely contested battle for the U.S. Senate and Governors (chapter 3, Geoffrey Skelley), and the race for the U.S. House (chapter 4, Kyle Kondik). Sandwiched in between those chapters is a deep demographic dive into the presidential results by David Byler of *RealClearPolitics* (chapter 2).

Veteran political reporter Rhodes Cook comes next (chapter 5) with a detailed look at the primary results in both the Democratic and Republican races, contests that stayed very competitive well into the spring. Robert Costa (chapter 6) and Greg Sargent (chapter 7), both of the *Washington Post*, follow with a rich recounting of, respectively, the Republican and Democratic primaries.

The growing Hispanic vote was the subject of much pre- and post-election scrutiny, with several analysts taking issue with the suggestion by the national exit poll that Clinton carried only two-thirds of the Hispanics, about on par with Barack Obama's 2008 and 2012 performances (or even a little worse). Matt Barreto, Gary Segura, and Tom Schaller of the polling firm Latino Decisions convincingly argue Clinton did better than the exit poll suggested as part of their analysis of Latinos in the election (chapter 8).

Ronald B. Rapoport of the College of William and Mary and Walter J. Stone of the University of California, Davis kept tabs on Republican identifiers throughout the election to measure how they felt about Donald Trump, and they explain how Trump, even in victory, had somewhat soft support from his own party (chapter 9).

National polls taken together got reasonably close to projecting the overall national vote in November, but many individual national surveys and surveys of quite a few battleground states gave the wrong impression that Clinton was leading. Ariel Edwards-Levy, Natalie Jackson, and Janie Velencia look at the evolving polling industry and what lessons 2016 provides to pollsters (chapter 10).

The role of the media and the role of money in the 2016 race (chapters 11 and 12) are explored by Georgetown University's Diana Owen, and former Federal Election Commission Chairman Michael Toner and former FEC analyst Karen Trainer, respectively. Alan Abramowitz (chapter 13) then makes the case that the rise of racial resentment among whites helped Trump to his narrow victory. *RealClearPolitics*' Sean Trende (chapter 14) diagnoses what went wrong with the theory of the "Emerging Democratic Majority" and how Republicans won the White House despite demographic changes that, at least on the surface, seemed to benefit Democrats substantially. Finally, Susan MacManus of the University of South Florida and Anthony A. Cilluffo bring us ten lessons from this crazy campaign.

Our University of Virginia Center for Politics wraps up each major national election with a volume that is released as soon as humanly possible the year following that election. We thank our authors for participating in this project and for meeting what can be challenging deadlines that coincide with the holidays. We also want to salute the Center for Politics staff for their support, particularly Associate Director Ken Stroupe, Chief Financial Officer Mary Daniel Brown, and Executive Assistant Tim Robinson.

We also want to thank the team at Rowman & Littlefield for their support of this project, especially our editors, Jon Sisk and Kate Powers.

At the dawn of the Age of Trump, millions of Americans are ecstatic, and millions more are mortified. We can be sure of but one thing: None of the days ahead will be boring, at least for those who follow and study politics.

This volume will be just a starting point for what will be one of the most intensely studied elections of all time.

Larry J. Sabato, Kyle Kondik, and Geoffrey Skelley
University of Virginia Center for Politics
Charlottesville, Virginia
January 2017

1

The 2016 Election That Broke All, or At Least Most, of the Rules

Larry J. Sabato[1]

All of us living in the twenty-first century now know how people felt in 1948, when the *Chicago Tribune* headline "DEWEY DEFEATS TRUMAN" was prematurely published, and the pundits and pre-election polls were dead wrong.

Yet 2016 was even worse than 1948. Instead of just a couple of prominent pollsters on the scene when President Harry Truman upset the heavily favored Republican Thomas E. Dewey, there were dozens of independent pollsters and hundreds of surveys taken nationally and in the battleground states. Some national surveys in 2016 did reasonably well, though many surveys—especially in the highly competitive states—did not. Rather than halting the polling weeks before the 1948 election (believing the result was a done deal), the 2016 pollsters continued measuring public opinion right up to election eve, which should have made surveys more accurate, but did not in many cases.[2]

Comparing Donald Trump's upset to Harry Truman's is not to equate the two, of course. Truman was the incumbent while Trump defeated the incumbent White House party. Truman had had a long career in politics and government, while Trump had never served a day in any public office. Truman won the popular vote by 4.5 percentage points; Trump lost it by 2.1 points However, their electoral vote totals were similar—Truman at 303 and Trump at 304.[3]

Their campaigning styles were also akin to one another. Truman loved to "give 'em hell," and Trump's incendiary (and often inaccurate or outright false) charges were a new form of hell, augmented by his frequent use of Twitter to incite his millions of followers. Additionally, both Truman and Trump were underdogs, a status that confers a kind of freedom to roll the dice, and their unpolished speaking styles and populist approach attracted the white working class disproportionately.

Their opponents were of a sort, too. Dewey and Hillary Clinton made the classic mistake of frontrunners, sitting on their leads and saying little of consequence. "The little man on the wedding cake," as Dewey was called, trafficked in platitudes and mainly attacked Truman. Reporters at the time noted the size and enthusiasm of Truman's crowds, a contrast with the desultory Dewey followers who appeared to be carrying out an obligation rather than joining a cause.[4] Trump's crowds were normally huge and boisterous, full-throatedly chanting "Lock Her Up" (referring to Clinton, of course—urged on by Trump's declarations that she ought to be in prison). The secondary target at Trump rallies were members of the working press, who were often attacked individually and collectively by Trump and then threatened personally by the candidate's most ardent backers.

Like Dewey, Clinton was swimming in overconfidence and fooled by her campaign's rosy internal polling—which turned out to be quite erroneous in many critical states. She took for granted the normally Democratic states of Michigan, Pennsylvania, and Wisconsin, waking up too late to impending losses behind the "blue wall" by tiny but decisive margins. Her husband, former President Bill Clinton, sensed the problem and urged a change in direction to appeal to the white working class that had powered his victories, but he was dismissed by the campaign leadership as stuck in the 1990s. Hillary Clinton never once traveled to Wisconsin after the Democratic convention—shocking political malpractice by her team. You never take your base for granted, especially when the demographics of a state such as Wisconsin (as well as Michigan and Pennsylvania) were not dissimilar from Ohio and Iowa, two states that even the Clinton team knew she was likely to lose.[5]

Both Hillary Clinton and President Obama, her foremost campaign surrogate, appeared hesitant to tout an economy that, while far from ideal, was dramatically better than the one Obama inherited in 2009. Trump defined the economy as in near-depression shape, yet Democrats were almost mute and failed to correct the record. A charge unanswered is a charge agreed to in the hothouse of a campaign.

Unlike Trump, most Clinton rallies were relatively small and the participants rarely stirred by her stilted rhetoric. Trump's slogan, "Make America Great Again," had far more power with his constituency than Clinton's bland

"Stronger Together" had with hers. Moreover, while both major-party con-tenders were unpopular, with high unfavorable ratings (and Trump more so than Clinton for much of the campaign), the Democratic campaign focused most of its energy on attacking Trump rather than trying to remake Clinton's scandal-burdened image. Her campaign, reflecting the candidate's ultra-cautious nature and entangling personal alliances, was layered with bureau-cracy and rival power centers, so much so that it could take a day for everyone to sign off on an innocuous tweet—quite a contrast to the always tweeting Trump who cleared his missives with no one. The structure of Clinton World was complex; Trump World often began and ended with Trump himself, and that yields a significant tactical advantage.[6]

Even though Republicans insist otherwise, racial resentment and hostility to undocumented immigrants were powerful forces benefiting Trump. It was no accident that white nationalists were lavish in their praise of Trump, who for years had led the outrageous "birther" campaign that sought to delegitim-ize America's first African American president by falsely claiming he wasn't born in the United States and was therefore ineligible to occupy the White House. Many in this movement also insisted Obama was secretly a Muslim—no sin, even if true, but a complete lie. Very belatedly and without any fervor or apology, Trump acknowledged after a torrent of criticism dur-ing the campaign that he had been totally wrong and President Obama was born in the United States.[7]

In the chapters that follow, our group of contributors will expand on these themes and many more, while slicing and dicing the 2016 election from quite a few perspectives.

THE 2016 POLITICAL CLIMATE

At this writing prior to the onset of the Trump administration, we cannot say which Donald Trump will take the oath of office. Will it be the Trump that inspired his troops, the one that wants to "drain the swamp" of Washington, frustrate the establishment, keep and create millions of jobs, and solve the complicated problem of illegal immigration? Or will the Trump who takes possession of the Oval Office fail because of a lack of relevant experience, poor temperament, too many right-wing lieutenants, unsolved ethical chal-lenges and conflicts-of-interest, and reckless policies? Will President Trump rise to the occasion and use his business background to become a shrewd deal-maker and effective chief executive, or will he validate the image critics have of him as a dangerous authoritarian and narcissistic con-man? There have been contrary indications during the transition.

What we can do at this juncture is try to understand the forces that produced one of the most shocking upsets in U.S. history. This election was Hillary Clinton's to lose, and she lost it to one of the most unusual and controversial candidates ever, the first president to have no prior elective office or military experience but rather a billionaire businessman and reality-TV star.

Other authors in this anthology will analyze in detail the Clinton and Trump candidacies. For our purposes here and as already mentioned, it is sufficient to say that Clinton was not a compelling candidate—despite being the first major-party woman nominee. She never developed a potent message, especially on the loss of jobs that troubled white working-class voters in key states. The accumulated scars from decades of Clinton scandals (real and invented) took a toll, too, especially her decision to use a private server for email during her tenure as Secretary of State from 2009 to 2013. The Clinton high command complained, with some justification, that the emails were overemphasized by the media—but it was their job to push back and create a better image for their candidate. An FBI investigation of the emails was a nagging problem for Clinton, and erupted twice just days before the election, thanks to questionable actions by FBI Director James Comey. These bombshells almost certainly had an effect on undecided voters and wavering independents and Republicans. (More to come about this in later chapters.)

Almost daily disclosures of embarrassing emails from people closely associated with Clinton were another unsettling distraction. These missives were released by WikiLeaks and very likely stolen by hackers associated with the Russian government, which wanted Trump to win for reasons including a belief that Trump would be a friendlier occupant of the Oval Office. (President Obama ordered an intelligence agency investigation of Russia's interventions in the U.S. election in December 2016.)[8]

Trump's contrast with Clinton was stark. He attracted millions of followers so devoted that they were unmoved by many unsavory revelations about their nominee. His backers enabled Trump to survive more scandals than any modern presidential candidate has ever faced, including Bill Clinton when he ran in 1992. Trump smartly concentrated on rural and exurban areas that were filled with voters who regarded him as heroic and would prove to be essential to his victory. His election was driven by noncollege whites living in outlying suburbs and small-town America; their high turnout and massive margins for Trump were a big part of the Election Day story. They loved Trump's rejection by the Republican governing class, which certified this billionaire as an outsider populist. Shunned by many respectable "establishment" GOP leaders, Trump made a virtue of his foes' opposition, both in the primaries and the general election.

Timing helped Trump. Only once since 1952 have Americans given a third consecutive White House term to the same party: in 1988, when Vice President George H. W. Bush benefited from President Ronald Reagan's popularity and the prosperity and peace that generally prevailed at the time. Despite the fact that President Obama had even higher job approval numbers than Reagan enjoyed in his final year as president, Obama and Clinton could not quite pull off an Electoral College majority. The no-third-term tendency was maintained.[9]

THE ELECTION BY THE NUMBERS

In examining the data, it is obvious just how tight the election was. A mere 77,744 votes *combined* in the states of Michigan, Pennsylvania, and Wisconsin gave Trump the 46 electoral votes that put him over the top. Clinton had millions of excess votes in New York, California, and the other 18 states (plus Washington, D.C.) she won—far more than Trump had from the 30 states he captured.[10] However fanciful it seems, her campaign might have done better to spend a fraction of its massive war chest to relocate a couple hundred thousand Californians and New Yorkers to Michigan, Pennsylvania, and Wisconsin! No doubt Clinton's team would have done precisely that, had they had an inkling of what was about to happen.

At least Clinton had the satisfaction of knowing she carried the popular vote, and by a record-setting plurality of 2.87 million in a solid turnout of 137 million votes total (59.3 percent of the eligible population—a bit larger than in 2012 (58.6 percent).[11] This was roughly five times the plurality enjoyed by Al Gore over George W. Bush in 2000 (547,000 votes), and meant that Clinton won 48.0 percent (65,853,625) to Trump's 45.9 percent (62,985,106). Clinton's margin was just 1.8 percentage points smaller than President Obama's 3.9 point edge over Mitt Romney four years ago, and because of the slightly larger turnout, Clinton received almost as many votes as Obama did in 2012 (Obama won 65,918,507 votes four years ago). However, Trump secured almost 2 million more votes than did Romney. Nonetheless, we have to reach back to 1876 to find a popular-vote winner, Democrat Samuel J. Tilden, who garnered a larger national lead (exactly 3 points) yet still lost. Winning Republican Rutherford B. Hayes, who lagged behind Tilden by 250,000 votes, was called "His Fraudulency" during his single term.[12]

Like it or not, the Founders' Electoral College still gets to pick the president. Trump was the undisputed champion there, with 304 votes to Clinton's 227. Both sides played the game with the same rulebook, and Trump came

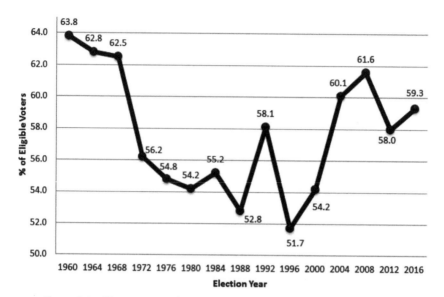

Figure 1.1. Voter turnout since 1960. *Sources:* Harold W. Stanley and Richard Niemi, *Vital Statistics on American Politics, 2011–2012* (Washington, DC: Sage/CQPress, 2011); Michael McDonald, "Voter Turnout," United States Election Project, http://www.electproject.org/home/voter-turnout/voter-turnout-data.

out ahead by a comfortable Electoral College margin. As president-elect, Trump and his staff declared his triumph to be "one of the biggest Electoral College victories in history."[13] This is patently untrue. Considering just the last ten presidential elections, Trump's winning College margin was only the eighth largest.[14] At the same time, Trump is much like Dr. Johnson's dog, which was hailed for the feat of walking upright, not criticized for how well he did it. The odds were so heavily stacked against Trump that his election by any margin counts as a remarkable achievement.

Democrats have garnered a popular-vote plurality in six of the last seven presidential contests, but lost the Electoral College, and thus the White House, twice. This may happen more frequently in future close elections since, as I just mentioned in the case of 2016, Democrats pile up more excess votes in their sure-win states. Along with the extra influence accorded small states thanks to each state, regardless of population, being given the same two senatorial electoral votes, the special GOP advantage in the Electoral College compared to the popular vote is another reason why attempts to abolish the archaic institution will not succeed.[15]

Regionally, the candidates drew support in about the usual pattern, with one exception—the often-Democratic industrial Midwest, where Trump narrowly edged Clinton thanks to his notable strength in the Rust Belt—Trump carried the South, the Mountain West, and the Plains easily, while Clinton swept the Pacific states (save Alaska) and the Northeast, though Maine and New Hampshire were tighter than expected. Trump won an extra electoral vote in Maine by carrying the northern Second District.

California deserves a special word. The state is predictably Democratic, but rarely as much as it was in 2016. Clinton's 61.5 percent exceeded Obama's percentages in both 2008 and 2012 (60.9 percent and 60.2 percent, respectively), while Trump's support in the Golden State was the GOP's all-time, post-Civil War low. Governor Alf Landon of Kansas previously held the record, receiving a mere 31.7 percent when he challenged President Franklin D. Roosevelt in 1936. Trump's proportion against Clinton was 31.5 percent. California alone provided Clinton with a plurality of over 4.2 million votes, which greatly exceeded her national lead of 2.9 million.[16]

That's not to say there weren't surprises in individual states. Trump won Arizona, Georgia, and Texas by smaller-than-usual percentages for a GOP nominee, and in Utah—where the Republican normally garners 60 percent or more—Trump couldn't even muster a majority. The 2012 GOP presidential nominee, Mitt Romney, and the state's dominant Church of Latter-day Saints made their objections to Trump quite clear, and an independent conservative candidate, Evan McMullin, a Utahan and a Mormon, secured 21.3 percent. Once reliably GOP Virginia prevented Trump from sweeping the South, and the Republican's decisive loss in the Old Dominion makes it three in a row for Democrats in presidential contests. The result solidifies the new classification of Virginia as being more Mid-Atlantic than Southern in its statewide politics.

Similarly, Clinton carried Colorado, Maine, Minnesota, and Nevada by smaller-than-expected pluralities. She lost Iowa and Ohio, both of which had voted twice for Obama, by wide margins. Her team had believed she would carry both Florida, which she lost by 1.2 points, and North Carolina, which she lost decisively (3.7 points). Until election night, the campaign never really thought Clinton would fall short in any of the northern tier of states she failed to carry—though they did understand that Michigan and Pennsylvania had become close. Wisconsin was a shocker for everyone, since Trump had shown weakness there even in the GOP primary and had never led in any of the established state polls.

Some of the reasons for the upset have already been mentioned, and others will be explored in subsequent chapters.[17] A combination of these factors pushed more of the late undecideds to Trump, many of whom were Republicans unhappy with Trump or weak backers of third-party candidates. In four critical states (Florida, Michigan, Pennsylvania, and Wisconsin) Trump

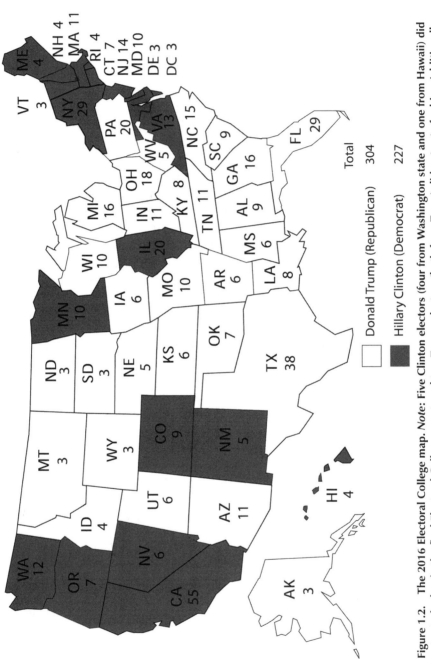

Figure 1.2. The 2016 Electoral College map. *Note*: Five Clinton electors (four from Washington state and one from Hawaii) did not vote for her in the final Electoral College count, and two Trump electors (both from Texas) did not vote for him. Additionally, Trump won an electoral vote from Maine's Second Congressional District.

scooped up the late undecideds by wide margins, easily enough to tip the states away from Clinton right at the end.[18] Some millennials, opposed to Trump but fans of Bernie Sanders rather than Clinton, also melted away in the final days to third parties or, mainly, to nonvoting status. Clinton's campaign manager has publicly blamed low turnout by young voters for his candidate's loss.[19]

WHO VOTED FOR WHOM?

A glance at the national exit poll's findings can flesh out some of the trends, though the pollsters stress, correctly, that the numbers for subgroups are not completely reliable.

Many pre-election polls had pointed to a record gender gap, with women substantially favoring the first female major-party presidential nominee. There was indeed a considerable gender gap: Clinton won women by 13 points, and Trump drew men 11 points. Depending on how one calculates the gap—adding together the net difference in support for the two genders or comparing the gender support of the winner—the 2016 cycle either set a record (24-point difference) or equaled the 1996 election (11-point difference as Trump won 52 percent of men and 41 percent of women). But the fact that the gender gap wasn't even more favorable for Clinton among women proved a major disappointment for Democrats, who have relied on female voters to power all of their victories in recent decades. Clinton also ran 4 points behind Obama's performance among men.

The role of gender will prove to be a fruitful subject for extended inquiry in the months and years ahead. Bias against women as political leaders has clearly diminished in modern times, and women have been elected to state governorships and other executive offices with some frequency. But the presidency is the ultimate executive office, and there are still many men, and some women, who have hidden (or not-so-hidden) gender prejudices. To what extent did gender, independent of party affiliation and other factors, influence the vote for and against Clinton? Throughout the campaign, an observer could not miss an assertion made frequently by women young and old: "I want a woman president, and I'm sure we'll have a woman president soon, but I don't want this particular woman (i.e., Clinton)."[20]

It is easy to see why Clinton depended on young voters. Those age 18–29 were the only age group to back Clinton with a sizable majority (55 percent), though she fell 5 points behind Obama in 2012 and 11 points behind Obama with this cohort in 2008. Clinton also won (by 10 points) those age 30–44— and mid-40s was the break point. Trump won voters 45 and up with 52 per-

Table 1.1.   Vote by Gender in Presidential Elections, 1972–2016

	Men		*Women*	
Election	*Dem %*	*GOP %*	*Dem %*	*GOP %*
1972	36%	**62%**	37%	61%
1976	**50%**	48%	**50%**	48%
1980	36%	**55%**	45%	**47%**
1984	37%	**62%**	44%	**56%**
1988	41%	**57%**	49%	**50%**
1992	**41%**	38%	**45%**	37%
1996	43%	**44%**	**54%**	38%
2000	42%	**53%**	**54%**	43%
2004	44%	**55%**	**51%**	48%
2008	**49%**	48%	**56%**	43%
2012	45%	**52%**	**55%**	44%
2016	41%	**52%**	**54%**	41%

Source: Exit poll data in each presidential election.

cent. Incidentally, young voters were about twice as likely as older voters to cast a ballot for a third-party candidate.[21]

A more diverse America has helped Democrats, because they get the lion's share of voters who belong to racial minority groups. Again, Clinton fared well with every racial minority, and minorities comprised 29 percent of the electorate (a bit higher than in 2012, if the exit poll totals are accurate). Her precise proportion of the vote with each group is a matter of some controversy. While the exit poll showed Clinton defeating Trump by 66 percent to 28 percent among Hispanics, more convincing data from the polling group Latino Decisions suggests the tally was closer to 79 percent to 18 percent. Latino Decisions explores the Hispanic vote later in this book.[22]

In any event, Trump's Electoral College majority was built overwhelmingly with the votes of whites—he received 57 percent to Clinton's 37 percent, about the same as in the Obama-Romney race. White men supported Trump 62 percent to 31 percent; white women backed him 52 percent to 43 percent, well under the white male margin but still quite healthy. Even young whites age 18–29 voted for Trump by 4 points.

Level of education emerged as a stark divider in 2016. Trump's unpolished speech and harsh positioning on a range of issues appealed disproportionately to people who were not college educated. Many in this category have been left behind economically, and they often blame other races, immigrants, and the establishment elite of both parties for their plight. Trump won non-college grads by 51 percent to 44 percent, and won whites with no college degree by a massive 66 percent to 29 percent. The vote was close among white college grads: Trump won 48 percent to 45 percent.

Meanwhile, Clinton won white female college grads by 51 percent to 44 percent. One of the largest Clinton margins among educational groupings came from those with some postgraduate college education: 58 percent Clinton to 37 percent Trump.

Despite all these variations in the 2016 vote, one factor remained the same—partisanship. Both Trump and Clinton received about nine of ten votes from those identifying with the candidate's party. In the case of Trump, this is astonishing because so many former and current GOP officeholders either refused to endorse Trump or publicly spoke out against his candidacy. Yet in the end, however reluctantly, Republicans came on board the Trump train. This is yet another measure of the intense partisan polarization that defines the current era. More self-identified Democrats voted (36 percent compared to 33 percent for the GOP), but Independents broke for Trump, 46 percent to 42 percent.

The 2016 contest didn't change much in some other respects. Those who are married tend to vote Republican and the unmarried voters are mainly Democratic. Trump's strongest social grouping was married men (57 percent), and Clinton's was unmarried women (63 percent).

Some fascinating evidence emerged that the era of personal scandals as decisive factors in elections may have ended, or at least the impact of such scandals going forward will be muted. Trump's life has been a tabloid dream—three marriages, multiple affairs, the *Access Hollywood* tape, dozens of X-rated appearances with Howard Stern, a dozen accusations of groping and sexual harassment, and so on. Granted, the Clinton family has had their share of disgrace, too, and Trump highlighted Bill Clinton's foibles whenever possible. But did anybody really expect white born-again Christians (26 percent of the electorate) to give Trump 80 percent of their votes? This was slightly higher than the share they awarded to George W. Bush, John McCain, and Mitt Romney.[23] Dislike of Hillary Clinton and the pending Supreme Court nomination must have done the trick. Trump secured a majority of the Catholic vote, too (50 percent to 46 percent), as well as 55 percent of those who attend church weekly or even more often.

The February 2016 death of conservative Supreme Court Justice Antonin Scalia may have been one of many factors that accounted for the difference in the election. The Scalia seat was viewed as critical to maintaining the current ideological balance on the Court (and of course it is possible that other seats will become open in the next four years). Had the Scalia seat not been open, evangelical Christians might not have been so willing to overlook

Trump's personal issues. But it was open, and Christians and conservatives considered the Court to be a top concern in determining their votes.

Clinton won the 74 percent of the country that did not identify as white born-again by 60 percent to 34 percent. In a continuation of the modern trend, the 22 percent of Americans who never attend religious services gave the Democratic nominee about a two-to-one majority.

Table 1.2 has much more from the national exit poll, including the impact of prominent issues and candidate characteristics; it is worth a close look. You can see that Trump did very well among military veterans, native-born Americans, and those disapproving of President Obama's job performance. Clinton scored very well with Obama backers, first-time voters, and LGBT voters.

Voting is an act that is both emotional and rational. Not all responses make sense, at least at first glance—the rational must be leavened by the emotional. More than half the voters said Clinton was qualified for the office and had the temperament to be president, while over 60 percent said Trump was not. Yet Trump received nearly one-fifth of the votes from the latter group. Undoubtedly, these were mainly reluctant Trump voters who were conservative, Republican, and anti-Clinton. As is their right, they decided to take a chance on Trump, given the alternative they detested.

TOWARD AN UNCERTAIN FUTURE

There cannot be any question that the United States is deeply divided; we may be more accurately termed the Disunited States. Red America and Blue America have very different cultural values and ideological politics, and the gulf is growing larger over time.

It is simply not obvious what we can do about it, or how the incoming president can hope to bridge the gap—especially *this* new president, whose favorability numbers are low and who is loved and hated in about equal measure by the nation's population. Much of what Donald Trump has done during the transition has underlined or even deepened partisan polarization, and the controversy over pro-Trump Russian involvement in the election can only accentuate our divisions. So too will his forthcoming reversal of much of President Obama's legacy, from Obamacare to immigration reform to climate change sensitivity. A change of party in the White House in these times means a sharp ideological shift, especially when accompanied by a Congress amenable to the president's agenda. Trump's loss of the popular vote may restrict his mandate somewhat and embolden Democrats, yet it will be difficult to derail most of the incoming White House's policies.

Fierce partisan battles are inevitable in the next four years, and the polarizing personality of President Trump as well as the intensified clash of cultural values between red and blue America could lead to turmoil in our society. Surely we aren't moving toward another civil war, though a lesser storm is already building. Widespread demonstrations and civil disobedience may well be in our future during the Trump administration. Perhaps this is too pessimistic a view. However, having lived through seventeen presidential elections and their consequences, I cannot see any equivalent to the passions we have already witnessed in the aftermath of November's outcome. Because the stakes are so high, neither the winners nor the losers have been particularly gracious—though President Obama and President-elect Trump were civil to one another during the transition. Compromise is a lost art for the most part, and it may be impossible to paper over the highly charged controversies that separate us.

For now, it might help a little to learn every possible lesson from the 2016 campaign. This book, we hope, is a start.

Table 1.2. 2016 National Exit Poll

Vote by Gender	Total % of electorate	Clinton 2016	Change from 2012	Trump 2016
Male	47%	41%	−4%	52%
Female	53%	54%	−1%	41%

Vote by Age	Total % of electorate	Clinton 2016	Change from 2012	Trump 2016
18–29	19%	55%	−5%	36%
30–44	25%	51%	−1%	41%
45–64	40%	44%	−3%	52%
65 and older	16%	45%	+1%	52%

Vote by Age	Total % of electorate	Clinton 2016	Change from 2012	Trump 2016
18–24	10%	56%	−4%	34%
25–29	9%	54%	−6%	38%
30–39	17%	51%	−4%	39%
40–49	19%	46%	−2%	49%
50–64	30%	44%	−3%	52%
65 and older	16%	45%	+1%	52%

Vote by Age	Total % of electorate	Clinton 2016	Change from 2012	Trump 2016
18–44	44%	53%	N/A	39%
45 and older	56%	44%	N/A	52%

Vote by Race	Total % of electorate	Clinton 2016	Change from 2012	Trump 2016
White	71%	37%	−2%	57%
African American	12%	89%	−4%	8%
Latino	11%	66%	−5%	28%
Asian	4%	65%	−8%	27%
Other	3%	56%	−2%	36%

Vote by Race	Total % of electorate	Clinton 2016	Change from 2012	Trump 2016
White	71%	37%	N/A	57%
Non-White	29%	74%	N/A	21%

Table 1.2. (continued)

Vote by Race and Gender	Total % of electorate	Clinton 2016	Change from 2012	Trump 2016
White Men	34%	31%	− 4%	62%
White Women	37%	43%	+ 1%	52%
Black Men	5%	82%	− 5%	13%
Black Women	7%	94%	− 2%	4%
Latino Men	5%	63%	− 2%	32%
Latino Women	6%	69%	− 7%	25%
All Others	6%	61%	− 5%	31%

Vote by Age and Race	Total % of electorate	Clinton 2016	Change from 2012	Trump 2016
White 18–29	12%	43%	− 1%	47%
White 30–44	16%	37%	− 1%	54%
White 45–64	30%	34%	− 4%	62%
White over 65	13%	39%	0%	58%
Black 18–29	3%	85%	− 6%	9%
Black 30–44	4%	89%	− 5%	7%
Black 45–64	5%	90%	− 3%	9%
Black over 65	1%	91%	− 2%	9%
Latino 18–29	3%	68%	− 6%	26%
Latino 30–44	4%	65%	− 6%	28%
Latino 45–64	4%	64%	− 4%	32%
Latino over 65	1%	73%	+ 8%	25%
All Others	6%	61%	− 6%	31%

Vote by Education	Total % of electorate	Clinton 2016	Change from 2012	Trump 2016
High School or Less	18%	46%	N/A	51%
Some College	32%	43%	− 6%	51%
College Graduate	32%	49%	+ 2%	44%
Postgraduate	18%	58%	+ 3%	37%

Are You a College Graduate?	Total % of electorate	Clinton 2016	Change from 2012	Trump 2016
Yes	50%	52%	+ 2%	42%
No	50%	44%	− 7%	51%

Education and Race	Total % of electorate	Clinton 2016	Change from 2012	Trump 2016
White College Graduates	37%	45%	N/A	48%
Whites No Degree	34%	29%	N/A	66%
Non-White College Graduates	13%	72%	N/A	22%
Non-Whites No Degree	16%	76%	N/A	20%

(continued)

Table 1.2. (continued)

Education among Whites by Sex	Total % of electorate	Clinton 2016	Change from 2012	Trump 2016
White College Grad Women	20%	51%	N/A	44%
White Non-College Women	17%	34%	N/A	61%
White College Grad Men	17%	39%	N/A	53%
White Non-College Men	16%	23%	N/A	71%
Non-Whites	29%	74%	N/A	21%

Vote by Income	Total % of electorate	Clinton 2016	Change from 2012	Trump 2016
Under $30K	17%	53%	N/A	40%
$30K–$49,999	19%	52%	N/A	41%
$50K–$99,999	30%	46%	N/A	49%
$100K–$199,999	24%	47%	N/A	48%
$200K–$249,999	4%	49%	N/A	47%
$250K or more	6%	46%	N/A	46%

Vote by Income	Total % of electorate	Clinton 2016	Change from 2012	Trump 2016
Under $50K	36%	53%	−7%	41%
$50K or more	64%	47%	+2%	48%

Vote by Income	Total % of electorate	Clinton 2016	Change from 2012	Trump 2016
Under $100K	66%	49%	−5%	45%
$100K or more	34%	47%	+3%	47%

Vote by Income	Total % of electorate	Clinton 2016	Change from 2012	Trump 2016
Under $50K	36%	53%	−7%	41%
$50K–$100K	30%	46%	0%	49%
$100K or more	34%	47%	+3%	47%

Vote by Party ID	Total % of electorate	Clinton 2016	Change from 2012	Trump 2016
Democratic	36%	89%	−3%	8%
Republican	33%	8%	+2%	88%
Independent	31%	42%	−3%	46%

Table 1.2. (continued)

Vote by Party and Gender	Total % of electorate	Clinton 2016	Change from 2012	Trump 2016
Democratic Men	14%	87%	N/A	9%
Democratic Women	23%	91%	N/A	7%
Republican Men	17%	7%	N/A	89%
Republican Women	16%	9%	N/A	88%
Independent Men	17%	38%	N/A	50%
Independent Women	14%	47%	N/A	42%

Vote by Ideology	Total % of electorate	Clinton 2016	Change from 2012	Trump 2016
Liberal	26%	84%	− 2%	10%
Moderate	39%	52%	− 4%	40%
Conservative	35%	16%	− 1%	81%

Vote by Marital Status	Total % of electorate	Clinton 2016	Change from 2012	Trump 2016
Married	59%	44%	+ 2%	52%
Unmarried	41%	55%	− 7%	37%

Marital Status by Gender	Total % of electorate	Clinton 2016	Change from 2012	Trump 2016
Married Men	29%	38%	0%	57%
Married Women	30%	49%	+ 3%	47%
Unmarried Men	18%	46%	− 10%	44%
Unmarried Women	23%	63%	− 4%	32%

White Born-Again or Evangelical Christian	Total % of electorate	Clinton 2016	Change from 2012	Trump 2016
Yes	26%	16%	− 5%	80%
No	74%	60%	0%	34%

Vote by Religion	Total % of electorate	Clinton 2016	Change from 2012	Trump 2016
Protestant	27%	36%	N/A	59%
Catholic	23%	46%	N/A	50%
Mormon	1%	28%	N/A	56%
Other Christian	24%	43%	N/A	54%
Jewish	3%	71%	N/A	23%
Muslim	1%	N/A	N/A	N/A
Other Religion	7%	58%	N/A	32%
No Religion	15%	67%	N/A	25%

(continued)

Table 1.2.   (continued)

Vote by Religion	Total % of electorate	Clinton 2016	Change from 2012	Trump 2016
Protestant	52%	39%	−3%	56%
Catholic	23%	46%	−4%	50%
Jewish	3%	71%	+2%	23%
Other Religion	8%	62%	−12%	29%
No Religion	15%	67%	−3%	25%

How Often Do You Attend Religious Services?	Total % of electorate	Clinton 2016	Change from 2012	Trump 2016
Weekly or More	33%	41%	N/A	55%
Monthly	16%	47%	−8%	49%
Few Times a Year	29%	48%	−8%	46%
Never	22%	62%	0%	30%

How Often Do You Attend Religious Services?	Total % of electorate	Clinton 2016	Change from 2012	Trump 2016
Monthly or More	49%	43%	N/A	53%
Less Often Than That	51%	54%	N/A	39%

Union Household?	Total % of electorate	Clinton 2016	Change from 2012	Trump 2016
Yes	18%	51%	−7%	42%
No	82%	46%	−3%	48%

Served in the US Military?	Total % of electorate	Clinton 2016	Change from 2012	Trump 2016
Veterans	13%	34%	N/A	60%
Non-Veterans	87%	50%	N/A	44%

Were You Born a US Citizen?	Total % of electorate	Clinton 2016	Change from 2012	Trump 2016
Yes	91%	45%	N/A	49%
No	9%	64%	N/A	31%

First-Time Voter?	Total % of electorate	Clinton 2016	Change from 2012	Trump 2016
Yes	10%	57%	N/A	38%
No	90%	47%	N/A	47%

Table 1.2. (continued)

When Did You Decide Presidential Vote?	Total % of electorate	Clinton 2016	Change from 2012	Trump 2016
Last Few Days	8%	43%	−7%	43%
Last Week	5%	41%	N/A	49%
In October	12%	37%	−12%	51%
In September	12%	46%	+1%	48%
Before September	60%	52%	−1%	45%

When Did You Decide Presidential Vote?	Total % of electorate	Clinton 2016	Change from 2012	Trump 2016
In the Last Week	13%	42%	−8%	45%
Before That	85%	49%	−2%	46%

When Did You Decide Presidential Vote?	Total % of electorate	Clinton 2016	Change from 2012	Trump 2016
In the Last Month	26%	40%	−10%	48%
Before That	73%	51%	−1%4	5%

Opinion of Presidential Candidate You Voted For	Total % of electorate	Clinton 2016	Change from 2012	Trump 2016
Strongly Favor	41%	53%	−1%	41%
Have Reservations	32%	49%	+7%	48%
Dislike Opponents	25%	39%	−2%	50%

Most Important Issue Facing the Country	Total % of electorate	Clinton 2016	Change from 2012	Trump 2016
Foreign Policy	13%	60%	+4%	33%
Immigration	13%	33%	N/A	64%
Economy	52%	52%	+5%	41%
Terrorism	18%	40%	N/A	57%

Which Candidate Quality Matters Most?	Total % of electorate	Clinton 2016	Change from 2012	Trump 2016
Cares About Me	15%	57%	N/A	34%
Can Bring Change	39%	14%	N/A	82%
Right Experience	22%	90%	N/A	7%
Good Judgment	20%	65%	N/A	25%

Illegal Immigrants Working in the U.S. Should be	Total % of electorate	Clinton 2016	Change from 2012	Trump 2016
Offered Legal Status	70%	61%	0%	33%
Deported to Home Country	25%	14%	−10%	83%

(continued)

Table 1.2. (continued)

View of U.S. Wall along the Entire Mexican Border	Total % of electorate	Clinton 2016	Change from 2012	Trump 2016
Support	41%	10%	N/A	85%
Oppose	54%	76%	N/A	16%

Effect of International Trade	Total % of electorate	Clinton 2016	Change from 2012	Trump 2016
Creates US Jobs	39%	59%	N/A	35%
Takes Away US Jobs	42%	32%	N/A	64%
Does Not Affect Jobs	11%	65%	N/A	30%

How is the Fight against ISIS Going?	Total % of electorate	Clinton 2016	Change from 2012	Trump 2016
Very Well	6%	85%	N/A	11%
Somewhat Well	35%	71%	N/A	24%
Somewhat Badly	28%	37%	N/A	55%
Very Badly	24%	12%	N/A	83%

How is the Fight against ISIS Going?	Total % of electorate	Clinton 2016	Change from 2012	Trump 2016
Well	41%	73%	N/A	22%
Badly	53%	25%	N/A	68%

In Your Vote, Were Supreme Court Appointments	Total % of electorate	Clinton 2016	Change from 2012	Trump 2016
The Most Important Factor	21%	41%	N/A	56%
An Important Factor	48%	49%	N/A	46%
A Minor Factor	14%	49%	N/A	40%
Not a Factor at All	14%	55%	N/A	37%

In Your Vote, Were Supreme Court Appointments	Total % of electorate	Clinton 2016	Change from 2012	Trump 2016
Important	70%	47%	N/A	49%
Not Important	28%	52%	N/A	39%

Does the Country's Criminal Justice System	Total % of electorate	Clinton 2016	Change from 2012	Trump 2016
Treat All Fairly	43%	23%	N/A	73%
Treat Blacks Unfairly	48%	72%	N/A	22%

Table 1.2. (continued)

View on Obamacare	Total % of electorate	Clinton 2016	Change from 2012	Trump 2016
Did Not Go Far Enough	30%	78%	N/A	18%
Was About Right	18%	83%	N/A	10%
Went Too Far	47%	13%	N/A	82%

Feeling about the Federal Government	Total % of electorate	Clinton 2016	Change from 2012	Trump 2016
Enthusiastic	6%	78%	N/A	19%
Satisfied	24%	76%	N/A	19%
Dissatisfied	46%	46%	N/A	48%
Angry	23%	18%	N/A	75%

Feeling about the Federal Government	Total % of electorate	Clinton 2016	Change from 2012	Trump 2016
Enthusiastic/Satisfied	29%	76%	N/A	19%
Dissatisfied/Angry	69%	36%	N/A	57%

Opinion of Government	Total % of electorate	Clinton 2016	Change from 2012	Trump 2016
Government Should do More	45%	74%	− 7%	22%
Government Doing too Much	50%	22%	− 2%	72%

	Total % of electorate	Clinton 2016	Change from 2012	Trump 2016
Strongly Approve	33%	93%	− 4%	4%
Somewhat Approve	20%	69%	− 11%	20%
Somewhat Disapprove	12%	14%	+ 5%	77%
Strongly Disapprove	33%	3%	+ 2%	93%

Opinion of Barack Obama as President	Total % of electorate	Clinton 2016	Change from 2012	Trump 2016
Approve	53%	84%	− 5%	10%
Disapprove	45%	6%	+ 3%	89%

Should the Next President	Total % of electorate	Clinton 2016	Change from 2012	Trump 2016
Continue Obama's Policies	28%	91%	N/A	5%
Be More Conservative	47%	13%	N/A	82%
Be More Liberal	17%	69%	N/A	23%

(continued)

Table 1.2.   (continued)

Opinion of Hillary Clinton	Total % of electorate	Clinton 2016	Change from 2012	Trump 2016
Favorable	43%	96%	N/A	3%
Unfavorable	55%	11%	N/A	81%

Opinion of Donald Trump	Total % of electorate	Clinton 2016	Change from 2012	Trump 2016
Favorable	38%	4%	N/A	95%
Unfavorable	60%	77%	N/A	15%

Opinion of Clinton and Trump	Total % of electorate	Clinton 2016	Change from 2012	Trump 2016
Both Favorable	2%	N/A	N/A	N/A
Only Clinton Favorable	41%	98%	N/A	1%
Only Trump Favorable	36%	1%	N/A	98%
Both Unfavorable	18%	30%	N/A	47%

Is Hillary Clinton Honest and Trustworthy?	Total % of electorate	Clinton 2016	Change from 2012	Trump 2016
Yes	36%	94%	N/A	4%
No	61%	20%	N/A	72%

Is Donald Trump Honest and Trustworthy?	Total % of electorate	Clinton 2016	Change from 2012	Trump 2016
Yes	33%	6%	N/A	94%
No	64%	71%	N/A	20%

Which Candidate is Honest?	Total % of electorate	Clinton 2016	Change from 2012	Trump 2016
Both Are	2%	N/A	N/A	N/A
Only Clinton Is	34%	97%	N/A	1%
Only Trump Is	31%	2%	N/A	98%
Neither Is	29%	40%	N/A	43%

Is Clinton Qualified to Serve as President?	Total % of electorate	Clinton 2016	Change from 2012	Trump 2016
Yes	52%	86%	N/A	9%
No	47%	5%	N/A	88%

Is Trump Qualified to Serve as President?	Total % of electorate	Clinton 2016	Change from 2012	Trump 2016
Yes	38%	4%	N/A	94%
No	61%	75%	N/A	17%

Table 1.2. (continued)

Who is Qualified to Serve as President?	Total % of electorate	Clinton 2016	Change from 2012	Trump 2016
Both Are	5%	22%	N/A	71%
Only Clinton Is	46%	94%	N/A	2%
Only Trump Is	32%	1%	N/A	98%
Neither Is	15%	15%	N/A	66%

Does Clinton have the Temperament to be President?	Total % of electorate	Clinton 2016	Change from 2012	Trump 2016
Yes	55%	83%	N/A	12%
No	44%	5%	N/A	88%

Does Trump have the Temperament to be President?	Total % of electorate	Clinton 2016	Change from 2012	Trump 2016
Yes	35%	5%	N/A	94%
No	63%	72%	N/A	19%

Which Candidate has the Right Temperament?	Total % of electorate	Clinton 2016	Change from 2012	Trump 2016
Both Do	5%	20%	N/A	77%
Only Clinton Does	49%	90%	N/A	5%
Only Trump Does	29%	2%	N/A	97%
Neither Does	14%	12%	N/A	67%

How Would You Feel if Clinton Wins?	Total % of electorate	Clinton 2016	Change from 2012	Trump 2016
Excited	17%	98%	N/A	1%
Optimistic	27%	92%	N/A	5%
Concerned	24%	19%	N/A	68%
Scared	29%	1%	N/A	94%

How Would You Feel if Clinton Wins?	Total % of electorate	Clinton 2016	Change from 2012	Trump 2016
Positive	43%	94%	N/A	3%
Negative	53%	9%	N/A	82%

How Would You Feel if Trump Wins?	Total % of electorate	Clinton 2016	Change from 2012	Trump 2016
Excited	13%	2%	N/A	97%
Optimistic	27%	3%	N/A	95%
Concerned	20%	54%	N/A	33%
Scared	37%	92%	N/A	2%

(continued)

Table 1.2. (continued)

How Would You Feel if Trump Wins?	Total % of electorate	Clinton 2016	Change from 2012	Trump 2016
Positive	40%	3%	N/A	95%
Negative	57%	78%	N/A	13%

Does Clinton's Use of Private Email Bother You?	Total % of electorate	Clinton 2016	Change from 2012	Trump 2016
A Lot	45%	7%	N/A	86%
Some	18%	68%	N/A	25%
Not Much	17%	88%	N/A	7%
Not at All	19%	93%	N/A	5%

Does Clinton's Use of Private Email Bother You?	Total % of electorate	Clinton 2016	Change from 2012	Trump 2016
Yes	63%	24%	N/A	69%
No	36%	91%	N/A	6%

Does Trump's Treatment of Women Bother You?	Total % of electorate	Clinton 2016	Change from 2012	Trump 2016
A Lot	50%	83%	N/A	11%
Some	20%	20%	N/A	73%
Not Much	13%	8%	N/A	88%
Not at All	16%	11%	N/A	86%

Does Trump's Treatment of Women Bother You?	Total % of electorate	Clinton 2016	Change from 2012	Trump 2016
Yes	70%	65%	N/A	29%
No	29%	10%	N/A	87%

Who Would Better Handle the Economy?	Total % of electorate	Clinton 2016	Change from 2012	Trump 2016
Clinton	46%	95%	N/A	1%
Trump	48%	3%	N/A	94%

Who Would Better Handle Foreign Policy?	Total % of electorate	Clinton 2016	Change from 2012	Trump 2016
Clinton	53%	86%	N/A	7%
Trump	42%	2%	N/A	96%

Who Would be a Better Commander in Chief?	Total % of electorate	Clinton 2016	Change from 2012	Trump 2016
Clinton	49%	93%	N/A	2%
Trump	46%	1%	N/A	95%

Table 1.2. (continued)

Opinion of the Democratic Party	Total % of electorate	Clinton 2016	Change from 2012	Trump 2016
Favorable	47%	88%	N/A	8%
Unfavorable	49%	9%	N/A	83%

Opinion of the Republican Party	Total % of electorate	Clinton 2016	Change from 2012	Trump 2016
Favorable	40%	11%	N/A	85%
Unfavorable	55%	73%	N/A	20%

Condition of National Economy	Total % of electorate	Clinton 2016	Change from 2012	Trump 2016
Excellent	3%	83%	N/A	16%
Good	33%	76%	−14%	18%
Not Good	41%	40%	−15%	53%
Poor	21%	15%	+3%	79%

Condition of National Economy	Total % of electorate	Clinton 2016	Change from 2012	Trump 2016
Good	36%	77%	−13%	18%
Poor	62%	31%	−7%	62%

Financial Situation Compared to Four Years Ago:	Total % of electorate	Clinton 2016	Change from 2012	Trump 2016
Better Today	31%	72%	−12%	23%
Worse Today	27%	19%	+1%	77%
About the Same	41%	47%	−11%	45%

Direction of the Country	Total % of electorate	Clinton 2016	Change from 2012	Trump 2016
Right Direction	33%	89%	−4%	7%
Wrong Track	62%	26%	+13%	68%

Life for the Next Generation of Americans Will Be:	Total % of electorate	Clinton 2016	Change from 2012	Trump 2016
Better Than Today	37%	59%	N/A	38%
Worse Than Today	33%	31%	N/A	63%
About the Same	25%	54%	N/A	38%

(continued)

Table 1.2. (continued)

Vote for President in Two-Way Race	Total % of electorate	Clinton 2016	Change from 2012	Trump 2016
Clinton	47%	97%	N/A	1%
Trump	47%	1%	N/A	97%
Would Not Vote	5%	16%	N/A	19%

How Confident are You in the Vote Count?	Total % of electorate	Clinton 2016	Change from 2012	Trump 2016
Very Confident	47%	68%	N/A	27%
Somewhat Confident	37%	33%	N/A	61%
Not Very Confident	11%	25%	N/A	68%
Not At All Confident	4%	28%	N/A	57%

Are You Confident in the Vote Count?	Total % of electorate	Clinton 2016	Change from 2012	Trump 2016
Confident	83%	53%	N/A	42%
Not Confident	15%	26%	N/A	65%

Are You Gay, Lesbian, Bisexual, or Transgender?	Total % of electorate	Clinton 2016	Change from 2012	Trump 2016
Yes	5%	77%	+ 1%	14%
No	95%	47%	− 2%	47%

Importance of Debates to Your Vote	Total % of electorate	Clinton 2016	Change from 2012	Trump 2016
Most Important Factor	25%	51%	N/A	47%
An Important Factor	38%	50%	N/A	45%
A Minor Factor	19%	37%	N/A	58%
Not a Factor	11%	41%	N/A	49%

Importance of Debates to Your Vote	Total % of electorate	Clinton 2016	Change from 2012	Trump 2016
Important	64%	50%	N/A	46%
Not Important	30%	38%	N/A	55%

Were Debates a Factor in Your Vote?	Total % of electorate	Clinton 2016	Change from 2012	Trump 2016
Yes	82%	47%	N/A	48%
No	11%	41%	N/A	49%

Table 1.2.   (continued)

Vote for US House	Total % of electorate	Clinton 2016	Change from 2012	Trump 2016
Democratic Candidate	49%	90%	− 3%	5%
Republican Candidate	50%	8%	+ 1%	87%

Area Type	Total % of electorate	Clinton 2016	Change from 2012	Trump 2016
Urban Area	34%	60%	N/A	34%
Suburban Area	49%	45%	N/A	49%
Rural Area	17%	34%	N/A	61%

Source: CNN, http://edition.cnn.com/election/results/exit-polls/national/president

NOTES

1. Note: The author would like to acknowledge the invaluable assistance of Timothy M. Robinson of the University of Virginia Center for Politics.

2. John Sides, "Which Was the Most Accurate National Poll in the 2016 Presidential Election?" *The Washington Post*, December 5, 2016, https://www.washingtonpost.com/news/monkey-cage/wp/2016/12/05/which-was-the-most-accurate-national-poll-in-the-2016-presidential-election/; Dhrumil Mehta, "How Much the Polls Missed By in Every State," *FiveThirtyEight*, December 2, 2016, http://fivethirtyeight.com/features/how-much-the-polls-missed-by-in-every-state/; Peter K. Enns, Jonathan P. Schuldt, Julius Lagodny, Alexander Rauter. "Why the Polls Missed in 2016: Was It Shy Trump Supporters After All?" *The Washington Post*, December 12, 2016, https://www.washingtonpost.com/news/monkey-cage/wp/2016/12/13/why-the-polls-missed-in-2016-was-it-shy-trump-supporters-after-all/; the national polls in the *RealClearPolitics* average right before the election had Clinton leading by 3.2 percentage points, and in the end she won by 2.1. That is reasonably close to reality, and below the variance in some other elections, including 2012. But many state polls were well off the mark, misleading everyone about the likely outcome in multiple battleground states.

3. Andrew E. Busch, *Truman's Triumphs: The 1948 Election and the Making of Postwar America* (Lawrence, Kansas: University Press of Kansas, 2012); Zachary Karabell, *The Last Campaign: How Harry Truman Won the 1948 Election* (New York: Vintage, 2001); David Pietrusza, *1948: Harry Truman's Improbable Victory and the Year That Transformed America* (New York: Union Square Press, 2011).

4. Richard Norton Smith, *Thomas E. Dewey and His Times* (New York: Simon and Schuster, 1982); Gary A. Donaldson, *Truman Defeats Dewey* (Lexington, Kentucky: University Press of Kentucky, 1999).

5. Glenn Thrush, "10 Crucial Decisions That Reshaped America," *Politico Magazine*, December 9, 2016, http://www.politico.com/magazine/story/2016/12/2016-presidential-election-10-moments-trump-clinton-214508.

6. *Ibid.*

7. Ashley Parker and Steve Eder, "Inside the Six Weeks Donald Trump Was a Nonstop 'Birther,'" *The New York Times*, July 2, 2016, http://www.nytimes.com/2016/07/03/us/politics/donald-trump-birther-obama.html; James Cook, "US Election: Trump and the Rise of the Alt-Right," *BBC News*, November 7, 2016, http://www.bbc.com/news/election-us-2016-37899026.

8. Tina Nguyen, "Obama Orders Investigation of Russian Hacking During 2016 Election," *Vanity Fair*, December 9, 2016, http://www.vanityfair.com/news/2016/12/obama-investigation-russian-hacking-election-2016.

9. Richard Ben Cramer, *What It Takes: The Way to the White House* (New York: Vintage, 1993).

10. Overall, Hillary Clinton had an excess of 11,226,189 votes. Donald Trump had an excess of 8,357,670.

11. Michael McDonald. "2016 November General Election Turnout Rates," United States Election Project, http://www.electproject.org/2016g.

12. Congress, not the Electoral College, awarded Hayes the disputed electoral votes that made him president, so the circumstances are not parallel. Incidentally, all five presidential candidates who have won the popular vote but been denied the White House have been Democrats: Andrew Jackson in 1824, Tilden in 1876, Grover Cleveland in 1888, Gore in 2000, and Clinton in 2016.

13. Kate Samuelson, "Donald Trump's Transition Team Dismisses Report on Russian Interference in U.S. Election," *Time*, December 10, 2016, http://time.com/4597274/donald-trump-russia-election-intervention-cia/.

14. The Electoral College vote totals for the past ten election winners are as follows: Ronald Reagan (1980): 489; Ronald Reagan (1984): 525; George H.W. Bush (1988): 426; Bill Clinton (1992): 370; Bill Clinton (1996): 379; George W. Bush (2000): 271; George W. Bush (2004): 286; Barack Obama (2008): 365; Barack Obama (2012): 332; Donald Trump (2016): 304.

15. Larry J. Sabato, *A More Perfect Constitution* (New York: Walker and Company, 2008), 121–153.

16. Political activists in the state have begun calling (again) for a Brexit-style "Calexit"; that is, the secession of California from the United States. Some have asked the states of Oregon and Washington to join with California in a new nation called Cascadia. Without question, this will not happen, and the matter of secession was essentially decided by the Civil War. Still, this suggests the deep division and extreme unhappiness after the 2016 election in some parts of the country.

17. David Robert, "Everything Mattered: Lessons from 2016's Bizarre Presidential Election," *Vox*, November 30, 2016, http://www.vox.com/policy-and-politics/2016/11/30/13631532/everything-mattered-2016-presidential-election.

18. According to the national exit poll, the 13 percent of voters who decided in the last week backed Trump 45 percent to 42 percent.

19. "Campaign for President: The Managers Look at 2016," Harvard Institute of Politics at the Harvard Kennedy School, December 1, 2016, http://iop.harvard.edu/get-inspired/campaign-managers-conference/campaign-president-managers-look-2016.

20. Jeffrey M. Jones and David W. Moore, "Generational Differences in Support for a Woman President," Gallup, June 17, 2003, http://www.gallup.com/poll/8656/generational-differences-support-woman-president.aspx; Clare Malone, "From 1937 to Hillary

Clinton, How Americans Have Felt about a Woman President," *FiveThirtyEight*, June 9, 2016, http://fivethirtyeight.com/features/from-1937-to-hillary-clinton-how-americans -have-felt-about-a-female-president/.

21. According to the exit poll, 18–29 year-old voters favored Hillary Clinton over Donald Trump 55 percent to 36 percent with 9 percent choosing another candidate; 30–44-year-olds favored Clinton over Trump 51 percent to 41 percent with 8 percent choosing another candidate; 45–64-year-olds favored Trump over Clinton 52 percent to 44 percent with 4 percent choosing another candidate; lastly, voters age 65 and older favored Trump over Clinton 52 percent to 45 percent with 3 percent choosing another candidate.

22. "Lies, Damn Lies, and Exit Polls," Latino Decisions, November 10, 2016, http:// www.latinodecisions.com/blog/2016/11/10/lies-damn-lies-and-exit-polls/.

23. In 2004, George W. Bush won 78 percent of white born-again Christians. In 2008, John McCain won 74 percent. In 2012, Mitt Romney won 78 percent.

2

Demographic Coalitions

How Trump Picked the Democratic Lock and Won the Presidency

David Byler

"Donald Trump Can't Win the White House Because [fill in the blank]."

Throughout this cycle, journalists, academics, bloggers, and analysts wrote countless pieces with titles like this. During the GOP primary, Trump attacked Republican elites rather than courting them and seemed unable to widen his appeal beyond 30 to 40 percent of the electorate, so many concluded he couldn't win. During the general election, Trump constantly generated controversies, lacked a traditional ground game, and had historically low favorability ratings—which again led many to argue that he would inevitably lose.

But perhaps the most popular argument in this genre was that demographics would keep Trump from winning the presidency. The basic idea was that Trump was toxic with too many groups—college graduates, Hispanics, African Americans, women, millennials, and more[1]—and he had no way to put enough votes together to win. This argument isn't new.[2] Since before the beginning of the Obama era, a number of political data wonks have argued that as America becomes more racially diverse and well-educated, Republicans (particularly those who take a hard line on illegal immigration) will find it difficult, if not impossible, to win the presidency.

Had Trump lost, analysts would still be arguing over this issue. Many liberals would have taken a Hillary Clinton victory as a sign that the Obama coalition was unstoppable, and many conservatives might have argued that a different presidential candidate would have been able to persuade Democratic voters or energize new voters enough to win back the White House.

But (despite losing the popular vote) the President won. If Trump or some other Republican can improve on his showing in some future election, he or she could win the popular vote as well as the Electoral College. So it's worth asking—what happened? How did Trump build a winning coalition in the face of demographic headwinds? How did the Democratic coalition change in this election? What do changes in both coalitions mean for the future of American politics?

I used a data-driven approach to tackle these questions. Essentially I found that Trump used a two-step process—consolidating the Republican base and then earning massive levels of support from whites without a college degree—to win, and that the parts of the Obama coalition that were supposed to doom Trump (African Americans, Hispanics, and college-educated whites) didn't show up in great enough number or force to beat him in the Electoral College. I'll go into detail on both of those points and then discuss what that means for politics in the coming years.

HOW TRUMP PUT TOGETHER
A WINNING GOP COALITION

Trump's process for winning the Electoral College can basically be divided into two steps.

First, he managed to keep the Republican base mostly in line. According to exit polls (note that exit polls are an imperfect measure, but they're useful for broad descriptions), Trump won 88 percent of self-identified Republicans. He also won 80 percent of evangelical Protestants and 81 percent of self-described conservatives.[3] Obviously there's significant overlap between these groups, but these numbers illustrate that Trump was able to keep the ideologically conservative parts of the GOP base behind him. Trump also did very well with white voters. He equaled 2012 Republican nominee Mitt Romney's twenty-point margin among whites while winning both college educated and noncollege whites.

These solid numbers with whites, evangelicals, and conservatives allowed him to keep the states that Romney won in 2012 as the base for his electoral map. In fact, all of the states that were deeply red in 2012 stayed in Trump's column.[4,5]

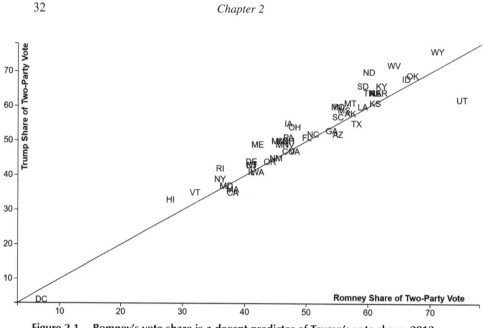

Figure 2.1. Romney's vote share is a decent predictor of Trump's vote share: 2012 versus 2016.

Figure 2.1 shows how Romney's share of the 2012 vote mapped onto Trump's share of the two-party vote. The right-hand side of the graphic essentially shows that red states remained red. Trump continued the tradition of Republican strength in the evangelical and heavily conservative South as well as the quadrennially Republican plains states.

In hindsight, it might seem obvious that Trump was going to win states like Texas, Georgia, South Carolina, and Utah. But for much of the 2016 election cycle, that wasn't so clear. During the Republican presidential primary, weekly church-attending evangelicals supported Trump at a much lower rate than other Protestants.[6] He was also squeezed on both the left and right—Texas Senator Ted Cruz's very conservative chunk of the Tea Party was wary of Trump, as were the affluent suburbanites who often opted for Ohio Governor John Kasich or Florida Senator Marco Rubio.[7] When Trump was reeling from various scandals and controversies during the general election (e.g., his public fight with a Gold Star father who spoke at the Democratic National Convention, his lackluster performance at the first debate, etc.), he lost the support of some reliable Republicans, and polls in red states like Arizona, Georgia, and even Texas tightened significantly.[8]

So this first step of his process—convincing skeptical parts of the GOP base that they should vote for him—was an important, ongoing task for the

Trump campaign. Ultimately, Trump won over these voters through a combination of avoiding scandal in the final weeks of the campaign, highlighting Clinton's recurring email issues (which reminded Republicans that they didn't like her) and emphasizing areas of policy agreement (like Supreme Court picks). But if Trump hadn't won over the base, he would have had a much more difficult time winning the White House.

Before moving on to the voters that Trump added to his base, it's worth looking quickly at two other features of the data—Clinton's base and whether the same *people* voted for Trump and Romney.

First, the left-hand side of the graphic shows that Hillary Clinton had strong support within her party. Exit polls and statewide results suggest that she was able to mostly secure liberals, Blacks, Hispanic/Latinos, Asians, young voters, and most other key Democratic constituencies. That helped her win quadrennially blue states like Massachusetts, California, Oregon, Washington, New Mexico, New York, Vermont, Connecticut, and more. While Clinton may not have fully matched President Obama's performance with racial minorities (more on that in the next section), the base of her coalition was similar in character to Obama's.

Second, this consistency from 2012 to 2016 persists when we zoom into smaller geographic subdivisions. Figure 2.2 shows how well the county-level results from 2012 map onto 2016 when third parties are excluded.

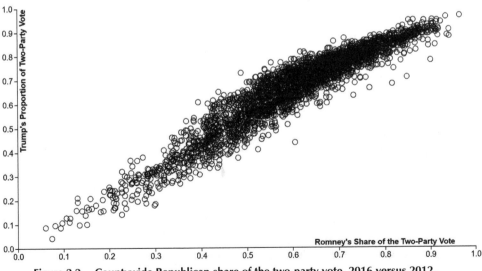

Figure 2.2. Countywide Republican share of the two-party vote, 2016 versus 2012, county data.

These data suggest (but don't by themselves prove) that Clinton and Trump won many of the same voters that Obama and Romney did in 2012. In other words, Clinton and Trump were both able to lay down familiar foundations before attempting to expand their coalitions.

This leads us to the second step of Trump's strategy—run up the score with non-college-educated whites. According to national exit polls, Trump won whites without a college degree 66 percent to 29 percent. That's a twelve-point shift in Trump's favor from 2012. But topline numbers like these are only so informative—in order to really understand Trump's coalition, we need to know where he gained, where he didn't, and why he gained these votes from this group specifically.

We'll tackle geography first—Trump's gains weren't evenly distributed across the country as figure 2.3 shows.[9]

The geographic pattern here is relatively clear. Trump made significant gains in the broad Midwestern/Mid-Atlantic region. He gained in large, less populous swathes of Michigan, Wisconsin, Ohio, Iowa, Minnesota, the Dakotas, New York, Pennsylvania, and Maine. In other words, Trump made significant strides in the heartland, Central Northern region, and the Northeast outside the DC-Philadelphia-New York-Boston "Acela" corridor.

In most of those states, Trump seemed to gain because he won over areas with large concentrations of whites without a college degree. Table 2.1 demonstrates this.

Most of table 2.1 is straightforward. Each row looks at the results in a state. The first column is the state's name. The second and third columns show the Republican's share of the two-party vote (excluding all third-party votes) in the 2016 and 2012 general elections. The fourth column is the difference between those numbers, and the table is sorted from largest Democratic gain to largest Republican gain.

The final column is the most important—it tracks how effectively the rate of college education among whites predicted Trump's gains over Romney within a state. This quantity (known to statisticians as R-squared for a simple linear regression) is measured on a percentage scale where larger percentages indicate that a larger amount of variance in the countywide results is explained by college education among whites. For example, the data show that education levels among whites powerfully explains where Trump gained on Romney in Ohio (72.5 percent) but it's less helpful in Kansas (37.2 percent). In states where there was insufficient data (too few counties) or extremely odd political divisions (Alaska) R-squared was not calculated.

In many of the most electorally important heartland states (e.g., Ohio, Pennsylvania, Iowa, Michigan, and Wisconsin), Trump improved on Romney's showing in areas with high concentrations of non-college-educated

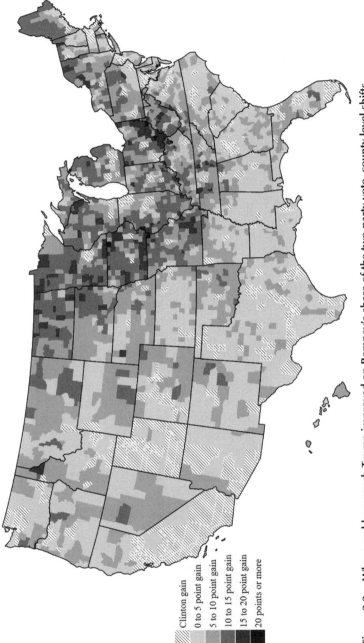

Figure 2.3. Where and how much Trump improved on Romney's share of the two-party vote, county level shifts.

Clinton gain

0 to 5 point gain

5 to 10 point gain

10 to 15 point gain

15 to 20 point gain

20 points or more

Table 2.1.   Which States Shifted Most and What Explains Those Shifts

State	Trump Two-Party Share	Romney Two-Party Share	Difference	How Much Does Education among Whites Explain?
Utah	62.4%	74.6%	−12.2%	65.2%
California	33.9%	38.1%	−4.3%	51.2%
Texas	54.7%	58.0%	−3.3%	48.2%
D. C.	4.3%	7.4%	−3.1%	NA
Massachusetts	35.3%	38.2%	−2.9%	69.7%
Arizona	51.9%	54.6%	−2.7%	52.9%
Georgia	52.7%	54.0%	−1.3%	57.1%
Washington	41.2%	42.4%	−1.2%	72.3%
Virginia	47.2%	48.0%	−0.9%	74.7%
Maryland	36.0%	36.7%	−0.7%	84.5%
Illinois	41.0%	41.4%	−0.4%	73.4%
Kansas	61.1%	61.1%	0.1%	37.2%
Colorado	47.3%	47.3%	0.1%	72.6%
Oregon	43.8%	43.7%	0.1%	71.6%
New Mexico	45.3%	44.7%	0.6%	53.4%
North Carolina	51.9%	51.0%	0.9%	56.2%
Florida	50.6%	49.6%	1.1%	65.6%
Alaska	58.4%	57.3%	1.1%	NA
Louisiana	60.2%	58.7%	1.4%	49.5%
Connecticut	42.9%	41.2%	1.6%	NA
New Jersey	42.7%	41.0%	1.7%	87.8%
Idaho	68.3%	66.4%	1.9%	36.0%
Nevada	48.7%	46.6%	2.1%	53.2%
Arkansas	64.3%	62.2%	2.1%	50.6%
South Carolina	57.5%	55.3%	2.2%	69.8%
Nebraska	63.5%	61.1%	2.4%	21.7%
New York	38.2%	35.7%	2.5%	77.7%
Oklahoma	69.3%	66.8%	2.5%	63.8%
New Hampshire	49.8%	47.2%	2.6%	92.1%
Vermont	34.8%	31.8%	3.1%	NA
Pennsylvania	50.4%	47.3%	3.1%	62.8%
Minnesota	49.2%	46.1%	3.1%	82.7%
Alabama	64.4%	61.2%	3.2%	48.2%
Tennessee	63.6%	60.4%	3.3%	61.4%
Mississippi	59.1%	55.8%	3.3%	39.1%
Delaware	44.0%	40.6%	3.4%	NA
Wisconsin	50.4%	46.5%	3.9%	82.8%
Montana	61.1%	57.0%	4.1%	41.3%
Kentucky	65.7%	61.5%	4.1%	31.6%
Hawaii	32.6%	28.3%	4.3%	NA
Wyoming	75.7%	71.2%	4.5%	52.3%
Indiana	60.1%	55.2%	4.9%	78.6%
Michigan	50.1%	45.2%	4.9%	87.5%

(continued)

Table 2.1. (continued)

State	Trump Two-Party Share	Romney Two-Party Share	Difference	How Much Does Education Among Whites Explain?
Missouri	59.8%	54.8%	5.0%	68.5%
Rhode Island	41.7%	36.0%	5.7%	NA
Ohio	54.3%	48.5%	5.8%	72.5%
Maine	48.4%	42.1%	6.3%	89.0%
South Dakota	66.0%	59.2%	6.8%	35.8%
Iowa	55.1%	47.0%	8.0%	75.8%
West Virginia	72.2%	63.7%	8.5%	37.2%
North Dakota	69.8%	60.1%	9.7%	13.3%

whites. Trump also appeared to make gains with these voters in Minnesota and Maine—normally safe blue states that Clinton won by a relatively small margin. Linear regressions on county level results, like every other part of statistics, has its limitations (e.g., this regression looks at county-level data, so it doesn't prove anything about individual behavior in the strictest sense), but it does strongly suggest that in key areas, Trump's increased strength came from newfound support among blue-collar whites.

But this strong statistical relationship didn't hold everywhere. In some states, longer-term trends complicated the picture.

For example, rightward trends in coal country threw off the predictive power of college education in Kentucky and West Virginia. Kentucky and West Virginia are perfect states for Trump—West Virginia has the lowest rate of college education among whites in the nation, and Kentucky has the second lowest. Both states have seen tough economic times, and neither has a large concentration of racial minorities that would push back on a heavily Republican white vote. Trump gained in both states, but education level among whites was not a particularly good predictor of where he gained. A quick look at the map in figure 2.4 shows why.

Voters in Kentucky coal country (southeastern portion of the state) didn't shift to Trump as much as the rest of the state, and the vote in coal-rich, economically damaged southwestern West Virginia shifted less than one might expect based on educational attainment there. That's partially because long-term trends allowed the GOP to pick up those regions before Trump even registered as a Republican.

The Democratic coalition has become more urban and cosmopolitan in recent decades (think about the difference in Bill Clinton's and Barack Obama's style and platform), and that has caused Appalachia to move toward the

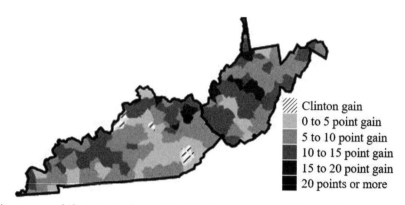

Clinton gain
0 to 5 point gain
5 to 10 point gain
10 to 15 point gain
15 to 20 point gain
20 points or more

Figure 2.4.   Shifts in Kentucky and West Virginia two-party GOP vote share: 2012–2016.

Republicans. As Democrats embraced a more environment-focused energy policy, voters in coal country may have seen Republicans as the more reliable ally of coal.[10] In other words, some of the most economically downtrodden white areas of the country were moving away from Democrats before Trump—in some cases so much that he had limited upside there.

A similar pattern explains why education wasn't as predictive in the South as in other regions. In Mississippi, Alabama, Georgia, Louisiana, Texas, and Arkansas, the predictive power of education was much lower than it was in many Midwestern and Mid-Atlantic states. That's probably partially because Republicans have been increasing their hold on white working class voters in the South for decades. The South's transition from a top-to-bottom Democratic stronghold to a supermajority Republican region is a complicated story that involves economics, culture, and race. But it's sufficient to say that voting in the South became racially polarized before Trump came onto the scene—that is, Republicans often win supermajorities of white voters, Democrats win supermajorities of African Americans, and that gives the GOP a substantial edge in almost all statewide and national elections across the region (apart from swing states Virginia, North Carolina, and Florida). In other words, non-college-educated whites in the South were already voting heavily for the GOP, so Trump could only gain so much with them.

There are other interesting geographic features of the vote (some of which we'll get into in the next section), but nongeographic aspects of the data also provide important insights into exactly who voted for Trump and why. Specifically, it's worth asking why education is a better predictor than economics and whether Trump gained by persuading Democrats or turning out new voters.

Throughout this chapter, I've used education rather than economics or racial resentment to predict the difference between the Trump and Romney versions of the GOP. That might seem odd to some—pundits, analysts, and even the politicians Trump ran against often told the story of the Trump phenomenon through those lenses. But statistical tools suggest that education is one of the best predictors of increased support for Trump—and that tells us a great deal about why some voters might like him.

I've tested a number of variables alongside education in an attempt to find out exactly what predicted increased support for Trump. After controlling for education, economic distress (whether measured by per capita income, percent under a certain income threshold, etc.) typically had almost no influence on whether Trump gained or lost support. In the few states where it did, education had a much stronger pull on election results than income did. It was also difficult to find a variable that measured racial resentment on the county level that didn't require significant amounts of additional theorizing (e.g., assuming that if an increase in minority population happened in a county, an increase in Trump vote was necessarily driven by whites feeling greater levels of racial apprehension).

But that doesn't mean those story lines were wrong. In fact, the predictive power of education alone suggests that economics, culture, and race all might play a role in Trump's rise. White voters without a college education tend to make less than those with a degree,[11] and they tend to feel greater levels of racial resentment.[12] Maybe most importantly, rural whites without a college degree live in a different cultural world than many who live in economically flourishing urban centers or prosperous suburbs—and Trump made explicit cultural appeals to that world. In other words, the statistics suggest that these competing narratives may be correct, and that Trump's rise was fueled by a combination of economics, race, and culture.

Finally, it's worth asking whether Trump gained votes by turning out new voters or chipping away at the Obama coalition. This question likely won't be fully answered for months. Some of the best data on turnout comes from government-collected as well as privately owned voter lists. These lists track who voted where and in what election, and they'll be able to provide a clearer picture of whether Trump won through persuasion or turnout.

But Doug Rivers of YouGov took an initial stab at the question and found that Trump benefited from turning out voters who skipped the 2012 election.[13] According to his polling, for every voter who voted for Obama in 2012 and Trump in 2016, five more voted for Trump after skipping the 2012 election. Additionally, in the key swing states, Rivers found that turnout was up in the most heavily Republican areas and down in Democratic strongholds. Again, it's important to wait for all of the data before coming to strong conclusions, and we're looking at this election only a couple of months after it was concluded. But it seems as if turnout played a leading role in Trump's victory, although persuasion helped him as well.

WHAT ABOUT EVERYONE WHO DISLIKED TRUMP?

So far in this chapter we've focused on the keys to Trump's victory—lining up the conservative base and adding on white working-class voters—but what about the rest of the country? Pre-election polling showed that Trump was unpopular with nonwhites, women, millennials, college-educated whites, and more. So why didn't these powerful, growing groups hand Clinton the White House?

This is a complex question that involves a wide range of interesting demographics. We don't have the space or (at this moment) sufficient data to analyze every group, so I'll focus on a few that were particularly large and influential: college-educated whites, Hispanic/Latino voters, and African Americans. While Clinton made gains with college-educated whites and won a supermajority of nonwhite voters, the backlash against Trump (where it materialized) simply wasn't strong enough to carry the right states for Clinton.

We'll look at college-educated whites first.

According to exit polls, Donald Trump performed worse with white college graduates than most recent Republicans. He won the group 48 percent to 45 percent, whereas Romney won them by 14 points. John McCain won college-educated whites by four points in 2008, but he was dragged down by a massive recession and President George W. Bush's unpopularity. When times were better for Republicans—in 2000 and 2004—Bush won the group by 8 points and 11 points.

But Clinton, despite outperforming past Democrats, failed to secure enough college-educated white voters to swing key states. For example, in Pennsylvania Clinton made gains in some of the counties where whites were most educated, but Trump's gains in less educated areas were significantly greater (see figure 2.5).[14]

The same pattern shows up in Wisconsin (see figure 2.6).

This was the case in many key swing states. Clinton was able to either hold Trump to Romney's numbers or decrease his vote share in some of the most well-educated areas, but that wasn't enough to overcome his massive gains in areas with many downscale whites.

Outside the swing states, Clinton's gains were mostly confined to cities and suburbs where many white professionals live and work.

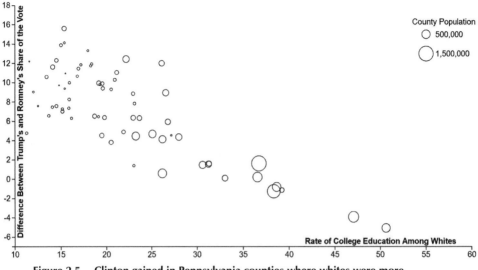

Figure 2.5. Clinton gained in Pennsylvania counties where whites were more educated.

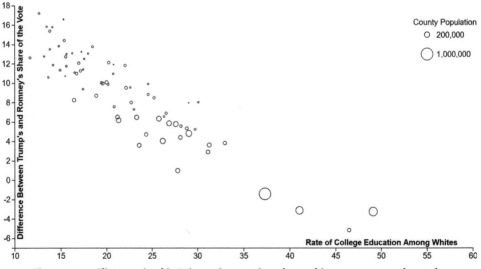

Figure 2.6. Clinton gained in Wisconsin counties where whites were more educated.

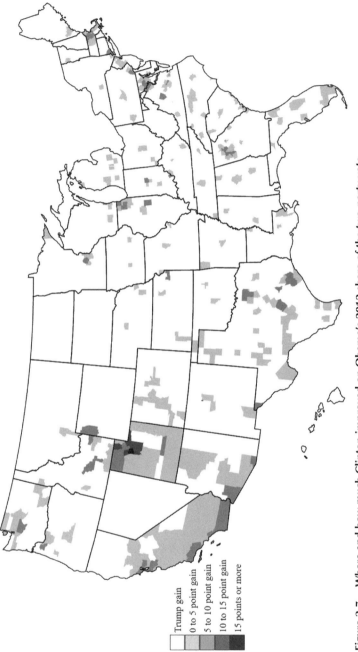

Trump gain

0 to 5 point gain

5 to 10 point gain

10 to 15 point gain

15 points or more

Figure 2.7.   Where and how much Clinton improved on Obama's 2012 share of the two-party vote.

Clinton gained in the Northeast Corridor—the stretch of cities and suburbs that runs diagonally from Boston through Philadelphia and New York down to Washington, DC, and Northern Virginia. In North Carolina, Clinton improved on Obama's vote share (see figure 2.7) in some "Research Triangle" counties—areas that include Duke University, North Carolina State University, and the University of North Carolina at Chapel Hill. In Georgia, Clinton's gains were mostly concentrated in the Atlanta area. Some of Clinton's best showings in Texas were in the Austin, Houston, and Dallas areas.

I could go on, but the pattern is clear—Clinton gained in major cities *as well as in the outlying areas.* That suggests that some of her gains came from grabbing a significant number of white, urban, or suburban professionals from the GOP.

Unfortunately for Clinton, these newly converted white professionals weren't particularly well-distributed. Clinton cut into traditional Republican margins in Georgia and Texas and roughly held onto Obama's margins in Colorado and Virginia in part by winning over white college graduates. But her improvements were insufficient in key swing states like Ohio, Michigan, Pennsylvania, Wisconsin, and Iowa. In other words, Clinton shaved a few points off Trump's margins in some red states and held onto a reasonably large margin in some light blue swing states, but Trump's success with non-college-educated whites offset her gains in the states that mattered most.

But college-educated whites weren't supposed to be Trump's only obstacle. Public pre-election polling showed that he was extremely unpopular with Hispanic/Latino and African American voters. This led many analysts (including myself)[15] to speculate that these groups might put Clinton in the White House. But these voters are distributed inefficiently throughout the country, and Clinton may have (depending on which data source you trust most) failed to create an anti-Trump wave amongst the nation's two largest racial minority groups.

Before getting into exactly how each group voted and whether or not they turned out in force, it's important to note that Hispanics and Blacks aren't evenly distributed across the country. Hispanics are heavily concentrated in the Southwestern states and large metro areas, and many Blacks are often scattered across the South or packed into dense urban centers. This dilutes the political influence of both groups.[16]

Table 2.2 shows the percentage of Hispanics in each state and how that state voted in the 2016 election. Most states don't have a large Hispanic population, and those that do are typically highly red or blue. New Mexico, California, New Jersey, and New York are reliably Democratic, while Texas and Arizona are typically at least light red. Hispanics exercise significant

Table 2.2. Statewide Vote and Hispanic/Latino Percentage of the Population

State	Percent—Hispanic or Latino	Trump Share
West Virginia	1.3	72.2%
Maine	1.4	48.4%
Vermont	1.6	34.8%
North Dakota	2.6	69.8%
Mississippi	2.8	59.1%
New Hampshire	3.1	49.8%
Kentucky	3.2	65.7%
Montana	3.2	61.1%
South Dakota	3.2	66.0%
Ohio	3.3	54.3%
Missouri	3.8	59.8%
Alabama	4.0	64.4%
Louisiana	4.6	60.2%
Michigan	4.6	50.1%
Tennessee	4.8	63.6%
Minnesota	4.9	49.2%
Iowa	5.3	55.1%
South Carolina	5.3	57.5%
Pennsylvania	6.1	50.4%
Alaska	6.2	58.4%
Wisconsin	6.2	50.4%
Indiana	6.3	60.1%
Arkansas	6.7	64.3%
Virginia	8.4	47.2%
Delaware	8.6	44.0%
North Carolina	8.7	51.9%
Maryland	8.8	36.0%
Georgia	9.1	52.7%
Oklahoma	9.4	69.3%
Wyoming	9.4	75.7%
Hawaii	9.6	32.6%
Nebraska	9.7	63.5%
District of Columbia	9.9	4.3%
Massachusetts	10.2	35.3%
Kansas	11.0	61.1%
Idaho	11.7	68.3%
Washington	11.7	41.2%
Oregon	12.1	43.8%
Rhode Island	13.3	41.7%
Utah	13.3	62.4%
Connecticut	14.3	42.9%
Illinois	16.3	41.0%
New York	18.2	38.2%
New Jersey	18.6	42.7%

(continued)

Table 2.2.   (continued)

State	Percent—Hispanic or Latino	Trump Share
Colorado	20.9	47.3%
Florida	23.3	50.6%
Nevada	27.2	48.7%
Arizona	30.1	51.9%
California	38.2	33.9%
Texas	38.2	54.7%
New Mexico	47.0	45.3%

influence in Florida, Colorado, and Nevada, but that's only three states out of arguably a dozen swing states throughout the country.

Table 2.3 shows that non-Hispanic Blacks also mostly live outside battleground states. Southern, heavily Republican states like Louisiana, Mississippi, South Carolina, and Alabama all feature large and heavily Democratic black populations. Some blue states like Maryland, Delaware, and the District of Columbia are home to a significant number of African Americans. Blacks make up a substantial share of the electorate in a few of the swing-ier states (e.g., North Carolina, light red Georgia, and light blue Virginia). But many of the most important swing states simply don't feature a large number of Black voters.

In other words, if Clinton uniformly increased her support with all Blacks and Latinos, many of those votes would be "wasted" in safe red or blue states. Clinton would have needed a wave of support from minority voters to carry her over the finish line in the Electoral College. While different data sources tell different stories, it appears as if no such wave materialized.

If the exit polls are to be believed (and there are reasons to doubt them), both Hispanics and Blacks supported Clinton at a lower rate than they did Obama. The 2016 exit polls have Clinton winning Hispanics 66 percent to 28 percent. That's a six-point shift from Obama's 71 percent to 27 percent victory over Romney. Clinton won African Americans in an 89 percent to 8 percent landslide, but her margin appears to be less than Obama's eighty-seven-point win with that group. The exit polls also show modest changes in turnout. Hispanics made up 10 percent of the electorate in 2012, and in 2016 they made up 11 percent. In 2012, Blacks made up 13 percent of the electorate, but they made up 12 percent in 2016.

These shifts aren't seismic. Clinton still won a large majority of Hispanics and Blacks. But the exit poll data suggest that an anti-Trump wave didn't materialize among nonwhites.

Table 2.3. Statewide Vote and Non-Hispanic Black Percentage of the Population

State	Percent Non-Hispanic Black	Trump Share
Montana	0.4	61.1%
Idaho	0.5	68.3%
Utah	1.0	62.4%
Vermont	1.0	34.8%
Wyoming	1.0	75.7%
Maine	1.1	48.4%
New Hampshire	1.1	49.8%
North Dakota	1.5	69.8%
South Dakota	1.5	66.0%
Oregon	1.7	43.8%
Hawaii	1.8	32.6%
New Mexico	1.8	45.3%
Iowa	3.0	55.1%
West Virginia	3.2	72.2%
Alaska	3.3	58.4%
Washington	3.5	41.2%
Colorado	3.8	47.3%
Arizona	3.9	51.9%
Nebraska	4.5	63.5%
Rhode Island	5.2	41.7%
Minnesota	5.3	49.2%
California	5.7	33.9%
Kansas	5.7	61.1%
Wisconsin	6.1	50.4%
Massachusetts	6.4	35.3%
Oklahoma	7.1	69.3%
Kentucky	7.8	65.7%
Nevada	8.0	48.7%
Indiana	9.0	60.1%
Connecticut	9.5	42.9%
Pennsylvania	10.5	50.4%
Missouri	11.4	59.8%
Texas	11.6	54.7%
Ohio	12.0	54.3%
New Jersey	12.8	42.7%
Michigan	13.8	50.1%
Illinois	14.2	41.0%
New York	14.4	38.2%
Florida	15.4	50.6%
Arkansas	15.5	64.3%
Tennessee	16.7	63.6%
Virginia	18.9	47.2%
Delaware	21.1	44.0%
North Carolina	21.2	51.9%

(continued)

Table 2.3. **(continued)**

State	Percent Non-Hispanic Black	Trump Share
Alabama	26.2	64.4%
South Carolina	27.4	57.5%
Maryland	29.0	36.0%
Georgia	30.4	52.7%
Louisiana	31.9	60.2%
Mississippi	37.2	59.1%
District of Columbia	48.7	4.3%

The county-level data tell a slightly better story for Clinton, but the data do not signal a pro-Clinton or anti-Trump wave either.

I used correlation to get a handle on whether counties with greater concentration of Black or Hispanic voters had increased turnout or spurred a jump in Democratic vote share from last cycle. Correlation is a simple statistical measure on a scale from -1 to $+1$ that shows how well two quantities track each other. If two quantities track each other closely (e.g., percent of white voters without a college degree in a county and Trump's improvements over Romney), then the correlation will be high and close to $+1$. If one quantity decreases as another increases (e.g., your weight decreases as the number of hours you spend at the gym increases), then the correlation will be closer to -1. And if there's no relationship, the correlation will be somewhere near 0.

In heavily Hispanic states, county-by-county correlations don't show much of a change between 2012 and 2016.

The third column of table 2.4 shows the correlation between Trump's gains in the countywide margin from 2016 to 2012 and the concentration of Hispanics in that county in selected states. These correlations are negative but not very strong. That suggests that Clinton may have gained ground compared to Obama with Hispanics (or at least gained ground in heavily Hispanic counties) in states like California, Arizona, Illinois, and New York. But the data are mixed, and in many states Clinton didn't seem to improve on Obama's showing in heavily Latino areas.

The story is even more muddled on turnout (see the fourth column). Clinton may have mobilized more Hispanics to vote in California and Arizona, but most of the rest of these correlations are relatively weak. This tracks with the exit polls, which only registered a one-point increase in the Hispanic/Latino share of the electorate from 2012 to 2016.

The patterns in the black vote are somewhat clearer (table 2.5).

Table 2.4.   How Well Hispanic/Latino Population Levels Predicted Turnout and
Vote Change in Selected States

State	Percent Hispanic or Latino	Correlation with Vote Change	Correlation with Turnout Change
Massachusetts	10.2	0.02	0.38
Kansas	11.0	−0.46	−0.13
Idaho	11.7	−0.15	−0.37
Washington	11.7	−0.21	0.14
Oregon	12.1	−0.29	0.16
Utah	13.3	−0.42	0.34
Connecticut	14.3	−0.50	−0.40
Illinois	16.3	−0.60	0.19
New York	18.2	−0.53	0.50
New Jersey	18.6	−0.15	0.21
Colorado	20.9	0.37	−0.31
Florida	23.3	−0.26	0.34
Nevada	27.2	−0.27	0.42
Arizona	30.1	−0.42	0.49
California	38.2	−0.45	0.74
Texas	38.2	−0.11	0.03
New Mexico	47.0	0.19	−0.25

In the many of the most African American states, turnout decreased as the non-Hispanic Black share of the countywide population increased. This was especially pronounced in Southern states like Georgia, South Carolina, Alabama, North Carolina, Tennessee, Mississippi, and Arkansas. This doesn't prove that black voters stayed home in those states, but it suggests that the historic levels of enthusiasm that President Obama generated among blacks are not necessarily a permanent feature of our politics.

The data on vote share are a bit less clear. Most of the correlations are negative but weak (see table 2.5). That suggests that Clinton was less likely to lose ground in counties with a higher percentage of black residents. But it doesn't conclusively prove that point. In fact, it mostly suggests that blacks voted similarly to how they voted in 2012 while turning out at a lower rate.

Taken together, these data seem to indicate that an anti-Trump wave didn't materialize among Black or Hispanic voters. Supermajorities of both groups cast their ballots for Clinton, but their support wasn't enough to win her the Electoral College—even if it was a substantial part of her strong showing in the popular vote.

It's critical to note here that some of the most important data on racial voting patterns have yet to be published. States and private firms are still working on voter lists. Additionally, other scientific surveys have claimed

Table 2.5. How Well Non-Hispanic Black Population Levels Predicted Turnout and Vote Change in Selected States.

State	Percent Non-Hispanic Black	Correlation with Vote Change	Correlation with Turnout Change
Pennsylvania	10.5	−0.33	−0.39
Missouri	11.4	−0.42	−0.39
Texas	11.6	0.08	−0.13
Ohio	12.0	−0.49	−0.42
New Jersey	12.8	−0.11	−0.48
Michigan	13.8	−0.32	−0.41
Illinois	14.2	−0.27	−0.36
New York	14.4	−0.55	0.30
Florida	15.4	−0.17	−0.53
Arkansas	15.5	−0.41	−0.69
Tennessee	16.7	−0.36	−0.74
Virginia	18.9	−0.18	−0.55
North Carolina	21.2	−0.26	−0.79
Alabama	26.2	−0.49	−0.86
South Carolina	27.4	0.10	−0.77
Maryland	29.0	−0.23	−0.70
Georgia	30.4	0.06	−0.77
Louisiana	31.9	−0.30	−0.63
Mississippi	37.2	−0.42	−0.87

that Trump's share of the Latino vote was significantly lower than Romney's already poor showing. It's important to wait for all of the data and carefully compare the results of these competing methods before making a final assessment of how racial minorities voted.

That being said, at the end of the day the vote totals have to add up. The data presented here tell a coherent story about how various demographic groups voted and turned out. So if we adjust one part of that story (e.g. claim that Latino vote share should be shifted toward Clinton) then it's important to adjust another part (e.g., increase turnout among blue-collar whites) of that story so that the popular vote and state-by-state results all still make sense.

WHERE BOTH PARTY COALITIONS GO FROM HERE

So where do both parties go from here? Can Democrats take back the White House despite their geographically inefficient coalition? Can Republicans use a Trump-like model to keep winning presidential elections?

The answer to the final two questions seems to be "yes."

A Democratic comeback in 2020 or 2024 is far from out of the question. Republicans won the Electoral College by running up the score in some key swing states. If Democrats manage to make small gains in the Midwest (not all of which need to be with working-class whites) without pushing another piece out of their coalition, they could win the presidency again. Alternatively, if Democrats manage to push Florida back into their column, they would only need one more state (possibly North Carolina or Arizona) to win the presidency without taking back any of the Midwestern states that they lost in 2016. Democrats have viable paths back into the White House, and they don't need to fundamentally alter their coalition to get there

Republicans could also continue to win by building on Trump's success. If Trump manages to keep his strong support among white working-class voters while winning back college-educated whites, he could add a popular vote majority to another Electoral College win. Alternatively, Republicans could try to make inroads with women, millennials, racial minorities, and other parts of the Obama coalition. But it's unclear now what part of Trump's policy agenda would help him gain those votes.

In other words, neither party built a permanent majority in 2016. No American political party ever has. So Republicans should neither spike the football nor dread the eventual arrival of an unbeatable Democratic majority. And Democrats shouldn't despair for the future or see 2016 as an aberration in their inevitable march to victory. Another presidential election is just around the corner, and it's anyone's guess which coalition will triumph.

NOTES

1. Jon Wiener's "Relax, Donald Trump Can't Win" in *The Nation* published on June 21 is a good example of this, but the articles that argued this are too numerous to list here.

2. Those unfamiliar with this debate might want to read *The Emerging Democratic Majority* by John Judis and Ruy Teixeira as well as *The Lost Majority* by Sean Trende. There are many good books and articles on the subject, but those provide a detailed, nuanced version of where this debate stood before the 2016 election.

3. CNN exit polls, last updated November 23, 2016: http://edition.cnn.com/election/results/exit-polls/national/president.

4. All election results in this chapter are taken from David Leip's *Atlas of U.S. Presidential Elections* except for Massachusetts, Maine, Mississippi, and Illinois. *Politico*'s counts were used for those states because Leip's data was not fully updated at the time of analysis.

5. Note that throughout this chapter I use Republican share of the two-party vote to measure election results. It's a simple measure—the Republican's vote total divided by the sum of the Democrat's and the Republican's vote totals. This measure omits third parties.

6. Gregory A. Smith, "Churchgoing Republicans, Once Skeptical of Trump, Now Support Him," Pew Research Center, July 21, 2016, http://www.pewresearch.org/fact -tank/2016/07/21/churchgoing-republicans-once-skeptical-of-trump-now-support-him/.

7. David Byler, "What's Driving Cruz-Mentum—and Why It Could Fade," *Real-ClearPolitics,* April 19, 2016, http://www.realclearpolitics.com/articles/2016/04/19/whats _driving_cruz-mentum_--_and_why_it_could_fade_130313.html.

8. Figuring out what causes shifts in public opinion can be tricky, but comparisons between the *RealClearPolitics* national and state averages on the date of these controversies and a week or two later suggests that these events may have had a strong pull on the polls.

9. This data is again taken from Dave Leip's *Election Atlas.* Demographic variables mentioned in this section come from the 2014 American Community Survey 5-year estimates. The five-year estimates are less current than some other numbers, but they are often more accurate. They were downloaded from the U.S. Census Bureau website using the American FactFinder tool.

10. Sean Trende, "Capito Win Could Cap GOP Transformation of W. Va.," *RealClear-Politics*, October 27, 2014, http://www.realclearpolitics.com/articles/2014/10/27/capito_ win_could_cap_gop_transformation_of_wva_124446.html.

11. The correlation between ACS estimates for college education among whites age 25 and older and per capita income among whites is high.

12. Michael Tesler, "The education gap among whites this year wasn't about education. It was about race," *Washington Post*, November 16, 2016, https://www.washingtonpost .com/news/monkey-cage/wp/2016/11/16/the-education-gap-among-whites-this-year-wasnt -about-education-it-was-about-race/?utm_term = .8dad2ff61401.

13. David Leonhardt, "The Democrats' Real Turnout Problem," *New York Times*, November 17, 2016, http://www.nytimes.com/2016/11/20/opinion/sunday/the-democrats -real-turnout-problem.html.

14. County population is taken from the 2014 ACS 5-year estimates.

15. David Byler, "Will Demographics Sink Donald Trump?" *RealClearPolitics*, March 28, 2016, http://www.realclearpolitics.com/articles/2016/03/28/will_demographics_sink _donald_trump_130095.html.

16. Data are again taken from Dave Leip's *Election Atlas* and the 2014 ACS 5-year estimates.

3

Straight Tickets for Senate, Split Tickets for Governor

The 2016 Senate and Gubernatorial Elections

Geoffrey Skelley

"Straight ticket" versus "split ticket" is an oversimplified way to contrast how the 2016 elections for the United States Senate (straight) and governor (split) related to the presidential contest that topped ballots around the country. Naturally, there is more complexity to unravel when examining these contests on a case-by-case basis, but the topline says something about how voters act in our politically polarized age. In all thirty-four states holding a Senate contest, voters backed the same party for president and Senate. Accordingly, Democrats picked up two net seats in the Senate by winning two seats in states that also went Democratic at the presidential level (Illinois and New Hampshire). However, because Donald Trump out-performed expectations in some battleground states, he provided a higher Republican support floor that benefited many GOP Senate incumbents, most of whom ran ahead of their presidential standard bearer. Meanwhile, voters chose a different party for president and governor in five of the twelve states that held gubernatorial elections. These split-ticket outcomes included a Republican gubernatorial win in Vermont, Hillary Clinton's sixth-best state by margin, and a Democratic gubernatorial win in West Virginia, Trump's second-best state by margin.

These two data points—100 percent straight-ticket for president and Senate, 58 percent straight-ticket for president and governor—reflect a subtle difference in how some voters regard federal and state-level elections. While 2016 data are not yet available, recent studies indicate slightly different voting patterns in these two sets of elections. For example, the 2008 and 2012 Cooperative Congressional Election Studies showed greater ticket splitting between president and governor than president and Senate. In both 2008 and 2012, 8 percent of voters who cast a ballot for both president and Senate split tickets between the two major parties in those races. Conversely, among the voters who cast ballots in both the presidential and gubernatorial elections, 15 percent split tickets between the Democrats and the Republicans in 2008 and 11 percent in 2012. These weren't large differences, but the data suggest that split-ticket voting was more common between president and governor than between president and Senate.[1]

Furthermore, the final outcomes in concurrent senatorial and gubernatorial elections in presidential cycles show more split-ticket outcomes for president-governor than president-Senate. Figure 3.1 lays out the percentage of straight-ticket president-Senate and president-governor outcomes over the past century, dating back to the first presidential election to take place after

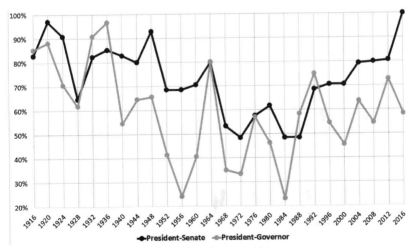

Figure 3.1.   Percentage of straight-ticket results for president and Senate versus president and governor, 1916–2016. *Note:* **Includes all states where both the presidential and Senate races and both the presidential and gubernatorial races were won by major-party candidates on the regular November election date.**

the establishment of popular Senate elections by the Seventeenth Amendment to the Constitution.[2]

As figure 3.1 shows, straight-ticket results tend to be more prevalent between president and Senate than between president and governor. From 1916 to 2016, a quadrennial average of 74 percent of Senate races were won by the same party that won the state at the presidential level while an average of 59 percent of gubernatorial elections were won by the same party that won the state at the presidential level. This difference also remains true in more recent times: from 1992 to 2016, 79 percent for Senate races and 61 percent for gubernatorial contests. To be clear, the number of gubernatorial races occurring in presidential years is now relatively small. Whereas thirty-five gubernatorial races took place in 1916, the movement of most states to four-year terms decided in midterm elections means that only eleven states now regularly conduct elections in presidential years, with Oregon's special election increasing the total to twelve in 2016. But from the data presented here, the straight-ticket phenomenon applies more readily to the federal-federal combination of president and Senate than to the federal-state combination of president and governor. While individual-level data sets will eventually offer evidence as to how much ticket-splitting occurred in 2016, the macrolevel outcomes in the Senate and gubernatorial contests indicate that this cycle also featured more straight-ticket voting between president and Senate than between president and governor.

A STRAIGHT-TICKET SENATE

Just how remarkable was it that the same party won the presidential and senatorial vote in all thirty-four states with Senate seats up in 2016? It had never happened before. Referring back to figure 3.1, 2016 marked the fourth occasion since the advent of popular elections for Senate where 90 percent or more of president-Senate results were straight-ticket. Prior to 2016, the previous record high happened in 1920, when the same party won both the presidential and Senate races in thirty-three of thirty-four states (97 percent).

Today's political environment is arguably the most polarized it has been in the post-Civil War era. Based on the well-known first dimension of the DW-Nominate measure that scores the left-right positioning of members of Congress, the ideological distance between the parties in the U.S. Senate and U.S. House has never been wider than it is today. But some argue this is a result of the public at large, suggesting that the increasingly polarized atmosphere in Washington and state capitals around the country reflects the public's divisions. Thus, our elections reflect these divides, too. For that reason, it's not surprising that we've seen an uptick in straight-ticket president-Senate results since the election of Bill Clinton in 1992, seen by many as the start of the modern, more polarized era of politics, especially with the "Republican Revolution" in 1994.[3]

Unsurprisingly, given the high levels of political polarization, the state-by-state vote percentages for president and Senate also moved together in 2016. In fact, based on the two-party vote for president and Senate in every cycle from 1916 to 2016, the 2016 election saw the second-highest correlation (.91) between the voting percentages for the two offices on Election Day, surpassed only by the 1916 cycle (.92). That means that about 83 percent of the variation (R-squared) in the two-party Senate vote in the 2016 election can be explained by the two-party presidential vote. The historical data for correlation (R) and the explained variance are presented in figure 3.2.

Understandably, the ups and downs of the correlation and fit data in figure 3.2 roughly mimic the straight-ticket president-Senate percentage data in figure 3.1. The more closely the votes for president and Senate hew to one another, the more likely the same party will win both in a given state. Considering what this may have meant for 2016, Trump's better-than-expected per-

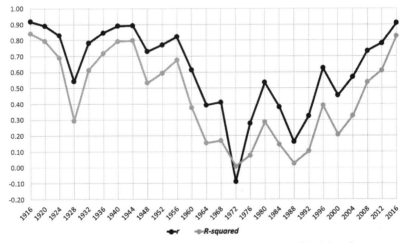

Figure 3.2.   Correlation and explained variance between presidential and Senate two-party election results on election day, 1916–2016. *Notes:* Excludes states where a major-party Senate candidate faced no major-party opposition, a third-party or independent candidate won the Senate race, or a third-party or independent candidate won the presidential race in the state in question. Also excluded are runoff elections that occurred after the regular November election day, decisive Louisiana open ("jungle") primary elections that took place before November, and Maine Senate races from before 1960 because they took place in September.

formances in some key battleground states meant that Republican support more-or-less started out at a higher baseline than some anticipated. From there, the individual appeal of candidates and idiosyncratic factors in each race helped all but one endangered GOP Senate incumbent to run ahead of Trump.

THE SENATE PLAYING FIELD

At the start of the 2016 cycle, Democrats were likely to gain seats in the Senate simply because the Republicans were highly exposed, holding twenty-four of the thirty-four seats that would be contested, which included seven in states that Barack Obama carried in 2012 and two others that he won in 2008. The map reflected the GOP's major gains in the 2010 midterm Republican wave, when it gained six net seats in the upper chamber. For Democrats, the seven-to-nine seat list of potential 2016 targets somewhat mimicked the GOP's circumstances in the 2014 midterm election, when the Republicans won all seven seats held by Democrats in states that Mitt Romney had won in 2012 and two battleground state seats in Colorado and Iowa. To top it all off, Democrats only had two seats to be concerned about losing: Colorado and Nevada, with only the latter starting out as a toss-up. Thus, Democrats had visions of winning at least the four net seats needed to achieve a fifty-fifty tie, which would give them a majority if the Democratic presidential nominee won the White House, and perhaps even more.

The news appeared to get even better for Democrats as the crowded Republican presidential field continued to develop and Trump entered the race in June 2015. By mid-July, Trump had taken the lead in the GOP primary polling averages. The media headlines soon began to offer what would become a refrain: some variant of "Republicans Worry Donald Trump Will Hurt Their Senate Chances," which was actually a headline in *The Hill* newspaper on August 25, 2015. With every controversial Trump statement and as Trump got closer to the GOP presidential nomination, the better Democrats' chances seemed to grow. Clinton led Trump in most early polling in key battleground states in the Electoral College that also had potentially competitive Senate seats held by Republicans. Considering the nation's sharp political polarization, increased straight-ticket voting, and straight-ticket president-Senate outcomes, there were reasons for Democratic confidence. But when the presidential race tightened in the autumn and some GOP Senate incumbents became more secure, the Democratic route to a Senate majority narrowed. Then on Election Day, Trump's stronger-than-expected performance in a number of key states not only won him the White House despite losing the popular vote, but it also helped Republicans hold onto a narrow

Senate majority. While state-level polling averages mostly got Clinton vote percentages right, they mostly undershot Trump, particularly in some states that also had important Senate races, such as Pennsylvania and Wisconsin. The higher-than-anticipated presidential floor helped GOP incumbents in close-run contests in those two states, and Trump's performance in Indiana and Missouri provided coattails that pulled up Republicans in those states even as they ran around five to eight points behind the GOP presidential standard bearer.[4]

With the Republican victory in Louisiana's December 10 runoff election, the final Senate tally for 2016 was fifty-two to forty-eight Republican, with a Democratic net gain of two seats. The fact that the Senate Democrats came up well short of expectations in 2016 has serious ramifications for the 2018 midterm cycle that will be discussed in the conclusion. But first, here is more on the most competitive and/or interesting races of the 2016 cycle, with certain themes connecting different sets of Senate contests.

NOTABLE 2016 SENATE RACES

The Illinois and New Hampshire Senate seats were the only two to switch party hands in 2016. In the Land of Lincoln, Republican Senator Mark Kirk began the cycle as the most vulnerable Senate incumbent, holding a seat in deep blue Illinois. The Senate matchup intriguingly featured two physically disabled nominees, with Democratic Representative Tammy Duckworth having lost both of her legs while serving as a helicopter pilot in the Iraq War and Kirk having suffered a stroke in 2012. In the end, Kirk was only able to run a point ahead of Trump, and Duckworth easily won by 15 points. The Granite State's contest featured two women candidates, incumbent Republican Senator Kelly Ayotte and Democratic Governor Maggie Hassan. Perhaps the most notable event in the campaign was the candidates' October 3 debate, when Ayotte made headlines for responding "absolutely" to a question about whether Trump could be a good role model for children, which became news fodder and fuel for Democratic attacks down the stretch. Coming into Election Day, major polling averages differed as to which candidate held a narrow lead of less than 2 points, with good reason: In the closest Senate contest of 2016, Hassan won by just 0.14 point (1,017 votes), 47.98 percent to 47.84 percent.[5]

For Democrats, the only other good news came from Colorado and Nevada. The latter was one of the year's marquee matchups. Senate Minority Leader Harry Reid decided against another run and his hand-picked choice, former state Attorney General Catherine Cortez Masto, won the Democratic nomination. Opposing her was Republican Representative Joe Heck, an Army Reserve doctor and three-term congressman. The polls bounced around, but by Election Day they showed Cortez Masto with a narrow lead of a point or two, and she edged Heck by 2.4 points, becoming the first Latina elected to the U.S. Senate. Because of Reid's retirement, Democratic Senator Michael Bennet of Colorado was the only Democratic incumbent viewed as potentially endangered at the start of the cycle. But top-tier Republicans passed on challenging Bennet, and Tea Party-favorite Darryl Glenn (R) won the Colorado GOP's nomination. National groups largely stayed away from the Centennial State race, and Bennet spent four times as much as Glenn en route to a six-point win.[6]

Underdog Republican Senate victories were the story in Pennsylvania and Wisconsin, where incumbent Republican Senators Pat Toomey of Pennsylvania and Ron Johnson of Wisconsin proved many pundits wrong. Katie McGinty, the Keystone State Democratic nominee, led Toomey in the polling averages by 2 to 3 points by Election Day, though a couple of late polls showed the race to be a dead heat. But just like the presidential race, the Republican outperformed the polls to win by 1.4 points, helped out to some degree by Trump's stronger-than-expected performance at the top of the ticket. Still, Toomey—a former president of the economically conservative Club for Growth—had a somewhat different path to victory compared to Trump. He outperformed Trump in more affluent areas, such as the three key Philadelphia collar counties of Chester, Delaware, and Montgomery, where he ran 6 to 9 points ahead of Trump. Meanwhile, he ran behind Trump in more blue-collar white areas of the state, such as parts of the southwest and in Lackawanna (Scranton) and Luzerne counties in the northeast. The Wisconsin race featured a rematch between Johnson and ex-Senator Russ Feingold, the Democrat Johnson beat in 2010. In his comeback bid, Feingold sought to become the first former senator to win back his old seat against the same candidate who beat him since Senator Peter Gerry, a Rhode Island Democrat, in 1934. For much of the cycle, Johnson looked unlikely to win. In fact, Johnson led only one poll over the course of the entire cycle in *RealClearPolitics'* polling database. Like Toomey in Pennsylvania, Johnson also took a slightly different path to victory compared to Trump. He ran ahead of Trump in the traditionally Republican and affluent Milwaukee "WOW" collar counties of Waukesha, Ozaukee, and Washington, as well as in Milwaukee County proper. Although Feingold performed better than Clinton in the western and northern reaches of the state, Johnson won 50.2 percent to 46.8 percent on Election Day.[7]

Late candidate entry—or reentry—played a role in the Florida and Indiana Senate contests. With Republican Senator Marco Rubio of Florida seeking the Republican presidential nomination, both parties expected to have competitive primaries. A crowded GOP field developed while Democrats prepared for a faceoff between fresh-faced Representative Patrick Murphy and Representative Alan Grayson, a wealthy bomb-thrower on the left. After Rubio lost badly to Trump in the March 15 Florida presidential primary, he suspended his campaign but looked unlikely to reenter the Senate race. In mid-May 2016, Rubio famously tweeted "I have only said like 10000 times I will be a private citizen in January [2017]." Perceiving the GOP field to be weak, leading Republicans pushed for him to reenter the race. On June 22, two days before the filing deadline, Rubio announced he would seek reelection, causing most other Republicans to drop out. Both Rubio and Murphy then went on to easily win their party primaries. During the general election campaign, Murphy took a hit when a local news exposé revealed that he had exaggerated his educational and business background. Rubio outraised Murphy and benefited from a massive outside spending advantage, likely promised to him as a part of reentering the race. In the end, Rubio won 52.0 percent to 44.3 percent, running three points ahead of Trump, in part because of stronger support among Latino voters: Rubio ran nearly ten points ahead of Trump in his home county of Miami-Dade. In Indiana, the race to replace retiring Republican Senator Dan Coats felt a seismic shock when former Democratic Senator Evan Bayh—who retired in 2010—announced his candidacy in mid-July 2016, just after the withdrawal of the Democratic nominee, former Representative Baron Hill. Facing Bayh was Republican Representative Todd Young, who started the race from behind. But Bayh's myriad political deficiencies marred his comeback run, including revelations that he made millions serving on corporate boards, from speaking fees, and from his partnership at a DC law and lobbying firm. He had also spent little time in Indiana since leaving the Senate, making his residency in the state an issue. Slamming Bayh as the consummate DC insider, Young's trajectory in the race improved throughout, and on Election Day the Republican won by nearly ten points.[8]

Many GOP insiders feared that the Republican incumbents in Missouri and North Carolina might falter. In the Show Me State, Republican Senator Roy Blunt had an establishment profile that did not fit the 2016 cycle. His opponent, Democratic Missouri Secretary of State Jason Kander, tried to make much of it, accusing the twenty-year D.C. veteran of paying heed to special interests, including the lobbying careers of Blunt's wife and children. Although it became clear that Trump would carry Missouri, internal polling and the few public polls suggested a close Senate race. A young Army veteran trying to run as an outsider, Kander had one of the most well-known television ads of the cycle, where he explained his support for gun control while assembling a rifle blindfolded. Kander ran eight points ahead of Clinton, but Trump's performance at the top of the ticket (he won 56.4 percent compared to Mitt Romney's 53.6 percent in 2012) helped Blunt, who won 49.2 percent to 46.4 percent. In the Tar Heel State, some Republicans complained that incumbent GOP Senator Richard Burr was not taking his race against Democrat Deborah Ross seriously enough. With Clinton marginally ahead in most polls from late September to late October and surveys showing Ross running close to Burr, GOP fears about possibly losing the seat were legitimate. Ross attacked Burr for not distancing himself from Trump, and Burr attacked Ross over her leadership of the state chapter of the ACLU from 1994 to 2002, where she defended the rights of flag-burning protestors and sex offenders. Trump's victory in North Carolina helped Burr, but he also managed to run a little more than 1 point ahead of the GOP presidential nominee, beating Ross by 5.7 points.[9]

Four other contests entered the Senate conversation at various times but lacked any drama by Election Day. Early on in the 2016 cycle, Democrats thought that Republican Senator Rob Portman of Ohio might be vulnerable. But Portman raised a huge war chest, reserved millions of dollars in TV ads, and put together an expansive field operation that overwhelmed the Democratic nominee, former Governor Ted Strickland. The ex-governor also proved to be very good at putting his foot in his mouth. In August, while talking about a Supreme Court case, Strickland joked that Supreme Court Justice Antonin Scalia died "at a good time." Portman crushed Strickland by 21 points. In Arizona, early polling suggested that Democratic Representative Ann Kirkpatrick might offer a competitive challenge to Republican Senator John McCain. The incumbent also had to deal with a primary challenge from the right for the second straight cycle. But once McCain won renomination in late August, he never seemed too endangered and ran nearly 6 points ahead of Trump in the presidential battleground. Two other races in Georgia and Iowa had moments when they appeared to be potentially interesting, but GOP incumbent Senators Johnny Isakson (Georgia) and Chuck Grassley (Iowa) each won handily.[10]

As for the other Senate elections in 2016, Democratic incumbents won reelection in Connecticut (Senator Richard Blumenthal), Hawaii (Senator Brian Schatz), New York (the new Senate Minority Leader, Chuck Schumer), Oregon (Senator Ron Wyden), Vermont (Senator Patrick Leahy), and Washington (Senator Patty Murray). Democratic newcomers also retained seats for their party in California (Kamala Harris) and Maryland (Chris Van Hollen), with the Golden State featuring its first Democrat-versus-Democrat statewide election since adopting an open primary system in 2012 where the top-two finishers advance to November regardless of party. Republican incumbents also won reelection in Alaska (Senator Lisa Murkowski), Alabama (Senator Richard Shelby), Arkansas (Senator John Boozman), Idaho (Senator Mike Crapo), Kansas (Senator Jerry Moran), Kentucky (Senator Rand Paul), North Dakota (Senator John Hoeven), Oklahoma (Senator James Lankford), South Carolina (Senator Tim Scott), South Dakota (Senator John Thune), and Utah (Senator Mike Lee). The GOP also won the open-seat race in Louisiana (John Kennedy), leaving Republicans in control of twenty-two of the thirty-four seats that were up in 2016, thus holding Democrats to a net gain of only two seats.

2018: DEMOCRATS ARE VERY EXPOSED

Looking ahead to 2018, the underwhelming Democratic performance in 2016 looms large because any additional seats they might have gained in 2016 could have offset possible 2018 losses on a much worse map for the party. Including the two independents who caucus with the party, Democrats control twenty-five of the thirty-three seats that will be up in 2018 (as of this writing). Of those, ten seats are in states that Trump carried in 2016, including some very red states: Indiana, Missouri, Montana, North Dakota, and West Virginia. To put that level of exposure in historical context, only three times in previous midterm cycles has a party been at least that exposed: Republicans at the start of the 1926 cycle and Democrats at the beginning of the 1938 and 1970 cycles. In the earlier two cases, the overexposed party also controlled the White House and suffered accordingly (net losses of seven and eight seats in 1926 and 1938, respectively). In 1970, Democratic exposure led to a net loss of three seats in part because the GOP controlled the White House. Two opposing forces will be at work in 2018: On the one hand, Republicans could benefit from the high degree of political polarization and take advantage of an expansive target list. On the other hand, Democrats could benefit—or at least limit their losses—because of the negative effect that usually afflicts the president's party in midterm cycles.[11]

THE GOVERNORS: SOME SPLIT TICKETS

As previously noted, a different party won the presidential and gubernatorial races in five of twelve states in 2016, differing notably from the Senate situation. In each case where the presidential party failed to win the concurrent governor's election there were some parochial factors that helped explain the results, as well as at least one case of incumbency coming into play.

In two of the split-ticket cases—Vermont and West Virginia—the party that won the state at the presidential level lost the gubernatorial race quite badly. The Green Mountain State contest featured Republican Lieutenant Governor Phil Scott and Democrat Sue Minter, Vermont's former state secretary of transportation. A moderate Republican—the only kind who can win in Vermont—Scott openly criticized Trump during the campaign and held socially liberal positions on issues such as abortion rights and gay marriage. Outside groups backing Minter went after Scott for being open to signing bills that could limit late-term abortions and abortion access for minors. But Minter struggled because of the unpopularity of outgoing Democratic Governor Peter Shumlin, whom the Republican Governors Association tied to Minter in TV ads. Scott won comfortably by 8.7 points even though Democratic and Progressive Party candidates carried every other statewide office. In the West Virginia contest to succeed Democratic Governor Earl Ray Tomblin, coal magnate Jim Justice ran as a conservative Democrat against Republican State Senate President Bill Cole. In some ways, Justice was the candidate most similar to Trump in the 2016 cycle: a billionaire businessman running a campaign based more on his personality than his politics. Justice also wisely—Trump won the state by nearly 42 points, the largest presidential margin in the state's history—voiced his opposition to Clinton at the top of the Democratic ticket. Cole ran a traditional Republican campaign centered on fiscal and social conservatism. The GOP made huge gains in West Virginia (and other parts of Appalachia) in the Obama era, but had yet to win the Mountain State governorship. But one of the Republicans' strongest pulls for voter support—Democratic opposition to the coal industry—could not work against a coal industry leader like Justice. In the end, the Trump-like Democrat won by about 7 points. In what was probably a shortsighted decision, the GOP-controlled state legislature passed legislation ending straight-ticket voting in 2015—supported by Cole—that became law prior to the 2016 election. While it may not have been decisive, that development likely helped Justice in a year where the GOP presidential nominee won West Virginia by a massive margin.[12]

In contrast to Vermont and West Virginia, two other split-ticket outcomes in New Hampshire and North Carolina proved to be close races. With crowded fields in both the Democratic and Republican primaries and a late primary date (September 13), the Granite State gubernatorial contest to replace outgoing Democratic Governor Maggie Hassan came and went quickly. Executive Councilor Chris Sununu won the GOP nomination by 1 point in a Republican primary race that had four notable candidates. A political scion—his father was governor and a White House chief of staff to President George H. W. Bush, and his brother was a one-term U.S. senator—

Sununu had strong name recognition by default. His opponent was a fellow member of the Executive Council, Democrat Colin Van Ostern. While Van Ostern won about the same percentage of the vote as Clinton at the top of the ticket, Sununu ran 2.4 points ahead of Trump and won the election 48.8 percent to 46.6 percent. Meanwhile, North Carolina had the most hard-fought gubernatorial contest of the cycle, with a fittingly extended ending. Crucial to the contest was incumbent Republican Pat McCrory's decision to sign the controversial House Bill 2 or HB2 into law in late March 2016. The most notable aspect of the new legislation was a provision mandating people to use the bathroom of the gender on their birth certificate, precipitated by a Charlotte's city ordinance that permitted transgender individuals to use the bathroom that matched whichever gender they identified with. In three polls taken from late August to early October, 50 to 55 percent of North Carolinians opposed the new law and 40 percent or fewer supported it. McCrory's electoral opponent, Democratic state Attorney General Roy Cooper, refused to defend the law in court. The incumbent's struggles clearly showed on Election Day compared to the presidential and Senate races: Trump won 49.8 percent, Burr won 51.1 percent, but McCrory only won 48.8 percent. He proved just weak enough to fall to Cooper, who won 49.0 percent (a 0.2-point margin) and ran 2.8 points ahead of Clinton, which meant he won a small but not-insignificant number of Trump and/or Burr voters to narrowly win. But the election didn't end quietly. By the time the final results were in, Cooper led by slightly more than 10,000 votes, the state's threshold for an automatic recount. But McCrory's team requested a recount, challenging results in a number of localities while making unsubstantiated allegations about widespread voter fraud. State and local boards rejected most protests, but the state board of elections ordered a recount in heavily-Democratic Durham County; when it concluded, Cooper gained two net votes. With that, McCrory conceded.[13]

Early in the cycle, Democrats felt somewhat bullish on their chances in Indiana and Missouri, only to see the Republicans win both once all was said and done. In the Hoosier State, 2012 Democratic nominee John Gregg sought a rematch against Republican Governor Mike Pence, who had narrowly defeated Gregg four years earlier. Spurring Gregg was the common view that Pence was somewhat vulnerable, in part because of controversy over a religious freedom bill that Pence signed into law in March 2015. But everything changed in July 2016 when Pence became the GOP's vice presidential nominee. The party's central committee picked Lieutenant Governor Eric Holcomb, who had only held the office since March 2016, to be Pence's replacement. Holcomb actually started the cycle running for the U.S. Senate, then dropped out of that race before becoming lieutenant governor. Gregg led Holcomb in the polls down the stretch, but the GOP nominee benefited from Trump's strong performance at the top of the ticket (and Mike Pence, too). Although Gregg ran 8 points ahead of Clinton, it was far from enough as Holcomb won by 6 points. In the Show Me State's race to succeed outgoing Democratic Governor Jay Nixon, Republicans had a brutal primary campaign that started out very ugly. Having declared his candidacy in January 2015, GOP state Auditor Tom Schweich committed suicide a month later, allegedly in part because of anti-Semitism aimed at him by someone associated with one of his primary opponents (Schweich was ancestrally Jewish, though a practicing Episcopalian). After that, the GOP race eventually developed into a competitive four-way race that ensured a heavily split vote. Perhaps appropriately for 2016, an outsider, nonprofit executive and former Navy SEAL Eric Greitens, won the party's nomination with 34.6 percent of the vote. As compared to the Republican nomination battle, the Democratic race was very straightforward: Attorney General Chris Koster easily won the nomination, which seemed like a smart choice in a red state. Koster was a former Republican and during the campaign he even garnered an unusual Democratic endorsement from the National Rifle Association. Throughout the general election, Koster held a narrow lead in most polls. But on Election Day, Greitens won 51.1 percent to 45.6 percent, likely helped by Trump's dominant win at the top of the ticket. Although Koster, like Kander in the Senate race, ran ahead of Clinton, it was not nearly enough to overcome the Republican edge in Missouri.[14]

Two of the three Democratic incumbents seeking reelection in 2016 were in Montana and Oregon. In Big Sky Country, Democratic Governor Steve Bullock defeated wealthy Republican businessman Greg Gianforte by about four points in 2016's other split-ticket race. Little public polling was available in the Montana contest, so the only expectation was a close race due to the countervailing forces of Bullock's incumbency and the sizable win Trump would have at the top of the ticket. In the end, incumbency narrowly won out, handing Democrats a fourth-straight gubernatorial term in Helena. To the west, appointed Democratic Governor Kate Brown beat Republican Bud Pierce in a special election to complete the term beginning after the 2014 election. In that cycle, then-Governor John Kitzhaber (D) won reelection, only to resign the office in February 2015 because of a public corruption scandal that involved Kitzhaber and his fiancée. Brown, then the Oregon secretary of state, became governor as that post is next in line for the governorship in the Beaver State. Considering Oregon's blue hue—it easily went Democratic at the presidential level and a Republican last won the governorship in 1982—there was never any doubt about the outcome. But Pierce's

2016 bid may simply be the opening act for a 2018 rematch with Brown, as Pierce originally intended to run in 2018 once Kitzhaber retired.[15]

Four other gubernatorial contests took place in 2016, and the incumbent party won in all four. Democratic Governor Jay Inslee won reelection in Washington, while Democratic Representative John Carney won the Delaware race to succeed outgoing Governor Jack Markell, a fellow Democrat. In Utah, incumbent Republican Governor Gary Herbert won reelection, and in North Dakota, Republican software executive Doug Burgum's victory made him the successor to retiring Republican Governor Jack Dalrymple. Overall, the GOP gained two net seats in 2016, leaving them with thirty-three governorships to Democrats' sixteen nationally, with an independent leading Alaska. At thirty-three, the GOP governorship mark is the party's highest total in the post-World War II era. In addition to their gubernatorial gains, Republicans also gained fifty-eight state legislative seats while Democrats lost twenty-seven (the discrepancy is mostly due to filled vacancies and party-switches). But Democrats did gain back one net legislative chamber, when accounting for coalition control in some chambers and a Democratic tie-breaker in the Connecticut State Senate.[16]

A LOOK AHEAD TO 2017 AND 2018

"Given the historical success of the out-of-White House party in gaining governorships, the only cure for what ails Democrats may be a Republican presidency." So went the concluding line of my chapter on the 2014 gubernatorial elections in *The Surge*, our previous post-election book. Now that scenario has possibly begun to take shape with Trump's victory. Looking ahead, the next gubernatorial battles will occur in New Jersey and Virginia in November 2017. The early assessment is that Democrats may be favored in the Garden State because of the unpopularity of outgoing GOP Governor Chris Christie, while Virginia's status is more uncertain. But for a party that suffered a net loss of thirteen governorships and around 950 state legislative seats from Barack Obama's first presidential victory in 2008 to the 2016 election that saw the election of a Republican presidential successor, there may be nowhere to go but up. In the 2018 midterm election, twenty-six Republican-controlled governorships will be up for election versus just nine Democratic ones (as well as one independent in Alaska). Should South Carolina Governor Nikki Haley indeed be confirmed as the new ambassador to the United Nations, half of those twenty-six GOP incumbents will be term-limited, including some in states that are traditionally competitive, such as Florida, Michigan, Nevada, New Mexico, and Ohio. With redistricting on tap after the 2020 census, both parties will be aiming to hold onto or gain important governorships to attain leverage in that vitally important process.[17]

NOTES

1. Author's analysis of data from Stephen Ansolabehere, Cooperative Congressional Election Study, 2008: Common Content, June 19, 2013 release, Cambridge, MA: Harvard University, http://cces.gov.harvard.edu; and Stephen Ansolabehere, Cooperative Congressional Election Study, 2012: Common Content, January 11, 2015 release, Cambridge, MA: Harvard University, http://cces.gov.harvard.edu.

2. Election data, historical and recent, come from three principal sources: *CQ Press Guide to U.S. Elections*, 6th Edition (Washington, DC: CQ Press, 2010); Dave Leip, *Dave Leip's Atlas of U.S. Presidential Elections*, http://uselectionatlas.org/; "Candidate and Constituency Statistics of Elections in the United States, 1788–1990 (ICPSR 7757)," Inter-university Consortium for Political and Social Research (Ann Arbor, MI: Inter-university Consortium for Political and Social Research, 1994). http://doi.org/10.3886/ICPSR07757.v5; state election websites were also used when needed.

3. "Party Polarization 1879–2015 Distance Between the Parties First Dimension" chart on "The Polarization of the Congressional Parties," *Voteview.com*, accessed December 14, 2016, http://voteview.com/political_polarization_2015.htm; for more about the public's role in political polarization, see Alan Abramowitz, *The Polarized Public: Why American Government is So Dysfunctional* (Boston: Pearson, 2012).

4. Ben Kamisar, "Republicans Worry Donald Trump Will Hurt Their Senate Chances," August 25, 2015, http://thehill.com/business-a-lobbying/251849-republicans-worry-trump-will-hurt-senate-chances; "2016 National Republican Primary," *HuffPost Pollster*, http://elections.huffingtonpost.com/pollster/2016-national-gop-primary; "2016 Republican Presidential Nomination," *RealClearPolitics*, http://www.realclearpolitics.com/epolls/2016/president/us/2016_republican_presidential_nomination-3823.html; Seth Masket, "Polls Got Clinton Right; They Got Trump Wrong," *Vox*, November 9, 2016, http://www.vox.com/mischiefs-of-faction/2016/11/9/13574824/polls-clinton-trump.

5. Donovan Slack, "Two Disabled Candidates Locked in Historic Battle," *USA Today*, May 18, 2016, http://www.usatoday.com/story/news/politics/elections/2016/2016/05/17/two-disabled-candidates-locked-historic-battle/84460720/; Paul Feely, "Ayotte 'Role Model' Comment About Trump in Debate Sets Off Internet Firestorm," October 3, 2016, http://www.unionleader.com/voters-first/ayotte-role-model-comment-about-trump-in-debate-sets-off-internet-firestorm-20161003; "2016 New Hampshire Senate: Ayotte vs. Hassan," *HuffPost Pollster*, http://elections.huffingtonpost.com/pollster/2016-new-hampshire-ayotte-vs-hassan; "New Hampshire Senate—Ayotte vs. Hassan," *RealClearPolitics*, http://www.realclearpolitics.com/epolls/2016/senate/nh/new_hampshire_senate_ayotte_vs_hassan-3862.html.

6. "2016 Nevada Senate: Heck vs. Cortez Masto," *HuffPost Pollster*, http://elections.huffingtonpost.com/pollster/2016-nevada-senate-heck-vs-cortez-masto; "Nevada Senate—Heck vs. Cortez Masto," *RealClearPolitics*, http://www.realclearpolitics.com/epolls/2016/senate/nv/nevada_senate_heck_vs_cortez_masto-5982.html; "Colorado Senate Race

Summary Data," Center for Responsive Politics, https://www.opensecrets.org/races/sum mary.php?id = COS1&cycle = 2016.

7. "2016 Pennsylvania Senate: Toomey vs. McGinty," *HuffPost Pollster*, http://elec tions.huffingtonpost.com/pollster/2016-pennsylvania-senate-toomey-vs-mcginty; "Pennsylvania Senate—Toomey vs. McGinty," *RealClearPolitics*, http://www.realclearpolitics .com/epolls/2016/senate/pa/pennsylvania_senate_toomey_vs_mcginty-5074.html; "Wisconsin Senate—Johnson vs. Feingold," *RealClearPolitics*, http://www.realclearpolitics .com/epolls/2016/senate/wi/wisconsin_senate_johnson_vs_feingold-3740.html.

8. Eli Stokols, "Rubio Suspends Presidential Campaign," *Politico*, March 15, 2016, http://www.politico.com/story/2016/03/rubio-suspends-presidential-campaign-220827; Marco Rubio, Twitter post, May 16, 2016, 10:44 p.m., https://twitter.com/marcorubio/ status/732401466066014209; Manu Raju, "Rubio Faces Pressure to Run for Re-Election as GOP Fears Grow Over His Senate Seat," CNN, May 28, 2016, http://www.cnn.com/ 2016/05/25/politics/marco-rubio-florida-senate-race/; Jim DeFede, "The Making of Patrick Murphy," CBSMiami, June 22, 2016, http://miami.cbslocal.com/2016/06/22/the -making-of-patrick-murphy/; "Florida Senate Race Outside Spending," Center for Responsive Politics, https://www.opensecrets.org/races/indexp.php?cycle = 2016&id = FLS2 &spec = N; Exit Poll, "Florida Senate," CNN, last updated November 23, 2016, http:// edition.cnn.com/election/results/exit-polls/florida/senate; Harper Neidig, "Bayh Jumps into Indiana Senate Race," *The Hill*, July 13, 2016, http://thehill.com/blogs/ballot-box/ senate-races/287526-bayh-officially-announces-senate-campaign; Seung Min Kim, "The Collapse of Evan Bayh," *Politico*, October 23, 2016, http://www.politico.com/story/2016/ 10/evan-bayh-indiana-senate-todd-young-230196.

9. Eli Yokley, "Will Kander's Attacks on Blunt's Family Business Work?" *Morning Consult*, October 4, 2016, https://morningconsult.com/2016/10/04/will-kanders-attacks -blunts-family-business-work/; Josh Kraushaar, "Exclusive: Senate Republicans Barely Surviving Trump Collapse," *National Journal*, October 18, 2016, https://www.national journal.com/s/643658/exclusive-senate-republicans-barely-surviving-trump-collapse; Scott Canon, "Jason Kander Wants You to Know He's Running for Senate as a Veteran," *Kansas City Star*, October 14, 2016, http://www.kansascity.com/news/politics-gov ernment/article108302532.html; Alexis Levinson, "Is Richard Burr Sailing into the Perfect Storm?" *National Review*, August 18, 2016, http://www.nationalreview.com/article/ 439132/richard-burr-reelection-campaign-struggles; "North Carolina: Trump vs. Clinton vs. Johnson," *RealClearPolitics*,http://www.realclearpolitics.com/epolls/2016/president/ nc/north_carolina_trump_vs_clinton_vs_johnson-59 51.html; "2016 North Carolina Senate: Burr vs. Ross," *HuffPost Pollster*, http://elections.huffingtonpost.com/pollster/2016 -north-carolina-senate-burr-vs-ross; "North Carolina Senate—Burr vs. Ross," *RealClearPolitics*, http://www.realclearpolitics.com/epolls/2016/senate/nc/north_carolina_senate _burr_vs_d_ross-5693.html; Mike DeBonis, "Burr's North Carolina Duel Could Determine Whether Republicans Keep the Senate," *Washington Post*, October 25, 2016, https:// www.washingtonpost.com/news/powerpost/wp/2016/10/25/burrs-north-carolina-duel -could-determine-whether-republicans-keep-the-senate/?utm_term = .20bed23e3029.

10. Andrea Drusch, "How Rob Portman Went from Unknown to Reelection Favorite," *National Journal*, September 6, 2016, https://www.nationaljournal.com/s/641379/how -rob-portman-went-from-unknown-reelection-favorite; Henry J. Gomez, "Ted Strickland Steps into Controversy by Cheering the Timing of Justice Antonin Scalia's Death," *Plain*

Dealer, August 10, 2016, http://www.cleveland.com/open/index.ssf/2016/08/ted_strickland_
steps_into_cont.html; "2016 Arizona Senate: McCain vs. Kirkpatrick," *HuffPost Pollster*,
http://elections.huffingtonpost.com/pollster/2016-arizona-senate-mccain-vs-kirkpatrick.

11. Kyle Kondik and Geoffrey Skelley, "2018 Senate: The Democrats Are Very
Exposed," *Sabato's Crystal Ball*, December 8, 2016, http://www.centerforpolitics.org/
crystalball/articles/2018-senate-democrats-are-very-exposed/.

12. David A. Lieb, "Governor Hopefuls Distancing Themselves from Clinton, Trump,"
AP, October 1, 2016, http://bigstory.ap.org/article/8c0b48477eb04b4fb8ff1f5feba59ab5/
governor-hopefuls-distancing-themselves-clinton-trump; Dave Gram, "Abortion Becomes
Issue in Race for Governor," *Burlington Free Press (AP)*, October 31, 2016, http://
www.burlingtonfreepress.com/story/news/politics/2016/10/31/abortion-issue-vermont
-governor-race/93091636/; Bob Kinzel, "In a Tight Race for Governor, Can Sue Minter
Distance Herself from Peter Shumlin?" Vermont Public Radio, October 24, 2016, http://
digital.vpr.net/post/tight-race-governor-can-sue-minter-distance-herself-peter-shumlin;
Mason Adams, "Is West Virginia Holding America's Weirdest Election?" *Politico Magazine*, http://www.politico.com/magazine/story/2016/09/west-virginia-2016-governor-coal
-cole-justice-214268; Shauna Johnson, "Ahead of General Election, Secretary of State
Reminds Voters Straight-Ticket Voting Is No More," *MetroNews*, September 15, 2016,
http://wvmetronews.com/2016/09/15/ahead-of-general-election-secretary-of-state-re
minds-voters-straight-ticket-voting-is-no-more/; "Senate Bill 249," West Virginia Legislature, 2015 Regular Session, http://www.legis.state.wv.us/bill_status/bills_history.cfm?
INPUT = 249&year = 2015&sessiontype = RS.

13. Will Doran, "Roundup of HB2 Fact Checks: North Carolina's Controversial New
LGBT Law," PolitiFact North Carolina, April 22, 2016, http://www.politifact.com/north
-carolina/article/2016/apr/22/roundup-hb2-fact-checks-north-carolinas-controvers/; "Prez
and Senate Races Tight; HB2 Drag on Gov. McCrory Re-Elect Bid," Monmouth University Polling Institute, August 24, 2016, https://www.monmouth.edu/polling-institute/
reports/MonmouthPoll_NC_082416/; "Elon Poll: N.C. Voters Oppose HB2, Razor-Thin
Margins in Governor, U.S. Senate Races," Elon University Poll, September 19, 2016,
https://www.elon.edu/E/elon-poll/poll-archive/091916.xhtml; "Results of SurveyUSA
Election Poll #23184," SurveyUSA-WRAL-TV poll, October 4, 2016, http://www.wral
.com/asset/news/state/nccapitol/2016/10/04/16082184/WRAL_News_poll.pdf; David A.
Graham, "The North Carolina Governor's Race Is Finally Over," *The Atlantic*, December
5, 2016, https://www.theatlantic.com/politics/archive/2016/12/north-carolina-governor
-pat-mccrory-concedes-to-roy-cooper/509603/.

14. Ed Payne, "Indiana Religious Freedom Restoration Act: What You Need to Know,"
CNN, March 31, 2015, http://www.cnn.com/2015/03/31/politics/indiana-backlash-how
-we-got-here/; Brian Eason, Tony Cook, and James Briggs, "Indiana GOP Panel Nomi-
nates Eric Holcomb for Governor," *Indianapolis Star*, July 26, 2016, http://www
.indystar.com/story/news/politics/2016/07/26/live-updates-indiana-republicans-meet-to
day-pick-pences-replacement/87540124/; "Indiana Governor - Holcomb vs. Gregg," *Real-
ClearPolitics*, http://www.realclearpolitics.com/epolls/2016/governor/in/indiana_governor
_holcomb_vs_gregg-6097.html; Tony Cook, "Eric Holcomb Defeats John Gregg for Indiana Governor," *Indianapolis Star*, November 9, 2016, http://www.indystar.com/story/
news/politics/2016/11/08/election-results-2016-indiana-governor-race-winner/93241306/;
Thomas Lake, "A Fragile Man, Political Whispers and a Pair of Suicides in Missouri,"

Washington Post, April 15, 2015, https://www.washingtonpost.com/national/a-fragile-man -whispered-innuendo-and-two-suicides-in-missouri/2015/04/15/fbb4c114-dedc-11e4-be40 -566e2653afe5_story.html; Nick Gass, "NRA endorses Democrat for Missouri governor," *Politico*, September 6, 2016, http://www.politico.com/story/2016/09/nra-endorses-chris -koster-227771; "2016 Missouri Governor: Greitens vs. Koster," *HuffPost Pollster*, http:// elections.huffingtonpost.com/pollster/2016-missouri-governor-greitens-vs-koster; "Missouri Governor - Greitens vs. Koster," *RealClearPolitics*, http://www.realclearpolitics.com/ epolls/2016/governor/mo/missouri_governorgreitens_vs_koster-5627.html.

15. Laura Gunderson, "Governor John Kitzhaber announces his resignation," *The Oregonian*, February 13, 2015, http://www.oregonlive.com/politics/index.ssf/2015/02/gover nor_john_kitzhaber_will_s.html; Chris Lehman, "When the 4-Year Plan Turns Into A 2-Year Scramble: Pierce's Run for Governor," Oregon Public Radio, October 24, 2016, http://www.opb.org/news/series/election-2016/bud-pierce-oregon-governor-campaign -who-is/.

16. "State & Legislative Partisan Composition (Pre-election)," National Conference of State Legislatures, November 7, 2016, http://www.ncsl.org/Portals/1/Documents/Elec tions/Legis_Control_2016_Nov7.pdf; "State & Legislative Partisan Composition (2016 Election)," National Conference of State Legislatures, December 15, 2016, http://www .ncsl.org/portals/1/documents/elections/Legis_Control_2016_Post12_15_11am.pdf.

17. Geoffrey Skelley, "It's Good to Be a Republican," in *The Surge*, ed. Larry Sabato (Lanham, Maryland: Rowman & Littlefield, 2015), 104.

4

House 2016: The Republicans Endure

But Does a Change in the White House Threaten Their Majority?

Kyle Kondik

Following the Republicans' huge wave election in the 2010 midterm, when they netted 63 House seats and won control of the U.S. House of Representatives back from Democrats after losing it in 2006, the GOP held 242 seats in the 435-seat chamber. Two presidential elections and one midterm later, they went into 2017 holding 241 seats. The Democrats have made little progress in breaking through in the House since 2010, although it may be that Donald Trump winning the White House will eventually provide to them the path they've been searching for back to the House majority. Or at least, that's what history suggests *could* happen.

But before looking ahead to 2018, let's look back at what happened in 2016.

As with the presidential race and the battle for the Senate in 2016, there's really no way to frame the race for the House as anything other than a disappointment for Democrats and a triumph for Republicans.

Democrats ended up gaining six net seats in 2016. While it never appeared the Democrats were ever close to winning the 30 net seats they needed to win the House majority, House generic ballot polling—national surveys asking voters which party they intended to vote for in their local House race—generally showed a modest lead for Democrats throughout the cycle, and many seat-by-seat analyses suggested a Democratic gain of more like somewhere in the low double digits. They ended up falling considerably short of even that.

Even the seemingly impressive feat of a party netting House seats during a presidential election their party is losing is rather common: The party that lost the White House actually netted House seats in many recent presidential elections: 1956, 1960, 1988, 1992, 2000, and 2016. That's a third of the eighteen presidential elections since the end of World War II. Three of those elections are among the closest of all time—1960, 2000, and 2016—and it's no surprise that a close presidential outcome could lead to seemingly contradictory results down the ballot.

Meanwhile, the Republicans held the Democrats to minimal gains and won the national popular vote for the U.S. House by about a percentage point, 49.1 percent to 48 percent.[1]

Republicans won 55.4 percent of all the seats with slightly less than half of the votes cast, continuing a fairly persistent trend over the last two decades where Republicans generally win a higher share of the seats than their share of the House popular vote would indicate. Democrats generally outperformed their share of the vote prior to 1994, the big Republican wave year that gave the GOP control of the House for the first time in forty years. Prior to 1994, the Democrats had held the House for sixty of sixty-four years; since 1994 and continuing at least through the end of 2018, Republicans will have held the House for twenty of twenty-four years. Part of the reason for this, at least in this decade, is redistricting: Republicans controlled the redistricting process in many more states than Democrats following the 2010 elections and census, which allowed them to reinforce the gains they made in the 2010 midterm.

The 6-seat Democratic improvement in 2016 might have been even less than that had it not been for (1) the fact that the Republicans were overextended in the House at 247 seats, which was their biggest majority since right before the Great Depression and (2) new court-ordered congressional maps in Florida and Virginia that helped Democrats make gains they might not have otherwise made on the prior maps in those states.

The redistricting in those two states is as good a place as any to start with the story of the 2016 House elections. They provided a glimmer of hope for Democrats in an election that would end up disappointing them.

COURT RULINGS IN FLORIDA AND VIRGINIA ALLOW DEMOCRATIC GAINS

Following big victories in gubernatorial, U.S. House, and state legislative races in 2010, Republicans were well-positioned after the decennial census to control redistricting following the reapportionment of the nation's 435 House seats. Two states where Republicans ended up drawing favorable maps were Florida and Virginia. Both states would vote for Barack Obama for president twice in 2008 and 2012, but following the 2014 midterms, Republicans held advantages of 8 to 3 in Virginia's 11-seat House delegation and 17 to 10 in Florida's 27 seat delegation.

However, court cases in both states would unwind the maps in both states and give Democrats some opportunities to make up ground.

In 2010, Florida voters approved a state constitutional amendment that prohibited state legislators from taking partisan data into account when drawing districts. The Florida Supreme Court ruled in 2015 that the Republican-controlled state legislature violated the "Fair Districts" parameters and eventually adopted a map that benefited Democrats. The map dramatically redrew the district held by Republican Representative Daniel Webster, the Tenth District, making it a Democratic district that Democrat Val Demings would ultimately win in November (Webster survived by running in the Eleventh District, held by retiring Republican Representative Richard Nugent).

The new map also made Republican Representative David Jolly's Thirteenth District more Democratic. Jolly, who was first elected in a nationally watched special election in early 2014, ran for the Senate, but then he decided to run for reelection after Senator Marco Rubio's belated decision to run for reelection following Rubio's failed Republican presidential primary bid. Jolly would end up losing a close race to Democrat Charlie Crist, a former Republican who had served as governor.

The Seventh District, held by Republican Representative John Mica, also became more Democratic following the redistricting, and he ended up losing to Democrat Stephanie Murphy in another very competitive November contest.

The map wasn't all good for Democrats, though: the district of Representative Gwen Graham, a Democrat who had won a very difficult race in a conservative-leaning district in 2014, became much more Republican in the remap, and she opted against running for reelection.

In Virginia, a federal district court eventually drew a new congressional map after Democrats successfully argued that Republicans had packed too many African-American voters into Democratic Representative Bobby Scott's Third District. This created changes to several surrounding districts in and around Greater Richmond and Hampton Roads, with the biggest change coming in Republican Representative Randy Forbes' Fourth Congressional District, which became a heavily Democratic district. Forbes decided to run for reelection in the Second District, which was open because Republican Representative Scott Rigell was retiring (Forbes would lose the Republican primary). Meanwhile, Democratic state Senator Donald McEachin would win the revamped Fourth.

Ultimately, one could argue that half of the Democrats' total 6-seat national net gain came from the two new maps in Virginia and Florida (a third state, North Carolina, also had to draw new districts, but the changes didn't lead to any net changes in the state's ten to three Republican congressional majority). Thanks in large part to the remap, Democrats picked up Florida's Seventh, Tenth, and Thirteenth districts while losing the Second, and they also netted the Fourth District in Virginia. That works out to a net gain of 3 seats, meaning that the Democrats likely would have had an even more disappointing general election had it not been for the courts throwing out the Florida and Virginia maps.

THE HOUSE PLAYING FIELD

Even under the new maps in Florida and Virginia, 2012 Republican presidential nominee Mitt Romney still carried 224 of the nation's 435 House districts despite losing to Democratic President Barack Obama by about four percentage points. Twenty-eight districts held by Republicans voted for Obama, while just five districts held by Democrats voted for Romney.

In order to try to win back the majority, Democrats identified many of the Obama-district Republicans to target. The Democratic Congressional Campaign Committee focused on several Republican incumbents whom they had either tried and failed to defeat in 2012 and 2014, such as Representative Mike Coffman of Colorado's Sixth District, or newer members from districts that appeared winnable, such as Representatives Carlos Curbelo of Florida's Twenty-sixth District or Barbara Comstock of Virginia's Tenth District, two first-term members who had won expensive, high-profile races in 2014. Coffman, Curbelo, and Comstock, among others, are good examples of the kinds of districts Democrats ended up prioritizing: districts that Obama had won or had come close to winning that were either suburban and/or had a high percentage of nonwhite residents. At the presidential level, Democrats often perform best in densely populated areas and among nonwhite voters.

In focusing on these districts, Democrats largely wrote off some of the less densely populated, whiter districts that at one time had been a vital part of their House majority. Even as late as 2014, Democrats were strongly competing for districts such as West Virginia's Second District and Arkansas's Second District, districts that had voted strongly for Mitt Romney in 2012. But Democrats would lose in both of those districts in 2014, and they lost a number of southern and Appalachian districts in 2010, 2012, and 2014, including 3 net seats in Arkansas, two in West Virginia, three in Tennessee, two in Mississippi, and five in North Carolina (thanks in large part to Republicans gerrymandering the state after 2010 after Democrats had redistricted the state to their advantage the previous decade). In 2016, Democrats did not really go after seats in any of these states, judging these districts to be too conservative to compete in. Instead, Democrats largely looked to Obama-won seats that were either diverse or suburban—seats like those held by the aforementioned Coffman, Comstock, and Curbelo.

The nomination of Donald Trump for president made this appear to be a shrewd strategy. Trump was strongest among white voters who did not hold a college degree, and he did not appear to be a candidate who would make any inroads with nonwhite voters, who were already overwhelmingly Democratic. Trump also seemed weak with white college voters, many of whom reside in swingy suburban House districts—precisely the kinds of districts the Democrats were now targeting.

Unfortunately for Democrats, Trump's nomination, which he effectively locked up in early May 2016, came too late for them to recruit challengers in some targeted districts in time to meet filing deadlines. But some candidates did enter the race late, such as Democrat Terri Bonoff, a Minnesota state senator who in April 2016 announced that she would run against Representative Erik Paulsen, a Republican who represented an affluent, highly educated swing district in the Twin Cities' suburbs. Democrats also hoped a Trump effect would help them spring upsets in some other similar districts, like that of Representative Kevin Yoder of Kansas, whose district in the Kansas City suburbs also seemed problematic for Republicans in the time of Trump. Democratic challenger Jay Sidie, a newcomer businessman, was another candidate who entered the campaign late and who ended up getting national attention.

At 247 seats, Republicans did not have that many opportunities to play offense. However, they did have a few places to target. Graham's seat in Florida seemed like an easy pickup thanks to redistricting, and her decision not to run for reelection made it even easier. Outside of redistricting, Democratic Representative Patrick Murphy's decision to run for U.S. Senate opened up his Eighteenth District, which had voted for Romney in 2012. Republicans also had a few Democratic incumbents to target who had won razor-thin victories in 2014: Representatives Brad Ashford of Nebraska's Second District, Ami Bera of California's Seventh District, and Rick Nolan of Minnesota's Eighth District. Ashford had defeated a very unpopular Republican incumbent, Lee Terry, in 2014, and Bera and Nolan had defeated Republican incumbents in 2012 and then hung on to be reelected in 2014. Nolan, in particular, would face a real challenge: It became clear after Trump won the nomination that he had particular appeal in Nolan's white, working-class district. That was just one of the many districts that would swing wildly from its 2012 presidential results in 2016.

THE PRIMARY SEASON

While Trump winning the Republican presidential nomination made 2016 a year of the outsider in presidential politics, nearly all House incumbents who sought renomination won it. Of 393 House incumbents who ran for reelection, just 5 lost primaries. And there are clear reasons for all of those primary losses.

The aforementioned redistricting in Florida, North Carolina, and Virginia accounted for three of the five incumbent losses. Representatives Corrine Brown of Florida's Fifth District, Renee Ellmers of North Carolina's Second District, and Randy Forbes of Virginia's Fourth District all saw their districts radically transformed, contributing to their losses against primary foes. The other two incumbent losers, Representatives Chaka Fattah of Pennsylvania's Second District and Tim Huelskamp of Kansas's First District, had unique problems. Fattah ran under indictment—he would eventually be sentenced to ten years in prison on bribery and federal corruption charges—and lost to longtime state Representative Dwight Evans in the Democratic primary. Huelskamp, meanwhile, angered agriculture interests in his farm-heavy district. His defeat turned the familiar Republican primary dynamic of the 2010s on its head: here was a very conservative member who was defeated by less conservative, establishment forces, as opposed to the other way around.

In all other districts, the incumbents won renomination.

One notable result near the end of the primary season came in California, which uses a "top-two" primary where all the candidates compete together and the top two finishers advance to the general election. Representative Darrell Issa of California's Forty-ninth District won his primary by only about five points over unheralded Democrat Doug Applegate, foreshadowing a very competitive reelection battle for Issa, one of the wealthiest members of Congress and a longtime antagonist of the Obama administration. Another noteworthy contest was Representative Debbie Wasserman Schultz's Democratic primary in Florida's Twenty-third district. Wasserman Schultz, who also served as chair of the Democratic National Committee before resigning right before the Democratic National Convention because of leaked emails that showed the party favoring Hillary Clinton over Bernie Sanders in the primary, faced Tim Canova, a Sanders-endorsed outsider who sought to turn the race into a proxy war between the Clinton and Sanders forces. Wasserman Schultz won, but by only a fairly weak 57 percent to 43 percent margin. It was fair to wonder going into 2017, as Democrats were exiled into the political wilderness, whether Democrats might see more of the party infighting in primaries that previously was more common on the Republican side during the Obama years.

Unrelated to primaries, one thing that 2016 lacked was an attention-grabbing, highly competitive special election. In recent years, there have typically been at least one big special election that generates headlines and is usually (over)interpreted to have meaning for the upcoming general election. These included dueling victories by a Democrat and a Republican in New York districts that favored the opposite party in 2011 and the aforementioned Jolly's upset win in his Tampa Bay-area seat that some argued foreshadowed the Republicans' successful midterm later in 2014. While there were a handful of special elections in the 2015–2016 cycle, including one for the seat of Republican House Speaker John Boehner in Ohio's Eighth Congressional District after he surprisingly left the House in late 2015, none of them were strongly contested by the two parties.

Of the 42 members who did not seek reelection—Boehner himself is not included in the tally because his Republican predecessor, Warren Davidson, was elected prior to the November general election and thus counted as an incumbent seeking reelection—25 were Republicans and 17 were Democrats, not exactly a lopsided total in favor of the Democrats once one remembers that Republicans won a 59-seat majority in the House in 2014. That Republicans ended up having so many incumbents running for reelection ended up helping them. Prior to the election, Emory University's Alan Abramowitz[2] and Brigham Young University's Michael Barber[3] both argued that incumbency, and not gerrymandering, accounted for most of the GOP's advantage going into the 2016 House election. Even taking into account the 25 Republicans who for one reason or another did not run for reelection and the 3 Republicans who lost primaries, Republicans had 219 incumbents running for reelection on Election Day 2016, one more than the bare minimum needed for a House majority (218). Ultimately, that alone left them well-defended against a potential Democratic wave, a wave that never materialized.

LITTLE CHANGE DESPITE MASSIVE SWINGS AT THE TOP OF THE TICKET

By the end of the national campaign the winds started to blow ever so slightly in the Republicans' direction. Of fifty-three surveys of the House generic ballot conducted in 2016 that were included in the *RealClearPolitics*' polling database, only seven did not show the Democrats leading. But two of those were among the last three released in the campaign—*Bloomberg* showed the Republicans leading by three points, and *Fox News* had the Republicans up one.[4]

It's difficult to prove with any certainty, but one wonders if the belief by prognosticators and the public that Clinton would win the presidency might have contributed to the Democrats' ultimately underwhelming performance in the House. In a pre-election article, Columbia University's Robert Erikson argued that "politically informed voters are more likely to vote for Congress against the party that they believe will win the presidency."[5] Betting markets had Clinton as a heavy favorite throughout the election. For instance, the PredictIt market listed Clinton as an 82 percent favorite to win on the eve of the election, and others had similar odds. Additionally, polls asking voters who they believed would win the election generally showed that the public perceived Clinton as a likely winner. For instance, University of Southern California Dornsife/*Los Angeles Times* "Daybreak" survey, which often showed better results for Trump than other surveys, had Trump leading by three points nationally right before the election. However, the poll also asked participants to predict the winner, and they favored Clinton by a ten-point margin. So it's possible that some voters thought Clinton would win and engaged in "anticipatory balancing," as Erikson calls it, to vote Republican down the ballot to put a check on Clinton, assuming she would win the White House.

In any event, Republicans won the national House popular vote by a little more than one point, meaning that in terms of margin, the combined GOP candidates ran about three points ahead of Trump, who lost nationally by two points. Again, there are probably lots of reasons for this: Republicans had more incumbents, more favorable maps in more places, and arguably had the political winds at their backs on Election Day.

As noted above, redistricting probably accounted for half of the Democrats' six-seat net gain. The other Republican incumbents they defeated in 2016 had problems specific to either them or their districts that left them exposed.

Republican Representative Robert Dold first won his Chicagoland Tenth District in the Republican wave of 2010. Democrat Brad Schneider narrowly defeated him in 2012, and then Dold came back and beat Schneider under more favorable conditions in 2014. Schneider again challenged Dold in 2016, and the incumbent, who was one of the most moderate members of the Republican caucus, was clearly hurt by Trump. Dold's affluent and highly educated district, which already had a significant Democratic lean, became even more Democratic in 2016: Barack Obama won it 58 percent to 41 percent, but Clinton carried it by almost thirty points.[6] Dold ran far ahead of Trump in the district, but the hole Trump put Dold in was too deep: He lost by five to Schneider. Democrats also defeated Representative Cresent Hardy, a somewhat accidental winner in Nevada's Fourth District in 2014. Hardy looked like one of the most vulnerable House members the whole cycle, although Democratic state Senator Ruben Kihuen ended up beating him by about four points, roughly matching Clinton's margin of victory in the district. Unlike Dold, Hardy wasn't able to generate much of any ticket-splitting.

Scandals of different sorts hurt two other Republican incumbent losers, Representatives Frank Guinta of New Hampshire's First District and Scott Garrett of New Jersey's Fifth District. Trump ended up narrowly carrying both districts in the presidential race, but that was not enough to save the incumbents.

Guinta, who faced Democrat Carol Shea-Porter for the fourth straight time in 2016 (Guinta beat her in 2010 and 2014, but lost to her in 2012), was dogged by a campaign finance scandal, and Shea-Porter beat him by roughly a point and a half. Garrett, meanwhile, found himself at odds with both national Republicans and his traditional backers on Wall Street—Garrett chaired a key subcommittee that dealt with the financial industry—by refusing to support the National Republican Congressional Committee because the NRCC had supported gay candidates. Colorful Democratic Representative Bill Pascrell of New Jersey once said, "I believe Scott, with all due respect, is to the right of Attila the Hun."[7] A spirited campaign by Democrat Josh Gottheimer, a former speechwriter for President Clinton who excited national Democrats, dislodged Garrett, who did not end up getting any support from the NRCC in his race.

Otherwise, Democrats came up short in several other targeted districts, such as an open seat in the Twin Cities' suburbs that appeared as though it might become more Democratic because of Trump (it did not, and Trump narrowly carried it), as well as their late-breaking challenge against Darrell Issa in California's Forty-ninth District. Issa hung on by a point despite his district swinging to Clinton. Overall, five districts that Mitt Romney had won in 2012 in California flipped to Clinton, meaning that Clinton won forty-six of the mega-state's fifty-three districts. But Democrats did not gain any House seats from California, though they did hold on to their already lopsided thirty-nine to fourteen advantage in the state's House delegation. Clinton ran significantly ahead of Obama's 2012 performance in districts the Democrats heavily targeted, like Mike Coffman's Sixth District in Colorado, Barbara Comstock's Tenth District in Virginia, and Carlos Curbelo's Twenty-sixth

District in Florida, but those incumbents all ended up winning fairly comfortable victories (Comstock's roughly six-point win was the smallest of the three).

Republicans contained their losses by defeating one Democratic incumbent, Brad Ashford of Nebraska's Second District, and also capturing an open seat, Florida's Eighteenth District (this district was not changed by redistricting, so it's not included in the redistricting calculations made above). They narrowly came up short against the two other Democratic incumbents they heavily targeted, Ami Bera of California's Seventh District and Rick Nolan of Minnesota's Eighth.

Nolan's victory was especially impressive given the massive shift at the presidential level in his district—indeed, Minnesota itself helped illustrate a dynamic seen across the Midwest. Obama had won Nolan's historically Democratic Iron Range district by six points in 2012, but Trump carried it by an eye-popping sixteen points, more than a twenty-point change in margin. Such huge swings were common in districts in white, working-class rural areas and small cities across the Rust Belt. Elsewhere in Minnesota, the First and Seventh districts swung sixteen and twenty-one points, respectively, toward the Republicans at the presidential level, leading to much closer-than-expected victories by the two districts' respective Democratic incumbents, Collin Peterson and Tim Walz. Elsewhere in Minnesota, Representative Erik Paulsen's Twin Cities-based Third District, which has a high median income and education level, went from a district Obama won by one point to one Clinton won by more than eight, though Paulsen won by fourteen points.

Overall, 97 percent (380 of 393) of incumbents who sought another term won both their primaries and general elections.

Despite big shifts across the nation's congressional map, both toward and away from the Democrats, the net change in the House, six seats for the Democrats, ended up being relatively minor. This has become the norm in recent presidential elections: in seven of the last eight presidential elections, the net change in the House elections conducted those years has been in the single digits. The exception was 2008, when Barack Obama and the Democrats netted twenty-three seats amidst President George W. Bush's massive unpopularity and a collapsing economy. In recent times, the years with bigger shifts in the House have been midterms, particularly 1994 and 2010, when Republicans netted fifty-four and sixty-three seats, respectively, to flip the House, and 2006, when Democrats netted thirty seats and took control of the House.

With that in mind, let's look ahead to the 2018 midterm.

PEEKING AHEAD AT 2018

In recapping the 2014 House elections in *The Surge: 2014's Big GOP Win and What It Means for the Next Presidential Election*, I suggested that in order to win back the House, House Democrats might actually have to "root for the other party in the 2016 presidential race . . . because given what we know about midterm elections almost always going against the president's party in the House, perhaps the next best chance for the Democrats to win the House will be in 2018—*if* a Republican in the White House."[8]

Midterm elections often end up being a negative referendum on the president's party. There have been thirty-nine midterm elections since the start of the Civil War in 1860. The president's party has lost ground in the House in thirty-six of those midterms, and the average seat loss is high: thirty-three seats. With a 241 to 194 majority in the House, Democrats need to net 24 seats to win the House. That's within the historical average, so hypothetically it's possible. Much will depend on the state of the nation and the economy and, perhaps most importantly, what President Trump's approval rating is. If Americans do not like the direction of his administration, it's possible that districts that seemed safe for Republicans could become competitive. At the same time, if Trump is doing well, Republicans could limit their losses or perhaps even gain seats, as Democrats did in 1998 with Bill Clinton in the White House and Republicans did in 2002 with George W. Bush as president, two of the rare instances where the president's party did not lose ground in the House during a midterm. Those years, admittedly, featured extraordinary circumstances: The public seemed to think Republicans were overreaching on impeaching Clinton over his affair with an intern, particularly in what otherwise was a time of peace and prosperity, and Democrats had a hard time making up ground in 2002 in the wake of the September 11 attacks and the lead-up to the war in Iraq. Will we see similarly extraordinary circumstances in 2018? Who knows?

One wrinkle, though, is that the Trump election may signal some changes in the House map. Republicans will have to decide whether they want to compete in some typically Democratic districts across the Midwest and Rust Belt that moved heavily toward Trump in 2016. That includes the aforementioned Minnesota districts as well as several others, including Illinois' Seventeenth District (held by Democratic Representative Cheri Bustos) and Pennsylvania's Seventeenth District (held by Democratic Representative Matt Cartwright).

On the flip side, Democrats will have to determine whether they can compete in some typically Republican suburban districts that swung heavily toward Clinton in 2016.

A good example is Georgia's Sixth District in the Atlanta suburbs. Romney carried the seat 61 percent to 37 percent in 2012, but Trump only won it 48 percent to 47 percent in 2016. Its representative, Tom Price, was as of this writing in line to become secretary of Health and Human Services in the Trump administration. Assuming Price was confirmed, a special election in early 2017 might provide some clues as to whether Democrats can compete in such a district in the Trump era.

As they prepare for 2018, Democrats might be wise to cast a wide net. In the party's successful 2006 midterm, hard-charging then-Representative Rahm Emanuel of Illinois, who later became the mayor of Chicago, aggressively recruited moderate candidates in Republican-leaning districts, which helped Democrats capitalize on Bush's unpopularity in the 2006 midterm. Some Democrats are upset with House Minority Leader Nancy Pelosi, who holds a seat in liberal San Francisco, who has presided over four straight disappointing House elections. The failure of Democrats to truly threaten the GOP majority in recent years prompted Representative Tim Ryan, who holds a white, working-class seat in Ohio's Mahoning Valley where Trump performed far better than Romney had four years prior, to challenge Pelosi in leadership elections held after the November election. Pelosi won, but Ryan won the support of about a third of the Democratic caucus, suggesting some dissension among the Democratic ranks.

Overall, twelve Democrats now sit in districts that Trump won in the presidential race, and twenty-three Republicans occupy seats that Clinton won. As both parties begin to recruit candidates for 2018 and determine where they are going to make investments, these seats are likely the ones that will be at the front of their minds. Unfortunately for Democrats, the Republicans are not that much more overextended into blue turf than Democrats are into red turf despite holding considerably more seats. Still, they can only hope that the midterm dynamic that broke so decisively against them in 2010 and 2014 works in their favor now that there is a Republican in the White House.

NOTES

1. David Wasserman, Ally Flinn, and Ashton Barry, "2016 National House Popular Vote Tracker," *Cook Political Report*, https://docs.google.com/spreadsheets/d/1oArjXS Yeg40u4qQRR93qveN2N1UELQ6v04_mamrKg9g/edit#gid = 0. All House results in this chapter are compiled from this document.

2. Alan Abramowitz, "Incumbency, Not Republican Gerrymandering, Is the Main Obstacle to a Democratic House Majority," *Sabato's Crystal Ball*, November 3, 2016, http://www.centerforpolitics.org/crystalball/articles/incumbency-not-republican-gerry mandering-is-the-main-obstacle-to-a-democratic-house-majority/

3. Michael Barber, "How incumbency, not gerrymandering, may protect the Republican House majority," *Washington Post*, October 27, 2016, https://www.washingtonpost .com/news/monkey-cage/wp/2016/10/27/how-incumbency-not-gerrymandering-may-pro tect-the-republican-house-majority/?utm_term = .4b483c0d8686.

4. "2016 Generic Congressional Vote," *RealClearPolitics*, http://www.realclearpoli tics.com/epolls/other/2016_generic_congressional_vote-5279.html.

5. Robert S. Erikson, "Congressional Elections in Presidential Years: Presidential Coattails and Strategic Voting," *Legislative Studies Quarterly*, May 24, 2016, http://online library.wiley.com/doi/10.1111/lsq.12127/abstract.

6. David Nir, "Daily Kos Elections' presidential results by congressional district for the 2016 and 2012 elections," Daily Kos Elections, http://www.dailykos.com/story/2012/ 11/19/1163009/-Daily-Kos-Elections-presidential-results-by-congressional-district-for -the-2012-2008-elections.

7. Herb Jackson, "Congressional culture clash: Conservative icon Scott Garrett and the liberals of his redrawn 5th District," NorthJersey.com, September 20, 2012, http:// archive.northjersey.com/news/congressional-culture-clash-conservative-icon-scott-garrett -and-the-liberals-of-his-redrawn-5th-district-1.394230?page = all.

8. Kyle Kondik, "The State of the House," *The Surge*, ed. Larry Sabato, Kyle Kondik, and Geoffrey Skelley (Lanham, Maryland: Rowman & Littlefield, 2015), 83.

5

Presidential Primaries: A Hit at the Ballot Box

Rhodes Cook

No matter what one thought of the turbulent and often surreal 2016 presidential primary campaign, it was a hit at the ballot box.

More than 9 million more votes were cast in the Republican primaries than ever before. Democrats posted their second-highest primary turnout ever in raw votes, behind only the "instant classic" in 2008 between Barack Obama and Hillary Clinton. And the combined total for both parties in 2016 surpassed 60 million, the largest number of voters that have ever participated in the nation's presidential primary process.[1]

A "boffo" business it was, and offered a preview of what was to come in the fall. Then, 137 million voters turned out, also a record. They elected the precocious Republican nominee, Donald Trump, in a surprising win over Democrat Hillary Clinton in a race that featured two of the most unpopular candidates for president in recent memory.

Given the latter, why then the considerable voter interest, especially throughout the nominating process?

First of all, it was an open race for the presidency in 2016, the first in eight years. No incumbent was gliding to easy renomination. Instead, both parties were choosing their nominees from "scratch," which often means more competition and greater interest in the nominating contest.

Second, the Democratic field featured the wife of a former president, who was also a former senator from New York and secretary of state in her own right. That candidate (Hillary Clinton) was seeking to make history as the first female president in American history. Her prime challenger (Senator

Table 5.1.   Presidential Primary Turnouts since 1972

In 1972 the presidential nominating process changed dramatically, from one where nominations were decided at the national conventions to one where choices were made in the primaries. There have been few exceptions to this dynamic over the last four decades, as the number of presidential primaries have swelled to around forty each election. Primary turnouts have tended to be highest in election years where both parties had open contests for their nominations, such as was the case in 2016. Overall primary turnouts have usually been lower in years when one party had an incumbent president running virtually unopposed for renomination, as was the case in 1972, 1984, 1996, 2004, and 2012. In 2008, the last open election for both parties before 2016, primary turnouts reached record highs, with nearly 37 million voting in Democratic primaries, almost 21 million in Republican primaries, and more than 57.5 million combined. In 2016, the number of votes cast in GOP primaries roared past their 2008 total, reaching a new record for the party in excess of 30 million votes. With a late surge of primary voters in Democratic-oriented states such as New York and California, Democratic primary turnout in 2016 approached 31 million, although that was well short of the number who participated eight years earlier.

	Number of Primary Votes Cast			*Party with Highest Primary Turnout*	*Party that Won Pres. Election*
Election	*Total*	*Democrats*	*Republicans*		
1972	22,182,246	15,993,965	6,188,281	D	R
1976	26,426,777	16,052,652	10,374,125	D	D
1980	31,438,276	18,747,825	12,690,451	D	R
1984	24,584,843	18,009,192	6,575,651	D	R
1988 (Open)	35,127,051	22,961,936	12,165,115	D	R
1992	32,935,932	20,239,385	12,696,547	D	D
1996	24,939,013	10,947,364	13,991,649	R	D
2000 (Open)	31,201,862	14,045,745	17,156,117	R	R
2004	24,122,770	16,182,439	7,940,331	D	R
2008 (Open)	57,689,496	36,848,285	20,841,211	D	D
2012	27,976,800	9,206,764	18,770,036	R	D
2016 (Open)	**60,992,225**	**30,805,736**	**30,186,489**	D	R

Sources: Race for the Presidency: Winning the 2004 Nomination (CQ Press) for presidential primary turnout numbers through 2000. The 2004, 2008, and 2012 editions of *America Votes* (CQ Press, a division of SAGE Publications) for primary election totals from 2004 through 2012. The 2016 presidential primary results are from the CNN Election Night in America Research Guide 2016.
Note: Presidential primary turnouts are based on results from those states (and the District of Columbia) that held presidential primaries. It does not include results from caucus states, where the turnout is traditionally much smaller than primaries.

Bernie Sanders of Vermont) produced a large and enduring donor base that surprised nearly everyone.

Meanwhile, the Republican field was viewed to be one of the party's strongest in years. It featured two young senators of Hispanic origin with prominent geographical bases (Ted Cruz of Texas and Marco Rubio of Florida), a battleground state governor (John Kasich of Ohio), a member of a famous political family (former Governor Jeb Bush of Florida) that already boasted two former presidents. Plus, there was a collection of other senators and governors, past and present, a couple of whom had made previous bids for the GOP presidential nomination.

And then there was Donald Trump. The billionaire New York real estate mogul was a brash political newcomer, making his first full-fledged bid for elective office. From the start of his campaign in June 2015, Trump was *sui generis*. He was entertaining to some, compelling to all, irreverent, and "in your face"—a one-of-a-kind candidate who drew attention to himself, proved a nightmare for much of the Republican establishment, and befuddled his primary opponents.

He was also catnip for the media. Trump rallies were regularly televised by cable news networks—such as CNN, MSNBC, and Fox News. As success breeds success, his boisterous rallies drew thousands, even tens of thousands.

A FOCUS ON TRUMP

For all practical purposes, the Republican campaign revolved around him, so much so that it was estimated that by the ides of March in 2016, Trump had received more than $2 billion worth of free media attention.[2]

For the networks, it was clearly worth it. The first GOP presidential debate, held in Cleveland in August 2015, drew a record viewership for a primary debate of nearly 24 million. Many voters clearly tuned in to watch Trump and to see if he might self-immolate. He didn't, although the debate featured several tense exchanges with the Fox News moderators, most notably Megyn Kelly.[3]

Viewership for the GOP debates declined a bit as they proceeded over the following months. But Republican audiences generally remained much larger than for the Democratic debates, which began in October with "only" 16 million viewers.[4]

There were numerous times during the opening months of the Republican campaign that Trump's seemingly intemperate, boorish, and over-the-top remarks would "deep six" his candidacy. Yet they never did.

Instead, his antiestablishment presidential bid grew steadily stronger as the months went by. In the *RealClearPolitics* rolling average of Republican presidential preferences, Trump was not even listed among the options in major polls taken in early spring of 2015. By early June that year, on the eve of his formal announcement, he drew less than 5 percent support, well behind in a GOP field that was led at the time by Jeb Bush.

Trump, though, quickly gained traction. By late July 2015, he was in the lead with a percentage approaching 20. Around Thanksgiving 2015, he was near 30 percent, and in January 2016, on the eve of the start of the presidential primary season, Trump's support in the *RealClearPolitics* average of GOP presidential preference polls exceeded 35 percent.[5]

Once the Republican primary season began in February, Trump continued to ride high, with his success achieved against a backdrop of large Republican turnouts. Trump won three of the opening four events in February (losing only Iowa), and in three of the four states more votes were cast on the Republican side than the Democratic. In the lead-off caucuses in Iowa, the GOP had a turnout edge of 15,000 votes; in the primary voting in New Hampshire, the Republican advantage was more than 30,000 votes. In South Carolina, it reached 370,000 votes, doubling the Democratic turnout total.

"There's no question about it: Donald Trump is the main cause of high Republican turnout," said Larry J. Sabato, director of the University of Virginia Center for Politics, about voter participation in the early events. "Love him or hate him, he's the center of attention."[6]

In the primary-heavy month of March, the Republican margin in the partisan ballot war with the Democrats swelled, as did Trump's number of primary victories. By the end of the month, he had won seventeen of the twenty-one Republican primaries, and the GOP turnout lead over the Democrats approached 5 million votes.

Trump continued to dominate the Republican race until the abrupt end of the contest in Indiana on May 3.

INDIANA ENDGAME

The GOP campaign in Indiana had its unusual moments. In a last-ditch effort to stop the GOP front-runner, Trump's leading challenger, Ted Cruz, took the nearly unprecedented step of naming a vice presidential running mate in the person of former Hewlett-Packard executive Carly Fiorina. Her own bid for the party's presidential nomination in early 2016 had quickly run aground. Cruz also bagged a primary-eve endorsement from Indiana's governor, Mike Pence, who barely two months later would emerge as Trump's running mate.[7]

Meanwhile, Trump had considerable momentum after sweeping through the Northeast and was boosted in the Hoosier State by a pantheon of Indiana's leading collegiate coaching legends. They included former Notre Dame football coach Lou Holtz and a trio of former basketball notables led by Indiana University's Bobby Knight, and joined by Notre Dame's Digger Phelps and Purdue's Gene Keady.[8]

Table 5.2. All-Time Leading Primary Turnout Years

Almost 61 million votes were cast in this year's major-party presidential primaries, breaking the all-time record for the two major parties of nearly 57.7 million ballots cast in 2008. More than 30.8 million votes were cast in the 2016 Democratic primaries, compared to nearly 30.2 million primary ballots cast in their GOP counterparts. The Republican total eclipsed the previous record for the number of GOP ballots cast in a single primary season by more than 9 million. The Democratic total this year was the second-highest number of primary votes cast in a single party's primaries, behind only that for the Barack Obama–Hillary Clinton contest for the Democratic nomination in 2008. The latter set the record for either party of 36.8 million primary votes.

	Primary Vote by Party					Combined Party Primary Vote	
Election	Party	Turnout	Nominee	Leading Challenger	Election	Turnout	Nominees#
2008	D	36,848,285	Barack Obama	Hillary Clinton	**2016**	**60,992,225**	**Trump (R)—H. Clinton (D)**
2016	**D**	**30,805,736**	**Hillary Clinton**	**Bernie Sanders**	2008	57,689,496	Obama (D)—McCain (R)
2016	**R**	**30,186,489**	**Donald Trump**	**Ted Cruz**	1988	35,127,051	Bush (R)—Dukakis (D)
1988	D	22,961,936	Michael Dukakis	Jesse Jackson	1992	32,935,932	B. Clinton (D)—Bush (R)*
2008	R	20,841,211	John McCain	Mitt Romney	1980	31,438,276	Reagan (R)—Carter (D)*
1992	D	20,239,385	Bill Clinton	Jerry Brown	2000	31,201,862	G. W. Bush (R)—Gore (D)

Sources: *Race for the Presidency: Winning the 2004 Nomination* (CQ Press) for presidential primary turnouts through 2000. The 2004, 2008, and 2012 editions of *America Votes* (CQ Press, an imprint of SAGE Publications) for primary election totals for 2004 through 2012. The aggregate primary turnout numbers for 2016 are based on state-by-state results published in the CNN Election Night in America Research Guide 2016.

Note: Voter turnouts are based on results from those states (and the District of Columbia) that held presidential primaries. An asterisk (*) denotes an incumbent president. A pound sign (#) indicates that the candidate elected president is listed first. In the elections of 2000 and 2016, the Democratic nominee won the popular vote but the Republican standard-bearer triumphed in the Electoral College.

The primary ended as so many before it, with Trump scoring a decisive victory. GOP turnout surpassed 1.1 million, a record for any Republican presidential primary in Indiana, and almost a half million more votes than were cast in the Democratic contest in which Sanders defeated Clinton.

Trump's last two active Republican challengers, Cruz and Kasich, quit the race after his decisive Indiana victory. At the time, Trump had won twenty-four of the twenty-nine Republican primaries, with close to 3.8 million more ballots cast in GOP primary contests than their Democratic counterparts.

With Trump wrapping up the Republican nomination early, and with deep blue states such as California and New Jersey holding their primaries at the end of the nominating calendar in June, Democrats eventually overcame the Republicans' advantage in the 2016 "battle of the primary ballots." In the final tally, 30.8 million votes were cast in the Democratic primaries to nearly 30.2 million in the GOP primaries.

Still, the Republican primary turnout was up significantly from any previous election cycle, including more than 9 million votes over the previous

Table 5.3.   Battle of the 2016 Primary Ballots by Month

One of the major story lines of the 2016 presidential primary season was the strong turnouts on the Republican side. That was truly the case, as GOP turnout this primary season eclipsed the previous Republican record, set in 2008, by more than 9 million votes. Yet by the end, more votes in 2016 were cast in the Democratic presidential primaries than the Republican. There were at least two basic reasons for this. First, the competitive stage of the Republican presidential nominating contest was concluded in favor of Donald Trump in early May, while the Democratic battle between Hillary Clinton and Bernie Sanders went to the end of the primary season in June. Second, a number of the late primaries from mid-April to June were held in states of the Northeast and Pacific West that boasted large Democratic registration advantages, and as a result, produced higher Democratic than Republican primary turnout totals.

| | Number of Primary Votes Cast (in thousands) | | | |
Time Period	Total Vote	Dem.	Rep.	Partisan Plurality	
Through February	1,651	624	1,027	R	403
Through March	35,526	15,280	20,246	R	4,966
Through April	46,056	21,384	24,672	R	3,288
*Through May 3**	*47,806*	*22,023*	*25,783*	*R*	*3,760*
Through May	51,428	24,245	27,183	R	2,938
Through June	60,992	30,806	30,186	D	620

Source: CNN Election Night in America Research Guide 2016, with primary results arranged into cumulative running totals by the author.
Note: Vote totals are rounded to the nearest thousand. An asterisk (*) indicates that May 3 was the unofficial end of the Republican primary campaign, when Donald Trump drove his remaining rivals from the race with a victory in Indiana.

GOP high in 2008, while the Democratic total was down by 6 million from the party's last contested presidential race in the same year.

Ultimately, Trump ended up as the party's all-time leading primary vote-getter with a nationwide aggregate of nearly 13.8 million votes. That far surpassed the previous GOP record of 10.8 million primary votes for George W. Bush in 2000. Republican nominees John McCain in 2008 and Mitt Romney in 2012 did not reach 10 million.

To be sure, Hillary Clinton drew more than 17.1 million votes in the 2016 Democratic primaries, almost 4 million more than her rival, Bernie Sanders. But theirs was essentially a two-way race, while Trump had to divide the Republican primary vote with multiple rivals.

SANDERS PROVIDES ENERGY FOR DEMOCRATS

On the Democratic side, the passion was not with the frontrunner, but with Sanders. The crusty septuagenarian socialist energized the progressive wing of the party by unapologetically championing its causes. He and Trump drew the largest, most enthusiastic crowds of the primary campaign, and Sanders boasted millions of contributions that as he liked to say, were on average "twenty-seven bucks."[9]

Sanders, though, was never a match for Clinton, who from the start boasted a wide lead among Democratic "superdelegates"—party leaders who have a say in the nominating contest and who are not pledged to any candidate through primary or caucus results—and scored landslide primary victories across the South, which further padded her comfortable delegate advantage. Backing from minorities and women also helped Clinton carry many of the nation's largest metropolitan areas in the primaries.

Yet Sanders combined strength in academic communities and small cities and towns to carry Democratic primaries in states such as New Hampshire, Michigan, and Wisconsin. The latter two would be lost again by Clinton in the fall.

SOME CAVEATS

Even in high-turnout years such as 2016, the number of votes cast in the presidential primaries has never reached 50 percent of the November presidential election turnout. There are several reasons for this.

First, not every state holds a presidential primary. Since 1980, the number of primaries has stayed largely in the thirty-five to forty range, with the rest of the states holding lower-turnout caucuses.

Second, in many of the states that hold primaries, not every registered voter can cast a ballot. In "closed" primary states, where only voters affiliated with a particular party can participate in that party's primary, the large swath of independent voters are excluded.

Third, in most election years the nomination in at least one party is settled long before the end of the primary season. That was the case for the Republicans in 2016, with Trump clearing the last of his sixteen rivals from the GOP race in the wake of Indiana's May 3 primary. With Trump essentially running unopposed in the later primaries, GOP primary turnouts declined far more than if Cruz and Kasich had remained in the race until the end of the primary season.

Still, those who do vote in the presidential primaries are often a decent cross-section of each party's base. They tend to be the most loyal of voters for each party, while the general election tends to attract many of those who are more casual in their voting habits.

CLUES FOR THE FALL

In any presidential election, a critical question is whether the turnout level for the primaries has any bearing on the fall election.

Often the answer is no. But in 2016, it was yes.

By March 2016, the basic outline of Trump's electoral coalition was already visible. "He is bringing new voters to the Republican contests and across the demographics," wrote Kelley Beaucar Vlahos of *Fox News*, "particularly among blue-collar, lower-income voters who have expressed an anger with the government and (are) seeking a political outsider for the White House."[10]

Ultimately, the basic geographical contours of the primary voting was reflected in the general election. Democrats won more votes nationwide in both, thanks to a large advantage over the Republicans in California, nearly 3 million votes in the primaries and more than 4 million in the fall.

But in both the primaries and the general election, Republicans drew more presidential votes than the Democrats in key battleground states such as Florida, Iowa, Michigan, North Carolina, Ohio, and Wisconsin. The Republicans' primary showing in these states proved a harbinger of Trump's success in these battlegrounds in the fall. Winning them in November enabled Trump to penetrate the Democrats' highly touted "blue wall" and win the White House.

Not always, though, do the primaries prove to be a harbinger of the fall. In only four of the twelve presidential elections held since the primary-

Table 5.4. Battle of the 2016 Primary Ballots by State

The pyrotechnics that Donald Trump brought to the GOP contest no doubt played a significant role in the more intense voter interest in the Republican primaries. Of the twenty-nine states that held presidential primaries through May 3, when Trump locked up the Republican race, more votes were cast on the GOP side in nineteen states, compared to ten states where the Democrats had the turnout advantage. Among the states where the GOP won more primary votes were battleground states such as Florida, New Hampshire, Ohio, Virginia, and Wisconsin. All of them helped Barack Obama to victory in the presidential elections of 2008 and 2012, but most turned to Trump in November 2016.

State	Number of Primary Votes Cast			Party Plurality (in votes)		Percentage by Party		General Election Winner
	Total	Dem.	Rep.			Dem.	Rep.	
AL	1,260,541	399,889	860,652	R	460,763	32%	68%	R
AZ	1,090,274	466,235	624,039	R	157,804	43%	57%	R
AR	631,940	221,020	410,920	R	189,900	35%	65%	R
CA#	7,400,644	5,173,338	2,227,306	D	2,946,032	70%	30%	D
CT	541,748	328,255	213,493	D	114,762	61%	39%	D
DE	163,532	93,640	69,892	D	23,748	57%	43%	D
DC*	97,763	97,763	—	D	97,763	100%	—	D
FL	4,070,988	1,709,183	2,361,805	R	652,622	42%	58%	R
GA	2,061,330	765,366	1,295,964	R	530,598	37%	63%	R
ID*	222,004	—	222,004	R	222,004	—	100%	R
IL	3,505,795	2,056,047	1,449,748	D	606,299	59%	41%	D
IN	1,749,322	638,779	1,110,543	R	471,764	37%	63%	R
KY*	454,565	454,565	—	D	454,565	100%	—	R
LA	613,017	311,776	301,241	D	10,535	51%	49%	R
MD	1,375,829	916,763	459,066	D	457,697	67%	33%	D
MA	1,852,233	1,215,970	636,263	D	579,707	66%	34%	D
MI	2,529,141	1,205,552	1,323,589	R	118,037	48%	52%	R
MS	643,434	227,164	416,270	R	189,106	35%	65%	R
MO	1,568,695	629,425	939,270	R	309,845	40%	60%	R
MT#	283,264	126,376	156,888	R	30,512	45%	55%	R
NE#	279,424	80,436	198,988	R	118,552	29%	71%	R
NH#	538,979	253,062	285,917	R	32,855	47%	53%	D

(continued)

Table 5.4. (continued)

State	Number of Primary Votes Cast			Party Plurality (in votes)		Percentage by Party		General Election Winner
	Total	*Dem.*	*Rep.*			*Dem.*	*Rep.*	
NJ#	1,342,257	894,305	447,952	D	446,353	67%	33%	D
NM#	320,702	216,075	104,627	D	111,448	67%	33%	D
NY	2,876,007	1,954,236	921,771	D	1,032,465	68%	32%	D
NC	2,292,446	1,142,916	1,149,530	R	6,614	50%	50%	R
OH	3,230,438	1,241,478	1,988,960	R	747,482	38%	62%	R
OK	795,765	335,843	459,922	R	124,079	42%	58%	R
OR#	1,035,515	641,595	393,920	D	247,675	62%	38%	D
PA	3,275,902	1,681,427	1,594,475	D	86,952	51%	49%	R
RI	184,072	122,458	61,614	D	60,844	67%	33%	D
SC	1,111,785	370,904	740,881	R	369,977	33%	67%	R
SD#	119,885	53,006	66,879	R	13,873	44%	56%	R
TN	1,227,951	372,222	855,729	R	483,507	30%	70%	R
TX	4,272,383	1,435,895	2,836,488	R	1,400,593	34%	66%	R
VT	196,266	134,838	61,428	D	73,410	69%	31%	D
VA	1,810,493	785,041	1,025,452	R	240,411	43%	57%	D
WA#	1,405,752	802,754	602,998	D	199,756	57%	43%	D
WV#	446,600	242,539	204,061	D	38,478	54%	46%	R
WI	2,113,544	1,007,600	1,105,944	R	98,344	48%	52%	R
2016 Total	**60,992,225**	**30,805,736**	**30,186,489**	**D**	**619,247**	**51%**	**49%**	**R**
2008 Total	**57,689,496**	**36,848,285**	**20,841,211**	**D**	**16,007,074**	**64%**	**36%**	**D**
2008 to 2016	**+3,302,729**	**−6,042,549**	**+9,345,278**					
	+6%	**−16%**	**+45%**					

Sources: America Votes 28 (CQ Press, a division of SAGE Publications) for 2008 presidential primary results. CNN Election Night in America Research Guide 2016 for presidential primary results in 2016.

Note: An asterisk (*) indicates that neither Idaho Democrats nor Republicans in Kentucky or the District of Columbia held a presidential primary in 2016. A pound sign (#) denotes that the GOP primary was held after Donald Trump drove his last rivals from the Republican race with his Indiana primary victory May 3, and hence, the GOP presidential primaries in these states were noncompetitive. Nebraska and Washington Democrats held nonbinding "beauty contest" primaries, with delegates allocated to reflect the results of a separate caucus process.

dominated era of the nominating process began in 1972 has the party that has drawn the most votes in the presidential primaries gone on to win the presidency.[11]

In the more limited number of open elections (those like 2016 without an incumbent on the ballot) that were held during this period, the correlation between primary and general election turnout has also been a mixed bag.

In the open election of 1988, nearly 11 million more ballots were cast in the Democratic primaries than the GOP, but Republican George H. W. Bush was elected president that fall.

In the open election of 2000, fully 3 million more primary votes were cast on the GOP side, and Republican George W. Bush won the White House. But it was an unusual election, much like 2016. In each, the Democratic candidate took the popular vote, while the Republican candidate won the all-important electoral vote, creating the first Electoral College "misfires" since the late 1800s.

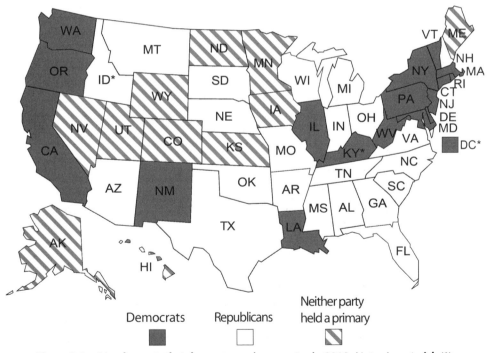

Figure 5.1. Map by party that drew more primary votes in 2016. *Note*: **An asterisk (*) indicates that neither Idaho Democrats nor Republicans in Kentucky or the District of Columbia held a presidential primary in 2016.**

Table 5.5.   All-Time Leading Primary Vote-Getters

Donald Trump liked to remind audiences that he won more votes in the 2016 presidential primaries than any other Republican candidate. Altogether, he drew nearly 3 million more votes than the party's previous primary record-holder, George W. Bush, did in 2000. However, Democrat Hillary Clinton won more than 3 million more primary votes in 2016 than Trump. That was due in large part to the fact that Clinton had only one significant challenger, Sen. Bernie Sanders of Vermont, while Trump had many and hence, the Republican primary vote was more divided. Clinton fell just short in 2016 of the all-time, single-year record of 17.7 million primary votes that she set in the 2008 Democratic primaries against Barack Obama. As for Sanders, he finished the 2016 primary season with more votes than any other candidate has ever won who was not named Clinton, Obama, or Trump.

Rank	Candidate	Election	Primary Votes	Nomination Outcome	General Election Outcome
1	Hillary Clinton (D)	2008*	17,714,899	Lost	—
2	Barack Obama (D)	2008*	17,423,314	Won	Won
3	Hillary Clinton (D)	2016	17,121,442	Won	Lost#
4	Donald Trump (R)	2016	13,757,263	Won	Won#
5	Bernie Sanders (D)	2016	13,210,249	Lost	—
6	George W. Bush (R)	2000	10,844,129	Won	Won#
7	Al Gore (D)	2000	10,626,645	Won	Lost#
8	Bill Clinton (D)	1992	10,482,411	Won	Won
9	John Kerry (D)	2004	9,870,082	Won	Lost
10	John McCain (R)	2008	9,862,865	Won	Lost
11	Mitt Romney (R)	2012	9,841,300	Won	Lost
12	Michael Dukakis (D)	1988	9,817,185	Won	Lost

Sources: Race for the Presidency: Winning the 2004 Nomination (CQ Press) for presidential primary vote data through 2000; various editions of *America Votes* (CQ Press, an imprint of SAGE Publications) for similar data for the primary contests in 2004, 2008 and 2012. CNN Election Night in America Research Guide 2016 for presidential primary results in 2016.
Note: The candidates' rankings are based on presidential primary results from states and the District of Columbia. Caucus results are not included. A pound sign (#) indicates that the candidates indicated as losers (Democrat Al Gore in 2000 and Hillary Clinton in 2016) actually won the popular vote but not the electoral vote, while candidates designated as winners (Republicans George W. Bush in 2000 and Donald Trump in 2016) won the all-important electoral vote but not the popular vote. An asterisk (*) reflects the controversial nature of the 2008 Democratic primary vote. If the vote that year is counted from all the primaries held in states and the District of Columbia—the tally that is listed above—Hillary Clinton had the higher total. But remove results from the unsanctioned Democratic primaries that year in Florida and Michigan, and Obama finished ahead with 16,847,100 primary votes to Clinton's 16,515,604.

In the open election of 2008, though, there was a clear relationship between the primary turnout and the November outcome. That year, the energized contest between Barack Obama and Hillary Clinton produced 16 million more votes in the Democratic primaries than in the Republican ones, which proved a precursor of Democratic success that fall.

That brings us to 2016, where there are pundits who can now say with conviction about the year's surprise outcome: "Oh, yes, we saw that coming in the primaries."

NOTES

1. The basic methodology of this chapter: Caucus votes are not included in the presidential primary vote. There are several reasons for this. First, primaries and caucuses are different. There are only about a dozen caucuses held every four years, and they are almost exclusively in smaller states. Turnout for them is much lower than presidential primaries. As well, the votes in caucuses are traditionally tallied by the state parties, not the states, as is the case in primary elections. As a consequence, the caucus tallies can sometimes be murky and incomplete. As a separate matter, the presidential primary turnouts mentioned in this chapter are based on the actual raw vote. The Pew Research Center has computed presidential primary turnouts since 1980 on the basis of voter-eligible population (citizens age 18 and older). The 2016 turnout rates featured results through early June that in some cases were nearly complete but unofficial. Even then, the turnout rate of 14.8 percent for Republican presidential primaries was higher than any other set of GOP primaries since 1980, while the turnout rate for Democratic primaries in 2016 of 14.4 percent was exceeded by 1980, 1984, 1988, and 2012. The combined turnout rate for both parties in 2016, listed by Pew as 28.5 percent of the voter-eligible population, was the highest for any year except 2008. Drew DeSilver, "Turnout Was High in the 2016 Primary Season, but Just Short of 2008 Record," Pew Research Center, June 10, 2016, http://www.pewresearch.org/fact-tank/2016/06/10/turnout-was-high-in-the-2016-primary -season-but-just-short-of-2008-record/.

2. Nicholas Confessore and Karen Yourish, "$2 Billion Worth of Free Media for Donald Trump," *New York Times*, March 15, 2016, http://www.nytimes.com/2016/03/16/up shot/measuring-donald-trumps-mammoth-advantage-in-free-media.html.

3. John Koblin, "Republican Debate Draws 24 Million Viewers," *New York Times*, August 7, 2015, http://www.nytimes.com/2015/08/08/business/media/republican-debate -draws-24-million-viewers.html.

4. Donovan Slack, "Presidential Debates, Ranked by Viewership," *USA Today*, January 15, 2016, http://www.usatoday.com/story/news/politics/onpolitics/2016/01/15/presi dential-debates-ranked-viewership/78867956/.

5. "2015–16 Presidential Polling: The Republicans," *The Rhodes Cook Letter*, January 2016.

6. Emily Schultheis, "What Do the Turnout Numbers Say about the 2016 Race?" CBS News, February 29, 2016, http://www.cbsnews.com/news/what-do-the-voting-turn out-numbers-say-about-the-2016-presidential-race/.

7. When seeking the Republican presidential nomination in 1976, Ronald Reagan also announced his choice for vice president in advance of his party's convention in a bid to overcome the delegate lead of President Gerald R. Ford. Reagan's choice of Republican Senator Richard Schweiker of Pennsylvania, however, failed to force Ford to announce his own vice presidential choice in advance of the presidential roll call or to prevent Ford's nomination.

8. Al Weaver, "Trump, Sports Legends Combine for Indiana Victory," *Washington Examiner*, May 4, 2016, http://www.washingtonexaminer.com/trump-sports-legends-com bine-for-indiana-victory/article/2590343.

9. Philip Bump, "Bernie Sanders Keeps Saying His Average Contribution Is $27, But His Own Numbers Contradict That," *Washington Post*, April 18, 2016, https://www .washingtonpost.com/news/the-fix/wp/2016/04/18/bernie-sanders-keeps-saying-his-aver age-donation-is-27-but-it-really-isnt/.

10. Kelley Beaucar Vlahos, "November Preview? Turnout Surging in Republican Primaries—and Sinking for Democrats," Fox News, March 3, 2016, http://www.foxnews .com/politics/2016/03/03/november-preview-turnout-surging-in-republican-primaries-and -sinking-for-democrats.html.

11. Sometimes high turnout in the primaries is due not to voter enthusiasm for a major contender but to antipathy between warring factions of the party that generates a lot of sparks (and interest). Also, when incumbent presidents seek reelection, they often run virtually unopposed for nomination and hence the primary turnout in the president's party is much lower than that for the opposition. That is particularly the case when the president is popular and a favorite for reelection.

6

Donald Trump and a GOP Primary Race Like No Other

Robert Costa

Six months before he descended down the golden escalators at his Manhattan skyscraper to announce his presidential candidacy, Donald Trump traveled to Iowa in January 2015 to address a land investment expo. The trip, made on a cold winter day, is little remembered. But it was the unofficial beginning of the real-estate mogul's extraordinary campaign for the Republican nomination.

As most pundits and GOP leaders ignored him, Trump met quietly with veteran Iowa conservative Chuck Laudner, one of the few high-profile consultants who was willing to take a meeting with a man whom so many in the party viewed warily. Aboard his private plane parked in Des Moines and backstage, Trump pressed Laudner about the state's political topography and the intricacies of the Iowa caucuses, all of which seemed almost foreign to him.[1]

By the time they parted ways, Laudner was convinced that Trump was going to run—that Trump's interest this time wasn't like his brief, birtherism-fueled flirtation in 2011.[2] The businessman may not have known much about Iowa politics, but he was engaged and deeply interested in what it'd take to mount a successful outsider-themed campaign, there and nationally, on a shoestring budget and unusually high media exposure.

Less than a month later, in a lengthy interview with *The Washington Post* that signaled much of what was to come, Trump said he was "more serious" than ever about pursuing a run for the White House in 2016 and announced

97

that Laudner and several other operatives had signed up for a likely campaign, including Corey Lewandowski, who would later become the Trump campaign's first manager.[3]

Trump also sketched out the themes that would be at the core of his message: frothing outrage over "people around the world [who] are laughing at us" and a promise to bring industrial jobs back from China and other global economic rivals.

Again, as they had with his Iowa visit, most Republican leaders and top Democrats shrugged off Trump's moves as more cringe-worthy attention seeking from a celebrity who reflected the worst of the Republican base's impulses. He was racially charged, incendiary, and antiestablishment. There was no way he'd actually run.[4]

Of course, Trump did run, and he won the nomination in historic fashion, winning over 13 million votes—more total votes than any Republican primary candidate in the history of Republican presidential primaries.[5] In the process, he outpaced sixteen major competitors who brought with them seasoned biographies, often better-funded campaigns, and pitches forged through decades of working within the party and within the conservative movement.

Trump's stunning victory in a party that had traditionally turned to whoever is "next in line"[6] and to a mainstream standard-bearer is a complicated story that will surely perplex and challenge historians for years to come, with possible clues found not only in the political sphere but in the economic and cultural orbits that festered the populist and nationalist-tinged frustrations of his supporters long before he stood before them at the Republican National Convention in Cleveland to accept the prize that he had won.[7]

Entering the contests as voters in the United Kingdom were pushing for "Brexit"—to leave the European Union amid fears of globalization and immigration—and as Republicans in the United States were animated by similar issues, Trump found himself in an environment that turned out to be especially fertile for him from the start, far more than he could have imagined in those early conversations in Iowa.[8] In spite of his numerous controversies[9] and haphazard decisions, he was routinely lifted back into contention by the raw passions of Republicans who saw in him a disruptor reflective of their own anxieties and convictions about the direction of the country and the world.[10]

But it took more than swirling and somewhat nebulous political winds to enable Trump and upend the Republican Party. For him to rise, other things had to fall—not just the candidates but the norms and assumptions that have long shaped the GOP.[11] Trump's path to the nomination was thus not so much about his brawling debate performances or his ground organization in certain states.[12] It was ultimately about a turbulent unraveling of a party—its political-donor class, its big-name stars, and its various orthodoxies. What was expected to happen in the twilight of Barack Obama's presidency—the ascent of a fresh-faced Hispanic senator or center-right governor who could lead them back to power and appeal to a diversifying electorate—did not happen.

Instead, Trump took the Republican Party by surprise, and over.

BUSH REDUX

By early 2014, five years after his brother George W. Bush left the White House with his popularity diminished, Jeb Bush was emerging as the favorite for the Republican presidential nomination—and reviving a certain kind of pragmatic, Bush-style Republicanism that had faded as the Tea Party and other forces had grown influential in Washington. Many of the GOP's most connected "insiders and financiers" had begun a "behind-the-scenes campaign to draft the former Florida governor," and Bush huddled with potential benefactors as he traveled the country giving speeches on income inequality, education, and foreign policy.[13]

For the overlapping donor and leadership wings of the GOP, Bush's move toward a campaign was a welcome development. Although Jeb Bush did not have the swaggering charisma of his older brother and he could be awkward and clipped while on the stump, he represented an iteration of the ideology and temperament with which they were most comfortable. Bush was supportive of comprehensive immigration reform, fluent in Spanish, and a proven vote-getter in a battleground state. He was hawkish on foreign policy and spoke with compassion about the poor.[14]

And he had the name: Bush. It was seen as politically gold-plated, with his father and brother both former presidents who had strong pockets of support. His late grandfather had been a senator. Looking ahead to a likely general election race against well-financed Democrat Hillary Clinton, establishment and elected Republicans were eager to have a candidate with a formidable network and a profile that could rally GOP voters together.

In other words, Bush looked like the surest bet in what was to be a crowded field, and his supporters worked to make sure that that status was preserved. Scores of loyalists and associates who had raised money for his family in the past began to raise tens of millions of dollars for his allied Super PAC, Right to Rise. A shadow campaign for Bush was evident by late 2014 and early 2015, with its fund-raising target eventually becoming $100 million, which it surpassed.[15] Many prominent donors who gave to Mitt Romney's 2012 campaign joined the effort. All of them were looking for a way back to the White House and a candidate who was in the center-right mode of Romney and Arizona Senator John McCain, the party's 2008 nominee—someone who fit the description of "electable."[16]

When Bush finally announced on a humid day in June 2015 at an event before a large and diverse crowd in Miami, he was still poised to be "someone with executive experience, conservative values and a reformer's instinct," and he had what seemed like a viable path to the nomination, if it had been any other year.[17]

But it fell apart. "If they're looking for an entertainer in chief, I'm probably not the guy," Bush said at one of the early GOP primary debates. He was, as David Frum noted, not only disconnected from the populism that was burbling throughout the party but temperamentally uncomfortable with the way the party was drifting.[18] The compassionate conservatism that carried his brother George into the White House in 2000 had lost its luster in the eyes of activists. They wanted a harder edge, and Jeb Bush, with his empathetic words for undocumented workers and nonconfrontational personality, never caught on with the GOP's base.

Ahead of the Iowa caucuses in late 2015, Bush found himself lost in a party that no longer seemed like the one he had known his whole life. His hawkish plan to combat the Islamic State did not generate the usual GOP applause, and Trump's noninterventionist instincts were resonating with voters weary of more than a decade of military engagements in the Middle East. His crowds were often half-full and veered older and white, with many supporters there out of loyalty to a family and party traditions now out of style.

Immigration, perhaps more than anything, haunted him. *The New York Times* observed in December 2015 that "large majorities in both Iowa and New Hampshire say they will only choose a candidate who agrees with them on the issue—and those majorities do not share" Bush's position.[19] He eventually stumbled badly in Iowa and New Hampshire and then hung on until South Carolina, where he stumbled again. Trump's "low energy" tag was much discussed at the time, but more apt was what Bush's mother, Barbara, had said months before about most voters: "We've had enough Bushes."[20]

THE CHALLENGE FOR CRUZ—AND THE RIGHT

Bush endorsed Senator Ted Cruz of Texas in March after ending his own bid for the Republican nomination. The gesture underscored how the mainstream wing of the Republican Party, while being outpaced by Trump, was also being outpaced by the conservative bloc within the party—the ideologically driven "movement conservatives" and religious voters who were distressed by the fast-changing culture as well as aspects of the globalized economy and government power that they perceived as threatening.

Cruz, an evangelical Christian and attorney with degrees from Princeton and Harvard universities, was elected to the Senate in 2012. He quickly made his name on the national stage by supporting the 2013 effort to shut down the federal government in defiance of President Obama's health care law, which made him a darling of activists who were resentful of establishment Republicans. He was a star in straw polls and on stage at conservative gatherings throughout 2014, racking up support as an unwavering follower of the Constitution and right-wing policies.[21]

By the time Cruz announced his bid on March 23, 2015 at the convocation ceremony at Liberty University in Virginia, he had also enlisted Jeff Roe, one of the party's rising strategists, to build a sprawling digital and field operation across the country that would tap into the support he had accrued as well as the coalitions within the broader conservative movement—a ready-made base and a powerful one, if it could be fully consolidated.[22] The scene at Liberty was telling: Cruz was getting into the race early not only to get name recognition and a jump start but because the path to the nomination seemed clear. Win over the evangelicals in conservative hotbeds like central Virginia and in states like Iowa, and you stood a real chance of being the nominee. After previous nominations going to the center-right and establishment, conservative leaders like Cruz felt like their time had finally come.

But first Cruz had to get over an expansive group of likely candidates who saw the same path and were adopting a similar profile as the way forward. This bloc was distinctly separate from Bush: fiercely conservative and more comfortable in the cadence of conservatism than in the Republican Party itself. They revered Ronald Reagan, saw the state as a looming threat, infused their politics with faith and wanted to be seen as outsiders from the party even as they appealed to its base. Wisconsin Governor Scott Walker was among them, following a fast ascent in early 2015 and a series of well-reviewed appearances in the early states. Then there was Libertarian-leaning Senator Rand Paul, Louisiana Governor Bobby Jindal, retired neurosurgeon Ben Carson, former Arkansas Governor Mike Huckabee, and former Silicon Valley executive Carly Fiorina. Senator Marco Rubio of Florida straddled the mainstream, Bush-type wing and the conservative wing, but never found traction in either.[23]

Trump, as ever, remained an enigmatic outlier to Cruz and others in this wing of the primary race, at least during this initial sprint. He was one of them in some ways, in terms of being an outsider, but he was, at his core, more about his own appeal and populism than anything. That was in many respects why Cruz decided for months to run in Trump's wake—to not tangle with him directly but instead to concentrate on bringing together his own base and clashing with those candidates who were more direct competition for him in his so-called lane or path to the nomination. This plan of action, as Cruz allies told me at the time, was boosted by how Trump and Cruz both argued for more hardline immigration policies. In their view, attacking Trump didn't make political sense because it risked eroding Cruz's support among conservative voters whose central and driving issue was border security and immigration.

"I like Donald Trump. I think he's terrific. I think he's brash. I think he speaks the truth," Cruz told *Fox News* in June 2015 as Trump was getting into the race and making comments about some Mexican immigrants being rapists.[24] The chumminess continued throughout the fall of 2015 as Cruz's campaign continued to believe that Trump would fade away and their own message and organization would lift the senator. The warm feelings, however, ceased by the winter as the Iowa caucuses were nearing and Cruz was ahead in that state and poised to win. Trump harshly turned on Cruz, questioning his citizenship due to Cruz's Canadian birth and berating him at every turn. He called Cruz, at various times, crazy, unhinged, and unqualified to be president. Cruz was never comfortable under fire from Trump during this period. He was slowly but effectively building a potential winning coalition, but every day turned into a media circus about Trump's latest remark. When Trump used a picture of Cruz's wife in a Twitter message that was derogatory, Cruz pushed back against Trump with force, but it was a messy ordeal that left Cruz rattled and deeply unsettled.[25]

Cruz's rivals eventually fell away, and his organization did prove to be formidable. Walker struggled in the debates and never seemed to take to the national scene in the same confident way he did in his Wisconsin efforts. Carson's boomlet was brief, and his campaign was in disarray during much of the winter. Huckabee and Jindal fell short on fundrasing and then fell apart. Fiorina had her own brief moment where she ticked up in the polls, but it did not last. Paul's failure wasn't so much his own failing but the inability of his live and let live credo to catch on with Republican primary voters, in spite of the significant groundwork laid by his father Ron Paul, the former Texas congressman, during the 2012 Republican presidential nominating contests.[26]

The usual allies of conservatives like Cruz in the press, such as *National Review* magazine and others, failed to give him much of a lift as the race narrowed to Cruz and Trump by the spring, with Trump picking up momentum by the day. They no longer had the capital with the base as a new galaxy of outlets like the Trump-friendly *Breitbart* gained notice and influence. So did outlets that promoted the "alt-right," which had figures detached from the mainstream GOP and trafficked at times in material that was shared and cheered by white nationalists. Cruz's financial advantages and Super PACs also were less powerful than most Republicans expected because Trump was drawing intense coverage on national cable channels and was ubiquitous even though he was not competing with Cruz on paid advertising.[27]

As he looked for a jolt, Cruz tapped Fiorina to be his running mate in late April, just before the must-win Indiana primary where he was pinning the fate of his campaign. But the move was widely panned and seen as a political Hail Mary pass.[28] Trump dismissed it, and a few days later, Cruz lost Indiana. For him, the race was over, but more stunning was the defeat of a consensus on the right that 2016 would be theirs and that the fractured nature of the Republican Party gave them an unparalleled opening. It did not. What it did was give an opening to Trump, who moved forward for months as conservatives battled among themselves and mainstream Republicans quarreled. While Trump's rivals were scrambling to hold down their own bases, Trump was surging ahead with a hard-charging populism that drew from all sides.[29]

A PARTY SPLINTERS

Beyond the unfulfilled political promises offered by the Bush track and the Cruz track in the Republican primary race, there were more fundamental policy fronts that kept those candidates and others from winning the nomination. There was a historic—and often barely discussed—splintering on the core issues that had defined the Republican Party. Social issues that had dominated were largely relegated to the back shelf of the GOP scene. Hawks who had defined the party since Reagan on foreign policy found themselves outpaced by Trump and his noninterventionist instincts. Economic conservatives who had embraced House Speaker Paul Ryan's sweeping fiscal reforms saw themselves contested by Trump, who argued for few, if any, changes to long-term federal spending programs.

The social conservative evolution from powerhouse within the Republican Party primary process to a more nuanced bloc that did not necessarily turn to one of its own was a long time coming. As conservative commentator John Hinderaker noted, "Social conservatives aren't paranoid: many in the party's business wing have been yearning to dump them for quite a while."[30] Feeling their own influence waning in a party that was less vocal about abortion and marriage, all as same-sex marriage was being legalized nationally in 2015, many of the leaders in the community did not turn to the expected names during the first phase of the race. Huckabee fizzled as did Rick Santorum, the hard-charging former Pennsylvania senator who captured Iowa four years earlier. Other evangelicals gave Cruz a look, and many moved toward him. But others, too, were tempted by Trump, whose swagger and comments were off-putting to some but seen as defiantly antiestablishment to those in the ranks who saw both the establishment and the state as a looming threat.[31]

A turning point came in January 2016 when Jerry Falwell Jr., the president of Liberty University (where Cruz had announced his bid), endorsed Trump. The son of the famed late Jerry Falwell, Falwell was a major name in the faith community. But his endorsement was about more than a name; it was about the changing way evangelicals were looking at Republican candidates and the waning interest they had in finding someone who was just like them. Trump didn't speak in their political language or cadence, and he had in the past backed liberal positions, but he was disruptive to the political class that they viewed uneasily, especially with regard to religious liberty. "Let's stop trying to choose the political leaders who believe we are the most Godly because, in reality, only God knows people's hearts," Falwell wrote. "You and I don't, and we are all sinners."[32]

Falwell's move was a culmination of sorts of how the faith community was becoming less of a political monolith, with significant consequences for the GOP primary race. As Michelle Boorstein wrote in *The Washington Post*, "for a decade, U.S. evangelicalism, which has no formal leadership or hierarchy, has been increasingly divided over who is fit to speak for those who choose that label."[33] Trump waded into this new environment and took advantage. While Cruz won Iowa on the strength of his backing of religious conservatives, it was not enough of a coalition to carry him to the nomination in Cleveland. Evangelicals and others in their sphere had changed "their tune on morality," to Trump's benefit.[34]

In the Republican Party's foreign policy community, the changing dynamic that enabled Trump was similar to the one among social conservatives: the GOP didn't change its core principles, but it changed how stakeholders and leaders on those issues exerted power in the primary race.

The usual patterns were wiped away for a variety of reasons, in particular by Trump's disruption. But there was also exhaustion regarding the consensus that had been practiced and preached by party elites since George W. Bush's presidency. "GOP voters are fed up, not just with President Obama and Democrats but also with their own party," wrote former Bush speechwriter Marc Thiessen in October 2015, commenting on the unrest on policy and politics that spilled into the congressional ranks when House Speaker John Boehner stepped down as he lost support among conservatives.[35] (Ryan would replace him.)

Foreign policy hawks, with their interventionist impulses and support for a military ramp up, saw their favorites like Senator Lindsey Graham of South Carolina and Jeb Bush stumble. So did New Jersey Governor Chris Christie and Ohio Governor John Kasich. These onetime boosters of the Iraq War, who were linked politically to the Bush wing of the party, encountered a Republican base that was far less inclined to the Bush view of the world and the hawkish approach to geopolitics. Rubio was perhaps the best example of how even when a hawk had a wealth of donor support and a sharp political profile, the traditional Republican foreign policy views did not translate to popularity.

"The breakdown occurred because we got into a cycle where policy didn't matter at all. Policy was not just secondary, but it was almost not even in the conversation. And when people tried to interject policy—whether it was Rubio or Bush or others—there was just no appetite for it. It didn't catch on," said Peter Wehner, a former official in George W. Bush's White House. Added former House speaker Newt Gingrich, in an interview with me in March 2016: "Rubio was prepared, much like Jeb Bush, for a reasonable dialogue in Washington policy language, offering positions that reflect 40 years of national security and foreign-policy experts. All of that disappeared. The market didn't care."[36]

Trump repeated his case against George W. Bush and the Iraq War in debate after debate throughout the primaries, such as when in February 2016 in South Carolina he said, "Obviously, the war in Iraq was a big, fat mistake, all right? We spent $2 trillion, thousands of lives, we don't even have it. Iran has taken over Iraq with the second-largest oil reserves in the world." He said later that night, "We should have never been in Iraq. We have destabilized the Middle East." These discussions and exchanges, notably with Bush, were a cold bucket of water tossed over the hawkish consensus and its proponents, who had thought their past positions and actions would largely be unchallenged through the 2016 primary race. Trump not only challenged them; he was incessant and made many primary voters rethink their own views in the process.[37]

The final and deep rupture in Republican policy during the primary race came on fiscal and economic policy. Trump's economic populism on trade was in direct opposition to the kind of policy agenda that congressional Republicans and Mitt Romney had run on in recent years. Trump's aversion to taking on the entitlement state and tweaking federal spending programs like Medicare and Social Security was another change. "This is the biggest fault line in the party: whether Republicans should be talking about reducing benefits," conservative economist Stephen Moore told me during the campaign. "Republicans have fallen on their sword for 30 years trying to reform

Social Security and Medicare, but the dream lives on—and it makes everyone nervous. Some see a political trap; others see it as necessary."[38]

As *Roll Call* observed, "Trump's candidacy is making plain an open secret in Washington—that Republicans aren't as committed to fiscal discipline as they pretend," and that extended to how Republican candidates talked about these issues on the campaign trail.[39] The proposals that had been pushed by the Romney-Ryan ticket four years earlier never made waves with GOP voters, even when presented by new faces like Christie and Walker, who both positioned themselves as fiscal hawks early on. On trade and immigration, Trump again and again backed away from the traditional manner Republicans spoke about those issues. Rather than appealing to the Chamber of Commerce wing of the party and to business leaders, he struck a populist chord and in the process made this once surefire way to burnish your conservative credentials a relic of campaigns past.

THE TRUMP SURPRISE

Donald Trump's unlikely presidential campaign was long in the making, and there were hints for years before he got into the race, from his appearances at conservative confabs to his rousing of the right-wing base with the "birther" charge against President Obama in the 2011–2012 period, which included a flirtation with a run for the presidency. He traveled to New Hampshire in the late 1980s, and he mulled a Reform Party bid in 1999.[40] Yet when Trump began once again to consider a campaign in late 2014 and early 2015, it was as if many Republicans were sleeping. The same goes for many reporters and media pundits. There was a widespread refusal to believe that he would actually run and that even if he did, that he could win. Because Trump had come close to running before but never really gotten into presidential politics, he was considered to be a bloviating salesman who was merely seeking publicity for his brand—an American character, not an American candidate.

But Trump was able to take them by surprise. With a small cadre of aides such as operative Samuel Nunberg and GOP veteran Roger Stone, he began to build a political operation from his office on the 26th floor of Trump Tower overlooking Central Park. At the start of the primary race, it was unlike most presidential campaigns, where well-known finance advisers were hired and the campaign began to look at a ground game in Iowa and New Hampshire. What Trump wanted was to build his name recognition with television appearances and speeches, but he didn't feel the need to build too many relationships in the traditional GOP. He saw that aspect of the party—the leadership and the donors—as something he could run against. Guided by Nunberg and Stone, and then Laudner and Lewandowski, he decided in early 2015 that if he did get in, he would run as an outsider who underscored his views on trade and immigration. It would be a campaign not only to win the nomination but to destroy the norms of the modern GOP. In a time when conservatism was supposed to be the way to power in the party, Trump saw the populist path.

"A builder, an entrepreneur and a capitalist versus a bunch of politicians who are clearly part of the problem" is how Stone framed the contest in a document obtained by *The Washington Post* in 2015 as Trump rose in the polls. The memo suggested a sound bite: "I'm running because when I look at this field—all perfectly nice people—I know that none of them could ever run one of my companies. They are not entrepreneurs."[41]

Nunberg and Stone would eventually part ways with Trump in 2015, but the model they established was crucial to Trump's success. His past political dalliances but also his limited operation made GOP rivals pay little attention to him for much of the race. Jeb Bush's Super PAC held off on attacking him, as did Cruz. Most party leaders privately said they thought he'd quit or would implode due to controversy or his flimsy campaign structure. But as Trump often told me in interviews throughout the race, that was projection by his opponents. Especially once Trump got in the race, he saw clearly that he could present himself as a different type of candidate than most of the others and have a relatively easy path to the final stage of the primary if he could keep his name in the headlines and his views and statements dominant in the political debate. In his mind, he didn't need much more than that. Armed with a Twitter account and a phone, he believed he could outmaneuver candidates who raised millions.[42]

Lewandowski, a New Hampshire-based consultant, was brought on to Trump's campaign in early 2015, as was Laudner, the Iowa-based consultant. Laudner started to build an unusual network for Trump in Iowa that foreshadowed the coalition to come: evangelicals looking for a warrior over a fellow-traveler and populist-leaning conservatives who were tired of the same kind of Republicans traveling through the state. Lewandowski was installed as campaign manager and ran the campaign with a "Let Trump be Trump" mantra that enabled the candidate to be unpredictable if often off-kilter in his message and presentation. There was also Hope Hicks, a youthful adviser who filtered the hundreds of press requests that arrived. A galaxy of friends and allies were around the campaign, never formally part of it but giving Trump advice over the phone in calls to his office or cell phone. It was an "unusual power grid in a capital city used to a hierarchical structure . . .

[Trump presided] over concentric spheres of influence, designed to give him direct access to a constellation of counselors and opinions."[43]

The family played a critical role as well, in particular Trump's son-in-law, Jared Kushner, who regularly traveled with Trump on the plane. Kushner, for example, worked closely with Paul Manafort, who replaced Lewandowski, and built relationships for Trump in a party he barely knew. Sons Donald Jr. and Eric, and daughter Ivanka, also were constants at Trump's side, making them as influential as any member of the campaign staff and trusted confidants for their father.

But as much as Nunberg, Stone, Lewandowski, Kushner, and others mattered in the primary race, it was always Trump at the center, Trump himself who in a sense willed his way to the nomination and remade the Republican Party in his image. It was Trump who ran a campaign on gut and instinct and little organization. His ability to climb over more than a dozen rivals and snag the nomination was a feat that was both historic and strange. Here was a man who saw a broken party in the wake of George W. Bush and Mitt Romney and saw an opportunity, almost as if the GOP was a building in foreclosure from his work in real estate. It was a leaderless and rudderless party in most respects, with ideologies that had calcified and grown brittle over time. Trump didn't necessarily have to make a better argument or run a better campaign throughout the race, he simply had to be someone who offered a different approach and had the ability to burst through the pack and do so with unrepentant swagger. There was a determination to win more than a determination to convince; a determination to do whatever was necessary even if it was abhorrent to others. In the process, it became a race like no other, and Trump found his way to the convention floor with balloons above—and a few months later, he found himself in the White House.

NOTES

1. Robert Costa and Philip Rucker, "How Ted Cruz outfoxed Donald Trump in Iowa," *Washington Post*, February 2, 2016, https://www.washingtonpost.com/politics/the-inside-story-of-how-ted-cruz-won-iowa/2016/02/02/238b0b94-c839-11e5-a7b2-5a2f824b02c9_story.html.

2. Ashley Parker and Steve Eder, "Inside the Six Weeks Donald Trump Was a Nonstop 'Birther,'" *New York Times*, July 2, 2016, http://www.nytimes.com/2016/07/03/us/politics/donald-trump-birther-obama.html.

3. Robert Costa, "Trump says he is serious about 2016 bid, is hiring staff and delaying TV gig," *Washington Post*, February 25, 2015, https://www.washingtonpost.com/politics/trump-says-he-is-serious-about-2016-bid-is-hiring-staff-and-delaying-tv-gig/2015/02/25/4e9d3804-bd07-11e4-8668-4e7ba8439ca6_story.html.

4. McKay Coppins, "How the Haters and Losers Lost," *Buzzfeed*, July 17, 2016, https://www.buzzfeed.com/mckaycoppins/how-the-haters-made-trump.

5. Will Doran, "Donald Trump set the record for the most GOP primary votes ever. But that's not his only record," *Politifact*, July 8, 2016, http://www.politifact.com/north-carolina/statements/2016/jul/08/donald-trump/donald-trump-set-record-most-gop-primary-votes-eve/.

6. Jonah Goldberg, "GOP voters are refusing to fall in line," *Los Angeles Times*, January 12, 2016, http://www.latimes.com/opinion/op-ed/la-oe-0112-goldberg-establishment-disorder-20160112-17-column.html.

7. Philip Rucker and David A. Fahrenthold, "Donald Trump positions himself as the voice of 'the forgotten men and women,'" *Washington Post*, July 22, 2016, https://www.washingtonpost.com/politics/in-speech-at-republican-national-convention-trump-to-paint-dire-picture-of-america/2016/07/21/418f9ae6-4fad-11e6-aa14-e0c1087f7583_story.html.

8. Stephen Collinson, "Brexit: The UK's Donald Trump moment," CNN.com, June 24, 2016, http://www.cnn.com/2016/06/22/politics/eu-referendum-brexit-donald-trump/.

9. David A. Graham, "The Many Scandals of Donald Trump: A cheat sheet," *The Atlantic*, October 13, 2016, http://www.theatlantic.com/politics/archive/2016/10/donald-trump-scandals/474726/.

10. Patrick Healy and Jonathan Martin, "Donald Trump and Bernie Sanders Win in New Hampshire Primary," *New York Times*, February 9, 2016, http://www.nytimes.com/2016/02/10/us/politics/new-hampshire-primary.html.

11. Clare Malone, "The End of a Republican Party," *FiveThirtyEight*, July 18, 2016, http://fivethirtyeight.com/features/the-end-of-a-republican-party/.

12. Philip Rucker and Robert Costa, "An Iowa surprise: Donald Trump is actually trying to win," *Washington Post*, August 13, 2015, https://www.washingtonpost.com/politics/an-iowa-surprise-donald-trump-is-actually-trying-to-win/2015/08/13/564a9f50-4142-11e5-8e7d-9c033e6745d8_story.html.

13. Philip Rucker and Robert Costa, "Influential Republicans working to draft Jeb Bush into 2016 presidential race," *Washington Post*, March 29, 2014, https://www.washingtonpost.com/politics/influential-republicans-working-to-draft-jeb-bush-into-2016-presidential-race/2014/03/29/11e33b06-b5f2-11e3-8cb6-284052554d74_story.html.

14. Gerry Mullany, "Jeb Bush on the issues," *New York Times*, June 15, 2015, http://www.nytimes.com/2015/06/16/us/politics/jeb-bush-on-the-issues.html?_r=0.

15. Eli Stokols, "Jeb's shock-and-awe number," *Politico*, July 9, 2015, http://www.politico.com/story/2015/07/jeb-bush-2016-fundraising-11-million-in-16-days-119908.

16. Kristen Soltis Anderson, "All the Electable Republicans are Losing," *The Daily Beast*, August 18, 2015, http://www.thedailybeast.com/articles/2015/08/18/all-the-electable-republicans-are-losing.html.

17. Dan Balz, Philip Rucker, Robert Costa, and Matea Gold, "One year, two races: Inside the Republican Party's bizarre, tumultuous 2015," *Washington Post*, January 3, 2016, https://www.washingtonpost.com/politics/one-year-two-races/2016/01/03/28f65044-b15e-11e5-b820-eea4d64be2a1_story.html.

18. David Frum, "The Man for One Season," *The Atlantic*, October 29, 2015, http://www.theatlantic.com/politics/archive/2015/10/jeb-bush-struggles/413014/.

19. Trip Gabriel and Ashley Parker, "Jeb Bush's New Show of Confidence Is Failing to Connect with Republicans," *New York Times*, December 2, 2015, http://www.nytimes

.com/2015/12/03/us/politics/jeb-bushs-new-show-of-confidence-is-failing-to-connect-with
-republicans.html.

20. The *Sun Sentinel* editorial board (Broward County, Fla.), "Jeb had it all—and it wasn't enough," *Sun Sentinel*, February 24, 2016, http://archive.tcpalm.com/opinion/editorials/jeb-had-it-all--and-it-wasnt-enough-2ab74926-bf8f-0399-e053-0100007f8286-
3699499
81.html.

21. David A. Fahrenthold and Katie Zezima, "For Ted Cruz, the 2013 shutdown was a defining moment," *Washington Post*, February 16, 2016, https://www.washingtonpost
.com/politics/how-cruzs-plan-to-defund-obamacare-failed--and-what-it-achieved/2016/
02/16/4e2ce116-c6cb-11e5-8965-0607e0e265ce_story.html.

22. Jonathan Martin and Maggie Haberman, "Ted Cruz Hopes Early Campaign Entry Will Focus Voters' Attention," *New York Times*, March 22, 2015, http://www.nytimes
.com/2015/03/23/us/politics/ted-cruz-to-announce-on-monday-he-plans-to-run-for-presi
dent.html.

23. Chris Cillizza and Aaron Blake, "Ranking the 2016 Republican field," *Washington Post*, February 15, 2015, https://www.washingtonpost.com/pb/politics/ranking-the-2016
-republican-field/2015/02/15/0aaafda2-b52d-11e4-9423-f3d0a1ec335c_story.html.

24. Ryan Bort, "A Timeline of Donald Trump and Ted Cruz's roller coaster relationship," *Newsweek*, July 21, 2016, http://www.newsweek.com/donald-trump-ted-cruz-his
tory-timeline-482765.

25. Aaron Blake, "9 truly awful things Ted Cruz and Donald Trump said about each other," *Washington Post*, September 23, 2016, https://www.washingtonpost.com/news/
the-fix/wp/2016/09/23/9-truly-awful-things-that-were-said-between-ted-cruz-and-the-man
-hell-now-support-donald-trump/.

26. "Here's Who Was Wrong about Rand Paul," *Politico*, February 3, 2016, http://
www.politico.com/magazine/story/2016/02/rand-paul-dropping-out-quotes-213590.

27. Justin Dyer, "The Decline of Movement Conservatism and the Rise of the Alt-Right," *The Public Discourse*, November 17, 2016, http://www.thepublicdiscourse.com/
2016/11/18253/.

28. Elaine Kamarck, "How Ted Cruz lost long before Indiana," May 3, 2016, Brookings Institution, https://www.brookings.edu/blog/fixgov/2016/05/03/how-ted-cruz-lost
-long-before-indiana/.

29. Eliana Johnson, "The Weaknesses That Doomed Ted Cruz," *National Review*, May 4, 2016, http://www.nationalreview.com/article/434916/ted-cruz-why-he-lost.

30. John Hinderaker, "The Reagan Coalition is Dead. What's next for conservatism?" *Power Line*, May 1, 2016, http://www.powerlineblog.com/archives/2016/05/the-reagan
-coalition-is-dead-whats-next-for-conservatism.php.

31. Laurie Goodstein, "Donald Trump reveals evangelical rifts that could shape politics for years," *New York Times*, October 17, 2016, http://www.nytimes.com/2016/10/17/us/
donald-trump-evangelicals-republican-vote.html.

32. Jerry Falwell Jr., "Here's the backstory of why I endorsed Donald Trump," *Washington Post*, January 27, 2016, https://www.washingtonpost.com/news/acts-of-faith/wp/
2016/01/27/jerry-falwell-jr-heres-the-backstory-of-why-i-endorsed-donald-trump/.

33. Michelle Boorstein, "Why Donald Trump is tearing evangelicals apart," *Washington Post*, March 15, 2015, https://www.washingtonpost.com/news/acts-of-faith/wp/

2016/03/15/evangelical-christians-are-enormously-divided-over-donald-trumps-runaway
-candidacy/.

34. William Galston, "Has Trump caused white evangelicals to change their tune on morality?" Brookings Institution, October 19, 2016, https://www.brookings.edu/blog/fix
gov/2016/10/19/has-trump-caused-white-evangelicals-to-change-their-tune-on-morality/.

35. Marc A. Thiessen, "Finding a consensus conservative for the GOP," *Washington Post*, October 12, 2015, https://www.washingtonpost.com/opinions/chaos-in-house-is
-good-for-gop/2015/10/12/c2765450-70e8-11e5-9cbb-790369643cf9_story.html.

36. Robert Costa and Philip Rucker, "Rubio's demise marks the last gasp of the Republican reboot," *Washington Post*, March 15, 2016, https://www.washingtonpost.com/politics/rubios-demise-marks-the-last-gasp-of-the-republican-reboot/2016/03/15/e0a6413c
-ea3d-11e5-a6f3-21ccdbc5f74e_story.html.

37. Byron York, "Trump forces GOP to take uncomfortable look at Iraq War," *Washington Examiner*, February 14, 2016, http://www.washingtonexaminer.com/byron-york
-trump-forces-gop-to-take-uncomfortable-look-at-iraq-war/article/2583262.

38. Robert Costa and Ed O'Keefe, "Debate over Medicare, Social Security, other federal benefits divide GOP," *Washington Post*, November 4, 2015, https://www.washington
post.com/politics/debate-over-medicare-social-security-other-federal-benefits-divides-gop
/2015/11/04/166619a8-824e-11e5-a7ca-6ab6ec20f839_story.html.

39. Shawn Zeller, "Not Your Father's GOP," *Roll Call*, September 26, 2016, http://
www.rollcall.com/news/politics/gop-deficit-debate-disappeared-trump.

40. Justin Curtis, "Demystifying the Donald Trump, past and present," *Harvard Political Review*, Feb. 15, 2016, http://harvardpolitics.com/united-states/demystifying-donald
-trump-past-present/.

41. Robert Costa and Philip Rucker, "Donald Trump struggles to turn a political fling into a durable campaign," *Washington Post*, August 9, 2015, https://www.washingtonpost
.com/politics/inside-trumps-orbit-growing-pains-for-a-sudden-front-runner/2015/08/09/
7672a8be-3ec6-11e5-9443-3ef23099398b_story.html.

42. Bob Woodward and Robert Costa, interview transcript, *Washington Post*, April 2, 2016, https://www.washingtonpost.com/news/post-politics/wp/2016/04/02/transcript-don
ald-trump-interview-with-bob-woodward-and-robert-costa.

43. Philip Rucker and Robert Costa, "In Trump's Washington, rival powers and whispers in the president's ear," *Washington Post*, November 16, 2016, https://www.wash
ingtonpost.com/politics/in-trumps-washington-rival-powers-and-whispers-in-the-presi
dents-ear/2016/11/16/50f3306c-ac03-11e6-a31b-4b6397e625d0_story.html.

7

"Feel the Bern"

Hillary's Agonizing Loss and the Future of the Democratic Party

Greg Sargent

When Senator Bernie Sanders of Vermont announced his presidential run to a handful of reporters outside the Capitol in April 2015, the moment was almost comically lacking in the hype and scripted theatrics that usually attend such moments. "Let me just make a brief comment," Sanders said, adding, without a hint of irony, that he had to make it quick because he had other, more pressing business to attend to—as if he were there to announce something as trivial as the introduction of a doomed message amendment.

Yet Sanders' "brief comment" foreshadowed a series of bruising arguments over the identity of the Democratic Party that not only produced a surprisingly contested nomination battle: they are the same arguments that will continue into the foreseeable future as the party tries to rebuild itself after its shattering and disorienting loss to Donald Trump.

Sanders articulated the message that would win the presidency well before Trump announced his own presidential run: the economy and political systems are rigged by elites, and as a result, ordinary hardworking Americans are falling farther and farther behind, struggling under the weight of stagnating wages even as worker productivity increases and the elites get richer. "For most Americans, their reality is that they're working longer hours for lower wages . . . despite a huge increase in technology and productivity,"

Sanders said. "At exactly the same time, 99 percent of all new income generated in this country is going to the top one percent." Sanders vowed to shake up our rigged political system—"billionaires are literally able to buy elections and candidates; let's not kid ourselves"—and revamp trade deals that enrich multinational corporations while shifting jobs overseas.[1]

To be sure, vast differences emerged between Sanders and Trump, who won by blaming people's economic struggles more on Washington elites and other countries who rip us off than on Sanders' "billionaire class." Trump also relentlessly scapegoated Muslims and immigrants, creating a toxic right-wing populism whose economic message derived much of its energy from white identity politics.

But Sanders anticipated the rise of key strains of Trumpism with remarkable prescience. Trump—like Sanders—decried a combination of trade deals and a rigged system that, in tandem, have badly shafted American workers. Yet Trump, not Sanders, won the presidency. How did a celebrity TV pitchman billionaire who offshored jobs and ripped off untold numbers of workers himself manage to become the candidate who won by emphasizing jobs, trade, economic populism, and political reform against the party of the New Deal? What does that mean for the future of the Democratic Party?

THE GRAND ARGUMENT OVER THE PARTY'S NEW DEAL LEGACY

The epic Democratic primary battle between Sanders and Hillary Clinton unfolded around a great argument over how to repurpose the party's New Deal legacy in the face of the challenges of a New 21st Century Gilded Age: soaring inequality; stagnating wages; and a political system paralyzed from addressing such challenges and thus badly in need of reform. Clinton reached for this legacy when she announced her own presidential run in June 2015 from Roosevelt Island in New York, drawing on FDR's Four Freedoms to call for a restoration of the fundamental American bargain in which work is rewarded with a rising standard of living. Clinton—like Sanders—decried inequality and stagnating wages as defining challenges of our time.

Yet early on, as the crowds swelled with young, curious faces at Sanders rallies in towns throughout Iowa and New Hampshire, it became clear that he was the one capturing outsized energy and enthusiasm. Sanders appeared to make his followers and rally attendees feel as if they had been swept up in a movement. A rumpled, cranky former mayor of Burlington, Vermont, who called himself a socialist and hectored and lectured his audiences in an accent straight out of 1950s Brooklyn, Sanders was an unlikely candidate to lead such a phenomenon. Yet his *lack* of affectation is precisely what caught on. Even the shape of Sanders' bald spot—reproduced in relief on innumerable posters—became something of a cultural icon, seemingly capturing his refusal to capitulate to a political culture awash in blow-dried, scripted inauthenticity.

Ultimately, however, Sanders's surprising appeal was not simply cultural. It was also rooted in the unabashed ambitiousness of his policy agenda. From the outset, Sanders vividly depicted a country whose future is in profound peril. Our middle class and our democracy are in danger of extinction at the hands of plutocracy, he warned, and the long-term climate threat poses an existential threat to future generations. He insisted on single-payer universal health care and free college, both *as a matter of societal right*; at least $1 trillion in new infrastructure spending; a $15-per-hour federal minimum wage; breaking up the big banks and restoring campaign finance limits to break the power of the plutocracy; and vastly ambitious actions to combat climate change.

The energy of Sanders's candidacy seemed to flow from his *refusal* to flinch from outlining an agenda commensurate with the scale of the challenges he depicted. While previous presidential cycles have produced a robust left-wing challenger to the Democratic establishment candidate in primaries, Sanders' success appeared ideologically different. It seemed to reveal the existence of an unexpectedly large audience for a form of European-style social democracy that is much more ambitious than the more incremental economic policies championed by Democrats from the 1990s onward. This certainly appeared to have great appeal to younger voters, enormous majorities of whom gravitated to Sanders over Clinton. His apocalyptic warnings about our future spoke to their angst over that future—over *their* future.

Clinton, it must be said, developed a much more ambitious and detailed economic agenda during the primaries than her campaign is commonly credited for. Some of the specifics of that agenda surely emerged in response to the Sanders challenge. But it is also true that the economic progressivism she embraced was comfortably in sync with genuinely progressive instincts on her part that had been on display at previous moments throughout her career, such as when, as First Lady in the early 1990s, she famously threw herself into an ill-fated campaign for universal health care.

Clinton's agenda did not go as far as that of Sanders, but she embraced a $12-per-hour minimum wage while lending rhetorical support to local movements toward $15; campaign finance limits and a plan to rein in reckless shadow banking; hundreds of billions in new infrastructure spending; investments in targeted manufacturing and struggling coal communities; student debt relief; and an expansion of Obamacare to achieve universal coverage.

On climate, Clinton did not embrace a carbon tax, as Sanders did, but she called for increased investments in renewable energy and pledged to achieve 50 percent clean energy by 2030.

Yet the differences between Sanders and Clinton ran deep. In retrospect, it appears those differences may have foreshadowed a failing on Clinton's part that would come to haunt her in the general election.

SIGNS OF TROUBLE EMERGE
FOR HILLARY CLINTON

As the Democratic Party seeks to rebuild, it will once again take up—in one form or another—the deep differences that unfolded between Sanders and Clinton once the primaries got seriously underway after the voting began.

One of these erupted over how to speak powerfully and convincingly to voters' economic disillusionment—and how to balance that with other, traditional Democratic appeals. In the first two contests of the nominating season, Sanders surged to a near-tie in Iowa and defeated Clinton soundly in New Hampshire. But these were overwhelmingly white states, and as the battle turned to more diverse states such as South Carolina and Nevada, Clinton argued that Sanders' single-minded focus on Wall Street was misguided. "If we broke up the big banks tomorrow," Clinton asked an audience of union members in Nevada that included many blacks and Hispanics, "would that end racism? Would that end sexism? Would that end discrimination against the LGBT community?"[2]

Clinton won an overwhelming victory in South Carolina and bested Sanders by five points in Nevada, setting a pattern that would hold throughout: Clinton's support among nonwhites gave her a broader coalition that Sanders simply could not overcome. This led to crushing Clinton wins on Super Tuesday, March 1, and again on March 15, which were fought out in multiple big, diverse states, setting Clinton on a path to building an insurmountable delegate lead.

Yet in the midst of that stretch of Clinton wins came an alarming loss that—in retrospect—may have anticipated her weaknesses as a general election candidate. Sanders won a surprise close victory in Michigan that raised the question of whether he might have identified—more perceptively than she—the need for a message focused relentlessly on trade, wages, and the need for political reform. His sizable win among blue-collar whites jolted many insiders. Stan Greenberg, the veteran Democratic pollster who first identified the 1980s "Reagan Democrat" phenomenon in Macomb County, Michigan, told this writer at the time that his research into struggling Rust

Belt voters persuaded him that Clinton might be missing something fundamental about the 2016 electorate. "These voters are very anxious, very uncertain about the country's future, very focused on the economy, and want
change," Greenberg said.

The economic argument between Sanders and Clinton also became a dispute over whether an establishment candidate would inevitably be too com-
promised a figure to convincingly make the case for serious political and
economic reform. Sanders relentlessly attacked Clinton as a creature of the
political and economic elite. He called on her to release private speeches to
Wall Street and excoriated her for benefiting from a Super PAC, hinting (with
varying degrees of forthrightness) that she was too beholden to the establishment to fight for real change. Clinton and her supporters reacted with
outrage—there was a disingenuous quality to his attacks. Sanders seemed
unwilling to quite say what he was implying.

But there were already signs that the Clinton team privately suspected that
Sanders might have successfully identified a core Clinton weakness. Even as
Sanders basked in his Michigan victory, another candidate was doing the
same on the GOP side, and he, too, appeared to be speaking to the anxieties
Greenberg had identified. Donald Trump's large victory in the state—he too
did extremely well among blue-collar whites—moved him closer to winning
the GOP nomination, and the resonance of his harsh anti-immigration, anti-
trade, antiestablishment message caught the attention of the Clinton team.

Even then, Clinton campaign manager Robby Mook had already privately
concluded that Trump's appeal was derived, at least in part, from a widespread belief that traditional politicians are no longer capable of addressing
profound economic anxieties, and that this could give Trump a huge advantage among white men.[3] Sanders' appeal was similar (though without
Trump's naked racial and xenophobic appeals).

Clinton did adjust her pitch in the face of the Sanders challenge. But the
focus was less on developing her reform message (perhaps because running
as an outsider was not a credible option) and more on emphasizing that she
was offering a more realistic assessment of how to address the domestic pain
of globalization and the limits of the politically possible in the face of likely
GOP control of Congress in 2017. Clinton argued that Sanders was making
unrealistic promises ("pie in the sky," she scoffed at one point, deeply anger-
ing his supporters) and that the clock could not be turned back on economic
change.[4] She presented herself as the more seasoned fighter who could wring
incremental concessions out of Republicans, essentially seeming to promise
little more than an era of more trench warfare and minuscule gains in the
face of major long-term challenges.

Clinton's argument was enough to secure the Democratic nomination, partly on the strength of her more diverse coalition. But that argument carried over into the general election in problematic ways, and Democrats are now reckoning with the deeper meaning of this for their party going forward.

THE FAILURE TO SPEAK TO WORKING-CLASS WHITES

"I think there needs to be a profound change in the way the Democratic Party does business," Bernie Sanders said in mid-November, as Democrats began sorting through the wreckage of their loss. "I come from the white working class," Sanders added. "I am deeply humiliated that the Democratic Party cannot talk to where I came from."[5]

Why does the Democratic Party continue to struggle so badly to appeal to working-class whites? Trump successfully smashed through the so-called "Blue Wall" by winning in Pennsylvania, Michigan, and Wisconsin, a feat that was powered in part by his crushing win among noncollege white voters—including many who had voted for Barack Obama four years earlier.

"Trump spoke to their aspirations and fears more directly than any Republican candidate in decades," a *New York Times* post-election analysis noted, concluding that "white Americans without a college degree voted decisively to reject the more diverse, educated, and cosmopolitan Democratic Party of the 21st Century" in the "onetime heartlands of 20th Century liberal populism—the Upper and Lower Midwest."[6] Making this worse, Trump also outperformed among *middle-class* whites, too, which may have helped him edge Clinton in Florida and hold her margin down in the suburbs of Philadelphia, allowing him to prevail in Pennsylvania.

The simplest way to describe what happened is that demographics did not deliver for Democrats. The party and the Clinton campaign had good reason to be confident that the vaunted "Obama coalition"—the nonwhites, young voters, single women, and college-educated whites who powered majority victories in the two previous national elections—would come through one more time, as Republicans had shown no signs of even trying to evolve culturally in sync with the preoccupations of those groups. But demographic destiny fell short of swamping Trump's margins among blue-collar and middle-income whites.

Some critics now argue that the party must revamp its economic message to rectify a crucial mistake on Clinton's part. Clinton, goes this argument, failed to connect with the economic anxieties of these white voters precisely because overconfidence in her demographic advantage led her campaign to get lost amid micro-targeted cultural appeals to various groups in the Obama coalition, thus neglecting a broader economic and reform message. The oft-heard refrain is that Clinton's initial economic push—for shared prosperity and an economy that works for all—got overtaken by "identity politics," which is to say, by the Clinton team's decision to spend a great deal of time and resources on attacking Trump's racially charged campaign, rather than on beating him in the argument over the economy and the need for political reform.

There may be some truth to the notion that Clinton de-emphasized her economic message in a damaging way. Although Clinton's convention speech was heavily laden with a programmatic economic agenda, political scientist Lynn Vavreck conducted a post-election analysis of the TV advertising by both campaigns and concluded that more than three-quarters of the appeals in Clinton's ads were about character traits. Only 9 percent were about jobs or the economy. In contrast, more than one-third of the appeals in Trump's ads were focused on economic issues, such as jobs, taxes, and trade.[7] And some Democratic operatives have groused that the Clinton camp was overly confident of victory in reliably Democratic Rust Belt states like Wisconsin and Michigan—meaning, perhaps, that Trump's economic message had even more resonance in them than the Clinton team had anticipated.

But, in defense of the Clinton campaign, there are important nuances here that should not get lost amid all the recriminations—and they are deeply relevant to the debate over where the party goes next. For one thing, it is plausible that Clinton might have won if it were not for important external events well beyond her control. As of this writing, the CIA had concluded that Russia actively tried to interfere in the election to swing the outcome to Trump—and may have been behind the hacking into the emails of DNC and Clinton campaign officials, which produced months of vaguely sinister-sounding headlines about Clinton.

What's more, the importance of FBI Director James Comey's discovery of new emails potentially relevant to the previously closed investigation into Clinton's server arrangement—eleven days before the election—cannot be minimized. As *Politico*'s Glenn Thrush reported, top officials in both the Clinton and Trump campaigns saw this as a game changer. Clinton's chief data analytics guru saw her numbers tank among a crucial demographic: educated white voters who had been alienated by Trump's videotaped boasts of lewd groping and subsequent allegations of unwanted advances.[8]

Without Comey and the Russia hacking, elections analyst Nate Silver concluded, states like Florida, Michigan, Wisconsin, and Pennsylvania—which Trump won by excruciatingly tight margins—might have tipped to Clinton.

"Comey had a large, measurable impact on the race," Silver said.[9] In other words, if Comey had never taken that step, we might currently be discussing the staying power of the Obama coalition and the success of the Clinton strategy—in particular, the emphasis on attacking Trump's dangerously unhinged temperament, and his campaign of racism, hate, and abuse directed at Mexican immigrants and women—in driving college-educated whites into the Democratic camp.

It is often argued that Comey is not responsible for Clinton's loss, because he did not force her to set up a private server, or de-emphasize her economic message, or neglect the Rust Belt. But this argument is weak. It can be true that Clinton was a very flawed candidate who made mistakes, even as it is *also* true that Comey's letter had a major impact on the outcome—and potentially a decisive one—without which the Clinton strategy might have prevailed. Given that the Comey revelations ended up amounting to nothing in substantive terms, the fact that his decision did have such a large impact reveals his handling of the whole mess to be indefensible and reflects terribly on our political process. Clinton's real failings should not be permitted to minimize the significance of that.

What's more, it was not unreasonable for the Clinton team to conclude that the strategy of casting Trump as temperamentally unfit to handle national security—and too hateful and divisive to lead our diverse country—was going to succeed. Polls indicated for months that Clinton was on track to become the first Democrat to win a majority of college-educated whites in over half a century. Many analysts across the spectrum had concluded that such an outcome would probably cripple Trump's ability to prevail by running up enormous margins among white voters.

Finally, whatever the Clinton team's motives in making a big issue out of Trump's race-tinged campaign, it was the right thing to do. For all the talk about Clinton playing "identity politics," the candidate who played "identity politics" to a far greater extent was Donald Trump. His campaign—which fused the relentless scapegoating of Muslims and undocumented immigrants with revanchist appeals to "Make America Great Again"—was all about encouraging and playing to a sense that white identity and white America were under siege. It was important for the country that Clinton call out Trump's white nationalist appeals for what they were—and that she defend the minority groups that he had targeted for vilification. *Not* doing so would have been an abdication.

None of this, however, should absolve the Clinton campaign and the Democratic establishment figures who rallied to her side from facing a reckoning over the ways in which they *are* responsible for the outcome.

WHY DID CLINTON LOSE? WHAT SHOULD
DEMOCRATS LEARN FROM IT?

One of the Clinton campaign's official public explanations for her loss is that she ultimately came to be seen as a creature of the establishment at a moment when the electorate craved change. Clinton campaign manager Robby Mook recently described this as a "head wind" that could not be overcome.[10]

Of course, if that is true, then Clinton herself—and Democratic establishment figures—are partially complicit in creating that perception. In retrospect, the early decision to limit the number of debates—which the Democratic National Committee made in part out of deference to the Clinton campaign, which apparently wanted to limit her exposure—may have been an early signal of an unhealthy establishment faith in Clinton's chances. So too was the lack of more primary challengers, which appeared premised on the sense that she could not be beaten precisely because she was the pick of so many party leaders. To be sure, it was reasonable for many leading Democrats to suspect that Clinton—with her deep knowledge and experience—gave the party a very good shot at winning the White House. Whether this assumption was subjected to rigorous enough scrutiny—and whether a failure in that regard represented a more systemic problem with the party establishment, such as overconfidence in its ability to win national elections—should be topics of debate in coming months.

Another question that must be settled is whether the Clinton campaign—and establishment Democrats—reckoned seriously enough with polling that revealed abysmal public perceptions of her on trust and honesty, and widespread concern with her handling of her emails and the Clinton Foundation. Taken together, all of this amounted to a red flag—a warning that Clinton might not be seen as a credible messenger if the campaign became a battle over who would shake up our corrupt political system, as Trump sought to turn it into. Clinton rolled out a detailed political reform agenda, but it's not clear whether she conveyed a *gut* sense that she really wanted to shake things up. As one Democrat sighed to me in August: *I wish Clinton would show more discomfort with our political system and with how business is done in Washington.*

This possibility—that Clinton did not show a gut level of *discomfort* with our current arrangements—is worth mulling. Trump's numbers were even worse than Clinton's on honesty, and his promises to bust up the system were crude and laughably absurd—he actually argued that he was well qualified to reform our corrupt system because he had milked it himself from the inside to great effect. But it's worth asking whether he somehow conveyed a *visceral* disdain for the way business is done in Washington that Clinton simply did not. In retrospect, that "brief comment" Sanders made in announcing his run so many months ago—with its angry, unvarnished, unscripted focus on our rigged system and the reality of economic stagnation for so many—seemed prescient in capturing what this whole campaign would be all about, on an emotional level. Future Democratic candidates will likely keep these lessons in mind.

Of course, even if one accepts that Clinton failed to marshal effective enough messages on the economy and political reform, it's hard to know how much that mattered. The polling evidence is mixed on whether Clinton's economic message even failed—exit polls showed she won among voters most concerned about the economy in many swing states. Clinton won the popular vote by nearly 3 million votes, and her extremely close losses in multiple states might not have happened if turnout had shaped up differently even on the margins.

Beyond this, if the party is going to work to sharpen up its economic and reform message—to working-class white voters in particular—the crucial challenge is how to do this *without* backing off of its commitment to being the party that fully embraces cultural and demographic change. Much of the post-election debate is on some basic level framed around a false choice—one pitting the need to minister to the Obama coalition versus the need for economic appeals to working-class whites. But these things needn't be in conflict with one another. The challenges faced by the nonwhites, young voters, and women who make up the Obama coalition are *also* in many respects economic ones. Debates over systemic racism, over how to create more opportunity and mobility for minorities and young people, over how to integrate undocumented immigrants who have been contributing to American life for years but remain consigned to the shadows, and over how to foster economic equality for women—all of these are, at bottom, about the need for reforms that make the economy fairer and render prosperity more inclusive, for everyone.

Most early indications are that senior Democrats *are not* falling into the trap that this false choice debate presents. Most of the chatter among Democrats is how to refocus the party's message on economic fairness in ways that have appeal *across* diverse constituencies. That will likely continue.

The Democratic Party is a diverse party. It should not weaken its commitment to defending minority rights, particularly in an age of resurgent Trump Era white backlash. The party must not back off of its defense of undocumented immigrants—both for substantive and strategic reasons. If Trump makes good on his promises, the plight of undocumented immigrants could worsen into a genuine humanitarian crisis, one that Democrats must resist. The GOP will continue alienating the fast growing demographic of Latino voters, potentially hastening Democratic gains in Sun Belt states, which, over time, could reconfigure the map in advantageous ways in future national elections.

This time around, demographic destiny did not materialize for Democrats. But demographic change marches on. While that is by no means alone a guarantee of future success, the party's big challenge going forward will be to work to maintain its position on the right side of it—while also speaking more effectively to the anxieties of those who feel it is leaving them behind.

NOTES

1. Chris Cillizza, "Bernie Sanders's presidential campaign announcement is sort of amazing to watch now," *Washington Post*, February 1, 2016, https://www.washingtonpost .com/news/the-fix/wp/2016/02/01/bernie-sanderss-presidential-campaign-announcement -is-sort-of-amazing-to-watch-now/?utm_term = .ec99e3b6799a.

2. Nicholas Confessore and Yamiche Alcindor, "Hillary Clinton, shifting line of attack, paints Bernie Sanders as a one-issue candidate," *New York Times*, February 13, 2016, http://www.nytimes.com/2016/02/14/us/politics/hillary-clinton-shifting-line-of-at tack-paints-bernie-sanders-as-a-one-issue-candidate.html.

3. Amy Chozick and Patrick Healy, "Inside the Clinton team's plan to defeat Donald Trump," *New York Times*, February 29, 2016, http://www.nytimes.com/2016/03/01/us/po litics/hillary-clinton-donald-trump-general-election.html.

4. Dan Merica, "Clinton casts Sanders as 'pie in the sky' in Wisconsin," CNN, March 29, 2016, http://www.cnn.com/2016/03/29/politics/hillary-clinton-bernie-sanders-wiscon sin/.

5. Samantha Reyes, "Bernie Sanders 'deeply humiliated' Democrats lost white work ing-class voters," CNN, November 14, 2016, http://www.cnn.com/2016/11/14/politics/ bernie-sanders-humiliated-democrats-loss-working-class-voters/.

6. Nicholas Confessore and Nate Cohn, "Donald Trump's victory was built on unique coalition of white voters," *New York Times*, November 9, 2016, http://www.nytimes.com/ 2016/11/10/us/politics/donald-trump-voters.html.

7. Lynn Vavreck, "Why this election was not about the issues," *New York Times*, November 23, 2016, http://www.nytimes.com/2016/11/23/upshot/this-election-was-not -about-the-issues-blame-the-candidates.html.

8. Glenn Thrush, "10 crucial decisions that reshaped America," *Politico*, December 9, 2016, http://www.politico.com/magazine/story/2016/12/2016-presidential-election-10 -moments-trump-clinton-214508.

9. Nate Silver tweets (based on a previous analysis at *FiveThirtyEight*), December 10 and 11, 2016, https://twitter.com/NateSilver538/status/807640627101900800 and https:// twitter.com/NateSilver538/status/807984392480161793.

10. Karen Tumulty and Philip Rucker, "Shouting match erupts between Clinton and Trump aides," *Washington Post*, December 1, 2016, https://www.washingtonpost.com/ politics/shouting-match-erupts-between-clinton-and-trump-aides/2016/12/01/7ac4398e -b7ea-11e6-b8df-600bd9d38a02_story.html?utm_term = .88cf29650b4e.

8

Latinos and the 2016 Election

Matt Barreto, Thomas Schaller, and Gary Segura

For Latinos, the 2016 presidential election cycle effectively began the same day it did for every other American: June 16, 2015, the day Donald Trump declared his candidacy. That morning, Trump descended the escalators at Trump Tower in Manhattan to announce he would seek the Republican nomination for president. His announcement attracted about as much attention as expected for a businessman-turned-reality-TV-star deemed to be a long shot to win the GOP nomination in a crowded field of far more experienced Republican contenders.

But later that afternoon, Trump made the first of what became daily, front-page headlines when he bluntly insulted and denigrated Mexican-American immigrants. "When Mexico sends its people, they're not sending their best," said Trump. "They're sending people that have lots of problems, and they're bringing those problems with us. They're bringing drugs. They're bringing crime. They're rapists. And some, I assume, are good people."

The media seized upon Trump's comments, with pundits climbing over each other to declare Trump's candidacy dead on arrival. "I'm going to go out on a limb and predict that Trump will not be the next president of the United States or even the GOP nominee," Jonathan Capehart wrote in *The Washington Post*. "[H]is harsh rhetoric and the way his opponents respond (not well, I suspect) to the xenophobic zingers he will hurl on the debate stage will hobble the next Republican nominee's effort to secure the keys to the White House."[1]

Capehart was hardly alone in his condemnation of Trump's rapists-and-murderers statement, nor in predicting that Trump and any fellow Republicans who embraced such inflammatory rhetoric were doomed. After all, a few months after Mitt Romney's 2012 presidential defeat, the Republican National Committee published a self-diagnosis in which the RNC called for greater inclusiveness, and specifically a renewed appeal to Latino voters. The party promised to expand its reach, not demean and exclude large swaths of the electorate.

Prior to 2016, Latino politics—including but not limited to immigration and border issues—had never been so salient, so front and center during a U.S. presidential election. Nor had such unusual and offensive attacks ever been leveled so directly on American Latinos, immigrant or otherwise. In this chapter, we examine how Latinos voted in 2016. We specifically consider: Latino turnout in 2016; the partisan preferences of Latino voters in the presidential contest and key, down-ballot races; and the attitudes expressed by Latinos on the eve and day of the 2016 election.

In contrast to national media exit poll results we believe were severely flawed, we show that Latinos were in fact mobilized by opposition to Republican presidential nominee Donald Trump's candidacy. They voted in record numbers and in record shares for Hillary Clinton. And, yes, Trump's comments and behavior during the 2016 campaign offended Latinos and soured their perceptions of him and the Republican Party generally.

LATINO POLITICS IN THE 2016 ELECTION CYCLE

Latino politics are emergent, and Latino electoral power is rising. Politicians have been forced to respond to Latino voices and inputs. A bit of context is needed to fully understand the state of Latino politics by the start of the 2016 presidential contest.

In the 2008 Democratic primary race, by roughly a two-to-one ratio Latino Democrats preferred then-New York Senator Hillary Clinton to then-Illinois Senator Barack Obama. During that very competitive primary, Obama promised that, if nominated and elected, he would push for comprehensive immigration reform during his first year in office. In the 2008 general election, 67 percent of Latinos voted for Obama. Since the Latino vote began to be tracked in presidential elections, only Democrat Bill Clinton had received a higher share, 72 percent.

During Barack Obama's presidency, immigration in particular posed significant challenges for both parties. In Washington, where polarization and gridlock prevail and cooperation is rare, immigration served as a flashpoint for some of the more notable confrontations between President Obama and Congress, and between Democrats and Republicans. By the end of 2009, it was clear that the new president had already abandoned his pledge to reform immigration policy.

Although Obama had many competing domestic and economic problems to address during his first two years in office, his broken promise set the stage for the remainder of his first term. If Latinos were disappointed by the administration's passive advocacy for comprehensive immigration reform, they were further angered by the administration's active support for increased deportations of undocumented immigrants. The number of deportations in 2009 and 2010 exceeded even the highest number of deportations during the preceding Bush administration.

Polled in late May and early June 2011, Latinos expressed conflicted feelings about the president's inaction on immigration. A slight plurality of Latinos, 46 percent, said it was "understandable" that the administration did not prioritize immigration reform, given the pressing economic concerns. But another 42 percent said Obama "should have prioritized" reform.[2] At that point, fewer than half of Latinos polled said they were certain to vote for the president's reelection. A Pew Hispanic Center poll taken six months later, in December 2011, similarly pegged the president's approval level among Latinos below half, at 49 percent. According to Pew, by a margin of more than two-to-one, 59 percent to 27 percent, Latinos disapproved of the administration's deportation policies.[3]

Despite growing wariness among Latinos toward the Obama administration's immigration policies, Latinos viewed Republicans with equal if not greater suspicion. Specifically, Latinos said Republicans too often focus on border security as a diversion or to stall accomplishing comprehensive reform. "Republicans will have to do more than change their tone to connect with these voters, and Democrats will have to fulfill the promises they made, or they will have a harder time mobilizing the vote in 2012," said Frank Sharry, president of the pro-immigration reform group America's Voice, in describing the partisan stakes in the upcoming presidential cycle.[4]

By the time his 2012 reelection campaign got underway, however, it became clear to President Obama's reelection team that the administration's decision to shelve immigration reform had jeopardized his support among Latinos and potentially his reelection. With Latinos wavering, on June 15, 2012, the Obama administration announced the executive action on Deferred Action on Childhood Arrivals (DACA). The DACA ruling instructed the Department of Homeland Security to defer action on deporting the children born to undocumented parents living in the United States.

Obama's Latino support immediately surged. By sheer coincidence, Latino Decisions happened to be in the field polling Latinos about their support for Obama when the president announced the DACA order. The natural experiment created a pre- and post-announcement split-sample, and the results were clear: enthusiasm among Latinos for Obama immediately spiked 35 percent following the DACA announcement. "The announcement on June 15 appears to have clearly erased Obama's enthusiasm deficit among Latinos," we wrote at the time.[5] According to national exit polls, five months later 71 percent of Latinos voters supported Obama during reelection, and their votes provided sufficient support to ensure he captured the electoral votes in enough states that, without them, he would otherwise have failed to amass the required minimum of 270 electors.

Immigration and border issues were yet again hotly contested issues early during Obama's second term. In 2013, the U.S. Senate's so-called "Gang of Eight"—a group featuring both former GOP presidential nominee John McCain and 2016 Republican presidential hopeful Marco Rubio—began to fashion what they hoped would be an immigration reform plan that could attract the support of a filibuster-proof, bipartisan majority of at least sixty senators. But President Obama hedged again. In the middle of the 2014 midterm cycle, and supposedly under intense pressure from national party officials to not force Democratic Senate candidates to take a public stance on the issue, Obama delayed signing any new executive orders related to the administration's deportation policy for undocumented adults. Given the Democrats' loss of their Senate majority that November, the president's choice to wait until after the election probably helped his fellow Democrats little, if at all.

As the invisible primary season of 2015 opened and the two parties' presidential aspirants began preparing their campaigns, policy fights over immigration and the broader battle for Latino voters were mostly dormant. Senators Marco Rubio and Ted Cruz were expected to declare their presidential ambitions, making them the two most serious Latino contenders for a major-party presidential nomination in history. Former Florida Governor Jeb Bush, the son and brother of former presidents and husband to a Mexican-American wife, was the early frontrunner and held a slim lead among a crowded and growing field of expected Republican contenders. Few other Republican contenders seemed likely to stake out their identity within the GOP field on issues like immigration.

Then came Donald Trump.

As the Republican primary unfolded, Trump escalated his anti-immigrant rhetoric far beyond his rapists-and-murderers announcement day statement —a comment, we should note, that helped immediately catapult him to a lead in the GOP primary polls he never relinquished.[6] Indeed, Trump's signature campaign pledge was his promise to construct a massive wall along the U.S.-Mexico border and force Mexico to pay for it. At Trump campaign rallies, "build the wall!" chants quickly became a crowd favorite. Soon Rubio and Cruz began attacking each other during Republican debates as too soft on border and immigration issues. In short order, Trump had changed not only the tenor of the 2016 campaign, but the Republican Party's posture toward Latinos and positions on immigration policy.

Once Trump won the nomination, his anti-Latino rhetoric continued unabated. In a statement Republican House Speaker Paul Ryan characterized as the "textbook definition" of racism, Trump charged an American-born, Latino federal judge of being incapable of ruling fairly in a lawsuit filed against Trump University because of his ethnicity. The former owner of the Miss Universe pageant, Trump falsely claimed that Alicia Machado, a Latina Miss Universe he publicly humiliated two decades earlier for gaining weight, had starred in a sex tape. A prominent Trump supporter, Marco Gutierrez, warned that if America didn't do something about immigration there would soon be "taco trucks on every corner." Even after Trump won an Electoral College victory on November 8, he and some of his supporters continued to assert that Trump had been deprived from winning the national popular vote because millions of noncitizens had illegally cast votes for Democratic presidential nominee Hillary Clinton.

On the Democratic side, Hillary Clinton was again the prohibitive favorite to be the party's nominee. Seven years after losing to Obama despite receiving the lion's share of the Latino vote, Latinos continued to express strong support for the former first lady and secretary of state. In a post-midterm November poll conducted by Latino Decisions for Presente.org, the National Alliance of Latin American and Caribbean Communities (NALAAC), and Mi Familia Vota, a combined 85 percent of Latinos indicated they were either very likely (68 percent) or somewhat likely (17 percent) to support Clinton for president. But their support was conditional on Clinton endorsing Obama's executive action on deportation.[7]

Clinton did, in fact, later announce she supported President Obama's executive action on immigration and that, if elected, she would renew it. (The order is temporary, and unless Congress passes permanent reform President Trump has the power to renew, alter, or even reverse DACA.) In December 2015—just six weeks before formal voting began in the 2016 Democratic primary—Clinton delivered a major speech on immigration in which she pledged to uphold and even extend Obama's immigration protections. "America was built by immigrants," Clinton said. "Our future will be always written in part by immigrants and every single one of us, no matter how long ago our ancestors arrived in this land, whether they came by foot or boat or plane, across the Pacific or the Atlantic or the Rio Grande."

If ever there were a clear contrast on Latino politics generally, and immigration policy specifically, the 2016 general election provided it. In 2008, the differences between the two major parties were slight: Democrat Barack Obama—who to that point continued to mostly pay lip service to comprehensive immigration reform—ran against "Gang of Eight" Republican John McCain. In 2012, the candidate gap widened slightly, as DACA-convert Obama ran against "self-deportation" Republican nominee Mitt Romney. But by late 2015, on issues of importance to Latino voters the candidate and partisan gap between Clinton and Trump had grown into a chasm.

ELECTION RESULTS AND POLLING CONTROVERSY

Donald Trump carried thirty states, winning 304 electoral votes. He held all of the states fellow Republican Mitt Romney won four years earlier, and flipped another six states from blue to red: Florida (twenty-nine electoral votes), Iowa (six), Michigan (sixteen), Ohio (eighteen), Pennsylvania (twenty), and Wisconsin (ten). Trump amassed an Electoral College majority despite losing the popular vote to Hillary Clinton by more than two percentage points.

Exit polls confirmed what pundits predicted all along: Trump won based on his strength of support among white voters (57 percent to Clinton's 37 percent), particularly white men (62 percent to 31 percent), and more specifically whites without a college degree (66 percent to 29 percent). According to exit polls, Trump also won 28 percent of Latino voters, better than Mitt Romney—a seemingly shocking result, given his issue positions and statements.[8]

This figure is demonstrably wrong. For eight weeks prior to the election, Latino Decisions' tracking poll never showed Trump above 18 percent; meanwhile, Clinton steadily grew her share from 74 percent to 79 percent by the final week before the election. That 79 percent matched exactly the results from Latino Decisions' separate Election Eve Poll, which also pegged Clinton's support among Latinos at 79 percent, to just 18 percent for Donald Trump.

The national exit poll estimate of 28 percent Latino support for Trump was a clear outlier that diverged dramatically from other high-quality, large sample pre-election polls. All of these polls showed Trump's percentage much closer to what Latino Decisions found throughout the pre-election tracking or election eve polls: *Univision/Washington Post*, 19 percent; *NBC/Telemundo* oversample, 17 percent: NALEO/*Telemundo* Tracking Poll; 14 percent; and FIU/New Latino Voice, 13 percent.

Ample circumstantial evidence further suggests that Latinos voted for Clinton at the same if not higher rates than they did for Obama four years earlier. Consider the data from table 8.1, which shows the two-party vote shares for both Clinton in 2016 and Obama in 2012 in the seven largest Latino population states.

The impact of third-party candidates Gary Johnson and Jill Stein mask the rather remarkable fact that Clinton's national two-party vote share (51.1 percent) wasn't much lower than Obama's (52.0 percent) four years earlier. Yet in five of the seven large Latino states—Florida and Nevada excepted—Clinton *over*performed her national, two-party decline of 0.9 percent relative to Obama. In three of those five overperforming states, Clinton bested Obama's two-party margin outright. Not coincidentally, those three states—Arizona, California, and Texas—alone account for about 60 percent of Latinos nationwide; the two states where she bettered Obama's two-party share by the widest margins, California and Texas, are home to roughly half of all U.S. Latinos.

Precinct-level analyses conducted by political scientists Stephen A. Nuño and Bryan Wilcox-Archuleta of all 1,288 Arizona voting precincts confirm that Clinton carried closer to 80 percent of Latino voters in the Grand Canyon State. "Relying on a social-science analysis called ecological inference developed by Harvard political scientist Gary King, our precinct analysis shows Latinos in Arizona voted at rates greater than 80 percent for Hillary Clinton in 2016," Nuño and Wilcox-Archuleta conclude. "An estimated 550,000 Latino voters providing record support for the Democratic candidate is likely why Arizona was a narrow 4-point margin in 2016." Their analysis pegged

Table 8.1.   Obama versus Clinton Two-Party Vote Shares in Key Latino States

State	Obama 2012	Clinton 2016	Difference
Nevada	53.4	51.3	−2.1
Florida	50.4	49.4	−1.1
US Average	**52.0**	**51.1**	**−0.9**
New Mexico	55.3	54.7	−0.6
Colorado	52.7	52.7	−0.1
Arizona	45.4	48.1	2.7
Texas	42.0	45.3	3.3
California	61.9	66.1	4.3

Source: Dave Leip's US Election Atlas
Note: Due to rounding, difference column may not add up.

Trump's Latino support at 15 percent, a figure perfectly in line with all the pre-election and tracking polls cited above.[9]

In a similar, ecological inference analysis of precinct-level data, Wilcox-Archuleta and Francisco Pedraza found that, contrary to state exit poll results, Clinton clearly outperformed Obama in Texas. Looking at the 864 precincts with at least 75 percent Latino population share, Pedraza and Wilcox-Archuleta conclude: "If we compare Clinton's vote margin over Trump to Obama's margin over Mitt Romney four years ago, Clinton had a higher margin than Obama in 692 of these 864 precincts—or 80 percent. The claim that Clinton somehow 'ran behind' Obama among Texas Hispanics is not consistent with the actual precinct data."[10]

Ditto for Florida: In their precinct-level ecological inference analyses of that state's results, political scientists Ali Valenzuela and Tyler Reny found that, in 88 percent of Florida precincts with at least 75 percent Latinos, Clinton won more net votes than Obama did four years ago. They also estimated that Clinton turned a 11.2 percent Latino deficit for Obama against Romney in Miami-Dade County in 2012 into a two-point victory over Trump in 2016. Echoing the results in Arizona and Texas, Valenzuela and Reny conclude that the statewide exit polls in Florida underestimated Clinton's Latino support. "When compared to the exit polls and Latino Decisions election eve poll, our overall estimate of 66.9 percent is a match to the [Latino Decisions] estimate of 67 percent for Clinton, while the exit poll estimate of 62 percent appears too low."[11]

Ecological inference analysis of voting results relies upon unusually uniform data points. Our own study of key precincts with very high if not uniformly Latino populations reinforce the precinct-level findings in Arizona, Florida, and Texas.[12] Table 8.2 shows specific precincts in Florida, New Mexico, Texas, and Wisconsin where both the presidential vote results and the Latino share of the population are known. Notice that even where the Latino population falls below 90 percent, Clinton's vote share is routinely above 80 percent, and sometimes closer to 90 percent. In the New Mexico and Texas precincts where nearly every voter is Latino—the closest case to pairing a pure Latino voter universe directly with partisan voting results—Clinton's shares are consistently in the high 70 percent to mid-80 percent range.

Down-ballot polling results affirm the partisan splits among Latinos in the presidential contest. In U.S. House contests, Latino Decisions' election eve poll showed 84 percent of Latinos voted for the Democratic candidate, just 15 percent for Republican House candidates. With the exception of Arizona, Florida, and Ohio, and the unusual case of California's blanket-primary contest, in all twelve of the poll's oversampled states with U.S. Senate races

Table 8.2. Partisan Results from Overwhelmingly Latino Precincts in Four States

Precinct	Latino%	Clinton%	Trump%
Las Cruces (#80), NM	99	85	9
Las Cruces (#13), NM	99	87	7
Starr County, TX	96	79	19
Las Cruces (#97), NM	96	85	10
Valencia (#24), NM	94	72	16
Jim Hogg County, TX	94	77	20
Maverick County, TX	94	77	21
Zavala County, TX	93	78	20
Kissimmee, (#210), FL	78	80	17
Milwaukee (12–232), WI	78	87	9
Milwaukee (12–233), WI	77	88	9
Kissimmee (#411), FL	71	80	18
Milwaukee (12–321), WI	72	90	8
Kissimmee (#200), FL	69	78	18

Source: Election results gathered by authors from county registrars of voters, November 9, 2016.

Latino support for Democratic Senate candidates also reached or exceeded 80 percent.

All of these results raise a rather thorny question: Does it really make sense that Hillary Clinton exceeded her national two-party margin difference in five of the seven most populous Latino states, and did better at the precinct level among Latinos in three of the biggest Latino states plus selected precincts in New Mexico and Wisconsin, yet she somehow captured a *smaller* share of Latino votes nationwide than Obama? To believe that requires the companion belief that Clinton made up the loss of Latino voters by compensating with higher support from among some combination of white, African-American, and, perhaps in the case of California, Asian-American voters. Believing that Donald Trump captured 28 percent of the Latino vote defies most everything that partisan demographers know, not to mention the exit poll results for non-Latino voters.

So, what explains why the national exit poll estimates indicate Latino support for Trump a full ten points higher than all other pre-election and election eve polls? The short answer is that the exit polls contain a variety of sampling problems for smaller and geographically concentrated populations like Latino voters.

First, exit pollsters interview too few respondents in Spanish. According to Census data, about 30 percent of Latino voters are foreign born; the share of Spanish-speaking respondents should be close to 30 percent. But during recent cycles, only about 6 percent to 7 percent of exit poll Latinos were interviewed in Spanish. Second, and overlapping with the English-language oversampling, exit polls had roughly 12 percent more Latino college graduates than the share indicated by the Current Population Survey, and 5 percent more Latinos with above-median incomes. Taken together, because the Latino sample skews toward more affluent, better educated, English-speaking respondents, of course the results will tilt more Republican—just as they would for a white voter sample that includes larger shares of high-income, college-educated, and English-speaking respondents.

OTHER 2016 RESULTS

Non-presidential results provide further compelling evidence of the record levels of Democratic support from Latinos in 2016—or, rather, record deterioration of the Republican brand under Donald Trump's stewardship in the eyes of American Latinos.

The evidence for declining Republican support among Latinos was evident well before Election Day. In a poll sponsored by the Latino Victory Project conducted during the Republican National Convention held in Cleveland in July, Latino Decisions reported how much the GOP brand had already collapsed because of Trump. Although 44 percent of Latinos in the sample reported that they had previously voted for at least one local, state, or national Republican candidate, fully 80 percent said they now had an unfavorable view of Trump: 13 percent "somewhat" unfavorable, and a whopping 67 percent "very" unfavorable. Similarly, 83 percent of Latinos described Trump as "racist," and 81 percent agreed that the "build the wall" chant at Trump rallies was "disturbing and encourages discrimination against immigrants and Latinos."[13]

Likewise, in an August national and battleground oversample poll of 3,729 Latinos conducted by Latino Decisions on behalf of America's Voice, when asked to describe the Republican Party, 45 percent of Latinos agreed with the statement that the GOP "doesn't care too much about Latinos" and another 28 percent described the party as "sometimes hostile" toward them. Fully 70 percent of Latinos agreed that Trump had made the Republican Party "more hostile" to Latinos.[14]

Results from 5,600 Latinos polled by Latino Decisions on the eve of the election also indicated deteriorating support and trust among Latinos for the Republican Party—and that the Trump campaign may have done permanent damage. Asked which statement best described their attitude toward the GOP, 17 percent of Latinos agreed with the statement, "I generally agree with the Republican Party on most issues and am likely to vote for them in future elections"; 33 percent said, "I disagree with the Republican Party on many issues, but I would consider voting for them in the future if they help pass immigration reform with a path to citizenship"; 41 percent agreed with the statement that "the Republican Party has now become so anti-Latino and anti-immigrant that it would be hard for me to ever consider supporting them in the future"; the remaining 9 percent agreed with none of these statements or did not know.[15]

The fact that two in five current Latino voters indicated they would find it hard to support Republicans in the future puts a hard ceiling on the party's Latino support. Donald Trump and his campaign have left an indelible imprint on a very large swath of the Latino electorate, which is much younger that the population overall and will be casting a growing share of votes in the future. Republican leaders will need a bold and concerted effort to change the party's immigration stance and end the party's overtly hostile rhetoric toward Latinos if it hopes to reverse the deepening Latino distrust and suspicion toward the GOP.

As for issues, immigration was the most important issue for Latino voters in 2016: A combined half of all Latinos polls cited either "immigration reform/deportations" (39 percent) or "anti-immigrant/Latino discrimination/ race relations" (10 percent) as one of the "most important issues" in their voting calculus this year. In a question allowing multiple responses, immigration-related issues surpassed "fix economy/jobs/unemployment" (33 percent), "education reform/schools" (15 percent), and "health care" (13 percent). Thirteen other issues received single-digit mentions as "most important" issues to Latinos in 2016.

LD's Election Eve Poll also indicated that one in five Latinos cast a presidential vote for the first time in 2016. Relatedly, more than one in three Latinos—35 percent nationally—said they were contacted by a campaign, political party, or community organizations during 2016 and asked to vote or register to vote. Although a much lower contact rate than for white or African American voters, the 35 percent contact rate represents a small increase over the 31 percent figure from LD's 2012 Election Eve Poll. Of the 35 percent of Latinos contacted during the 2016 campaign, 66 percent said they were contacted by a representative of the Democratic Party; 51 percent were contacted by a nonpartisan community organization; and 32 percent reported contact from a member of the Republican Party.

CONCLUSION

Lost amid the incessant focus on Donald Trump and working-class white voters is the fact that a record number of Latinos turned out to vote in 2016.

Flawed exit poll data to the contrary, by a record share—four out of every five—Latino voters supported Democrat Hillary Clinton for president. At similar rates, Latinos supported Democratic candidates for Congress as well. As a result of Donald Trump's anti-immigrant campaign promises and rhetoric, Latinos expressed a growing mistrust toward the Republican Party.

These levels of support make perfect sense in an election year in which Latinos and especially immigration and border policy were front and center, and xenophobic statements and anti-immigrant sentiment were commonplace. From "rapists-and-murderers" to "build the wall" to Alicia Machado, Trump and the Republican Party's response to his racially tinged campaign made for a memorable 2016 election that American Latino voters will not soon forget.

NOTES

1. Jonathan Capehart, "Donald Trump's 'Mexican rapists' Rhetoric Will Keep the Republican Party Out of the White House," *The Washington Post*, June 17, 2015, https://www.washingtonpost.com/blogs/post-partisan/wp/2015/06/17/trumps-mexican-rapists-will-keep-the-republican-party-out-of-the-white-house/.

2. Pilar Marrero, "Latinos Divided on Obama and Immigration," Latino Decisions, June 13, 2011, http://www.latinodecisions.com/blog/2011/06/13/latinos-divided-on-obama-and-immigration/.

3. Mark Hugo Lopez, Ana Gonzalez-Barrera, and Seth Motel, "As Deportations Rise to Record Levels, Most Latinos Oppose Obama's Policy," Pew Research Center, December 28, 2011, http://www.pewhispanic.org/2011/12/28/as-deportations-rise-to-record-levels-most-latinos-oppose-obamas-policy/.

4. Marrero, "Latinos Divided on Obama and Immigration."

5. Matt Barreto, "New Poll: Latino Voters in Battle Ground States Enthusiastic about Obama DREAM Announcement, Oppose Romney 'Self-Deport' Alternative," Latino Decisions, June 17, 2012, http://www.latinodecisions.com/blog/2012/06/17/new-poll-latino-voters-enthusiastic-about-obama-dream-announcement-oppose-romney-policy-of-self-deport/.

6. "2016 Republican Presidential Nomination," *RealClearPolitics*, http://www.realclearpolitics.com/epolls/2016/president/us/2016_republican_presidential_nomination-3823.html.

7. "Presente.Org/NALACC/Mi Familia Vota Poll on Executive Action—Nov 2014," Latino Decisions, November 20–22, 2016, http://www.latinodecisions.com/files/7714/1756/2260/Presente_Poll_-_Clinton.pdf.

8. 2016 National Exit Poll for President, CNN, last updated November 23, 2016, http://www.cnn.com/election/results/exit-polls.

9. Stephen A. Nuño and Bryan Wilcox-Archuleta, "Why Exit Polls Are Wrong about Latino Voters in Arizona," *Arizona Republic*, November 26, 2016, http://www.azcentral.com/story/opinion/op-ed/2016/11/26/exit-polls-wrong-latino-voters-arizona/94288570/.

10. Francisco Pedraza and Bryan Wilcox-Archuleta, "Donald Trump Did Not Win 34% of Latino Vote in Texas. He Won Much Less," *Washington Post*, December 2, 2016, https://www.washingtonpost.com/news/monkey-cage/wp/2016/12/02/donald-trump-did-not-win-34-of-latino-vote-in-texas-he-won-much-less/.

11. Ali Valenzuela and Tyler Reny, "Study: Trump Fared Worse than Romney in Florida Hispanic Vote," *The Hill*, December 16, 2016, http://thehill.com/blogs/pundits-blog/presidential-campaign/310760-study-finds-trump-faired-worse-than-romney-with.

12. Gary Segura and Matt Barreto, "Lies, Damn Lies, and Exit Polls . . . ," *Huffington Post*, November 11, 2016, http://www.huffingtonpost.com/latino-decisions/lies-damn-lies-and-exit-p_b_12903492.html.

13. "Latino Victory Project—RNC Reaction Poll—Full Results," Latino Decisions, July 18–22, 2016, http://www.latinodecisions.com/files/9814/6924/6980/LVP_RNC_Full_Toplines_July_18–21.pdf.

14. "America's Voice/LD 2016 National and Battleground State Poll," Latino Decisions, August 19–30, 2016, http://www.latinodecisions.com/files/5914/7318/6856/AV_Wave_2_Wave_2_Natl_7_State_Svy_Release.pdf.

15. "Latino Decisions 2016 Election Eve Poll," *Latino Decisions*, November 4–7, 2016; http://latinodecisions.com/files/2514/7864/5282/National_and_State_by_State_Toplines.pdf.

9

The Sources of Trump's Support

Ronald B. Rapoport and Walter J. Stone

In 2016 the Republican Party nominated possibly the most divisive candidate in its history. At the very least, Donald Trump was the most divisive candidate in the field. In the years leading up to 2016, the party had experienced defeat in two presidential elections and declining prospects because of long-term demographic changes in the American electorate. After the 2012 defeat, the GOP issued a reflective report—the "Growth & Opportunity Project"—stressing the need to appeal to more ethnic and racial minorities, and other ways of softening its image.[1] Despite these prescriptions, Trump became the party's 2016 nominee, running a campaign totally at odds with the 2012 post-mortem report. Most of the other leading contenders for the 2016 GOP nomination followed the harsh tone Trump set on immigration.

As part of an effort to understand how the Republican Party was coping with changes in the electorate and pressures from within its own ranks, most notably by the Tea Party faction, we conducted a panel survey of a national sample of Republican identifiers beginning with a nomination wave conducted in the week before and immediately after the Iowa caucuses.[2] We followed respondents into the general election stage with a second wave conducted in October 2016. This chapter reports on some of our findings from these two waves of the study.

The first part of the chapter focuses on support for Trump in the nomination stage (the first wave of the survey), and then we turn to examining bases of Trump support during the general election campaign (utilizing the October wave). For each, we examine both attitudinal and demographic bases of Trump support.

THE NOMINATION STAGE

The divisiveness of the Trump candidacy is apparent in our nomination-wave data. While in January 2016 Trump attracted more than twice the level of support of any other candidate, Republicans also rated him dead last among the other ten candidates they were asked to rank. While Trump led by twenty percentage points over the next most favored candidate in top choice rankings, he was simultaneously rated last by 23 percent of respondents—seven points more than any other candidate. Senators Ted Cruz and Marco Rubio, two leading alternatives to Trump, provide interesting contrasts: 18 percent ranked Cruz as their first choice, and 14 percent had Rubio as their first choice while neither was ranked last by even 5 percent of our respondents (see figure 9.1).

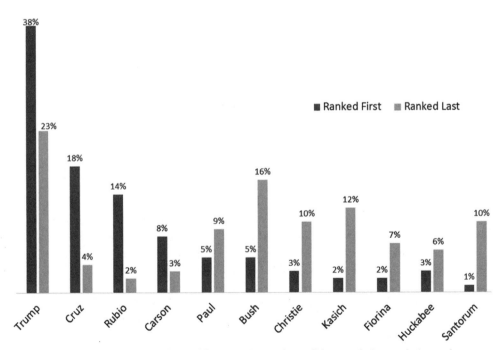

Figure 9.1. Percentage of Republicans rating each candidate as their top choice and percentage rating each as last choice.

Trump's unpopularity was also evident when Republicans were asked to rate each candidate on a scale running from poor to outstanding. Trump had a higher percentage rating him "poor" than any other candidate, while at the same time he had more rating him "outstanding." Even with a plurality of Republicans choosing him as their top choice for the nomination, Trump's average favorability rating was worse than either Rubio's or Cruz's.

Trump made his appeal on a variety of specific issues, but the most prominent were his positions on policy questions related to immigration. "Build the Wall" was probably the most common chant at Trump rallies, and his proposals to ban Muslims from entering the country and deport illegal immigrants rounded out his immigration policy. Given how divided the party was over Trump, and especially given the post-2012 Republican "autopsy" report, which called on the party to be more welcoming to diverse populations, we might expect the party to show significant division on this set of issues.

However, there was remarkable agreement across all three immigration issues within the party. While Trump supporters were consistently more in favor of his policies than were supporters of other candidates, at least two-thirds of non-Trump supporters favored each of the three, with 85 percent supporting the proposal to deport illegal immigrants immediately. As an indication of the high level of support for Trump's immigration agenda, 59 percent of non-Trump supporters favored all three proposals (among Trump supporters, 82 percent favored all three), providing across-the-board support.

But Trump's campaign had a populist focus that extended beyond immigration exemplified by his promise not to cut Social Security, his flirtation with increasing taxes on the wealthy, and his support for raising the minimum wage "to at least $10." On each of these three issues, Trump's supporters were more supportive of these policies than were supporters of his opponents. In fact, his supporters were almost as distinctive on these issues as they were on immigration issues (his supporters differed from non-Trump Republicans by an average of 15 percent on these domestic populism issues versus an average difference of 17 percent on immigration issues). Almost three-quarters of Trump's supporters favored protecting Social Security and Medicare from budget cuts, and almost two-thirds were supportive of raising taxes on high-income Americans. They were split down the middle on increasing the minimum wage, while only a third of other candidates' supporters favored this. Figure 9.2 compares support for different immigration and domestic populism measures among Trump supporters and Republicans who opposed the business mogul.

For both the three immigration issues and for the three domestic populism issues, we created indices utilizing all three questions and then divided the

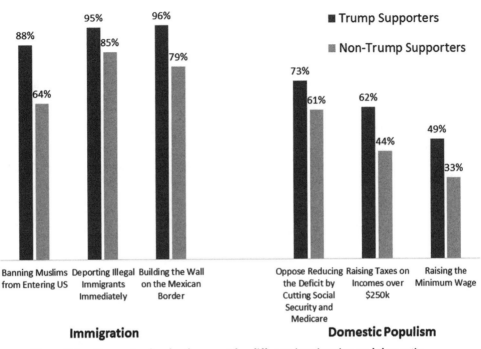

Figure 9.2. Comparing levels of support for different immigration and domestic populism measures between Trump and non-Trump Republicans.

sample in three groups: those most supportive of the set of policies, those least supportive, and those in the middle.

Figure 9.3 shows that both the immigration and domestic issues do well in predicting support for Trump as the GOP nominee. As we might expect, immigration has a stronger effect on Trump support, but both issue areas are important.

Among those in the least anti-immigrant group, only 20 percent supported Trump. In contrast, in the most anti-immigrant group, fully 60 percent supported Trump. The ability of the immigration scale to distinguish among levels of Trump support is remarkable. Another candidate who tried to take a hard line on immigration, Ted Cruz, showed only a small increase in support when we compare those who were least anti-immigrant with those who were most anti-immigrant (from 13 percent to 22 percent).

The effects of the two issue areas are independent of each other as table 9.1 shows. We divided the sample into those above and below the median on each index. Only 15 percent of Republicans who were below the median on anti-immigrant sentiment and below the median on support for domestic

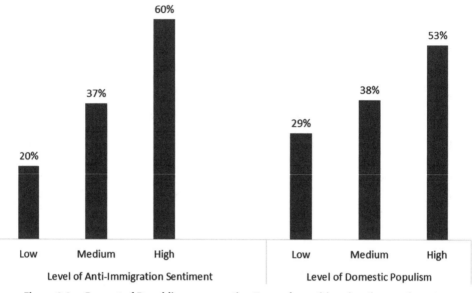

Figure 9.3.   Percent of Republicans supporting Trump by anti-immigration sentiment and domestic populism.

populist issues preferred Trump as the GOP nominee, while 68 percent of those above the median on domestic populism who were also most anti-immigrant preferred Trump. The difference in Trump support between those most in favor and those most against his two most important issue area commitments was more than four to one.

At the same time, the independent effect of each issue is apparent in table 9.1. Among Republicans relatively low in support for his immigration policies there is nonetheless a twenty-four percentage point difference in support for Trump between those above and below the median on domestic populism policies. Among those who agreed most strongly with Trump on immigra-

Table 9.1.   Percentage of Republicans Favoring Trump by Anti-immigration and Domestic Populism Sentiments

		Domestic Populism	
		Low	High
Anti-immigration	Low	15%	39%
	High	43%	68%

tion, the bump in support attributable to domestic populism issues is twenty-five points.

Immigration attitudes are even more strongly related to Trump support. Among Republicans more supportive of domestic populism, those more anti-immigrant were 29 percent more likely to support Trump than those who were less supportive of his hardline stance on immigration. Among those less supportive of economic populist issues, the anti-immigrant group was almost three times as likely to support Trump then the less anti-immigrant group.

Although hardline positions on immigration (even if less extreme than Trump's) have been popular with Republican voters and members of Congress, Trump's positions (and those of his supporters) on domestic populism issues have not found support within the Repubican Party. This is particularly true for its influential Tea Party faction, where large majorities have also favored more restrictive immigration policies while also favoring lower taxes, economic austerity, and wages set by market forces.

Therefore, the mix of domestic populism and anti-immigrant sentiment peculiar to Trump's campaign created significantly cross-pressure for the Tea Party movement and its supporters. Ted Cruz would be expected to be the Tea Party favorite because he seemed to check all the boxes, but Trump's outspokenness on immigration issues and his even stronger rejection of politics as usual (another tenet of Tea Party ideology) had clear appeal to much of the Tea Party. The split over Trump between Trump-hating Glenn Beck and Trump supporter Rush Limbaugh—two Tea Party icons—exemplified this tension. On the other hand, the view of much of the media can be summarized in the headline from the *Washington Times*: "Donald Trump enjoys support of tea party movement that refuses to fully embrace him." So where did Tea Party support go?

At the time of the Iowa caucus and New Hampshire primary, Tea Party support for Trump was fairly weak. Trump did best among respondents with an unfavorable or neutral view of the Tea Party, getting 38 percent and 42 percent respctively from these groups. But among those who viewed the Tea Party movement as either "excellent" or "well above average," Trump received support from only slightly more than a quarter of the group (28 percent), well below the percentage he received from Republicans as a whole.

DEMOGRAPHIC FACTORS

Although the populist appeal of Trump, combining anti-immigration attitudes with support for social programs, was the most discussed aspect of his campaign, there was also a great deal of discussion about demographic factors of

Trump support. In figure 9.4 we show Trump support associated with differences in age, religiosity, gender, education, and income.

Apparently, there was good reason for Trump to "love the poorly educated" (to quote the man himself), as support for Trump varied more by education level than by any other demographic factor. He was the first choice of almost half of the respondents without a college degree, but just over a quarter of those with a college degree. However, both age and church attendance also had strong effects, with the less religious and the elderly significantly more likely to support Trump than the young or more religious.

On the other hand, there is no consistent effect of income with Trump getting his lowest level of support from the under $30,000 group and the over $100,000 group, and his highest support among the $30–100k group. Notably, gender has no effect at all, with 40 percent of Republican men, and 39 percent of Republican women selecting Trump as their first choice.

However, demographic effects are almost entirely mediated by attitudes toward immigrants and domestic policy. When both sets of factors are included in a multivariate logistic regression analysis, it is the domestic populism and anti-immigration attitudes that dominate (with anti-immigration

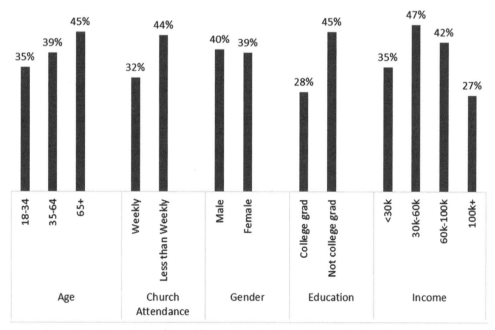

Figure 9.4.   Percentage of Republicans favoring Trump for nomination by demographics.

showing twice the effect of domestic populism). In fact, once we control for domestic populism and anti-immigration attitudes, no demographic factor (nor Tea Party favorability) has a significant effect on Trump support.

So although Trump was an extremely controversial and divisive candidate, his populist appeals, especially on immigration, resonated sufficiently with enough Republicans to secure the nomination.

Could Republicans have coalesced around one of the other candidates such that an alternative nomination contender could have defeated Trump head-to-head? The answer, based on our data, is "no." Because we had Republicans rank the eleven most viable candidates early in the nomination contest, we can determine the favored candidate in one-on-one races by assuming that each individual would prefer the candidate she ranked higher. Comparing Trump's ranking with that of every other candidate, we find that Trump was preferred by a majority of Republicans in our sample in every single head-to-head matchup.

It is not surprising, therefore, that the John Kasich-Ted Cruz effort to coalesce the "Never Trump" faction within the Republican Party ultimately fell apart. Although significant numbers of Cruz supporters disliked Trump, many preferred Trump to Kasich; and similarly, many anti-Trump Kasich Republicans preferred Trump to Cruz. Every candidate had his limitations, and despite Trump's unorthodox and divisive style, he was the choice that emerged principally because he formed a winning coalition on immigration and domestic populism issues.

THE GENERAL ELECTION STAGE: TRUMP'S FAVORABILITY

Once a candidate is nominated by his party, partisans tend to rally around him as the disappointment of the nomination campaign recedes and the race is reframed as between the nominee and that of the opposing party. In fact, we have found in the past that activists supporting unsuccessful nomination candidates transfer that activity directly to support for the nomination winner. But the 2016 Republican nomination contest was uniquely divisive. Never before had so many high-profile members of a party refused to endorse the nominee of their party.

As soon as Trump appeared to be unstoppable in the delegate race, the "Never Trump" group began to mobilize under the leadership of Mitt Romney. None of the Bush family (including two former Republican presidents) ever endorsed Trump, and numerous Republican establishment figures mobilized via letters, petitions, and op-eds to make their opposition to Trump well-known.

By interviewing the same Republicans in October whom we had surveyed in January, we can assess the movement in their level of support for and favorability toward Donald Trump. Unlike the usual tendency among partisans (especially Republicans) to rally around their party's nominee no matter whom they supported during the nomination fight, Republicans' evaluations of Trump were decidedly mixed in October, months after he had secured the party's nomination. Overall, Republicans evaluated Trump significantly more negatively in the October wave of our panel than in January. In January, Trump's positive to negative ratio was 2.5:1, whereas by October it had dropped to less than 2:1. As figure 9.5 shows, the percentages giving him negative or neutral ratings increased slightly between January and October. Remarkably in October, only 40 percent of Republicans gave Trump a positive rating of either "outstanding" or "well above average" compared with 47 percent who had rated him that positively nine months earlier.

To investigate the decline in favorability toward Trump among subgroups of Republicans, in figure 9.6 we compare the percentage of subgroups whose rating of Trump was "positive" (i.e., those rating Trump as either "outstanding" or "well above average") in January, with those whose October ratings of Trump were "positive." By doing this, we can assess both the change from January as well as the level of support in each subgroup at both points in time.

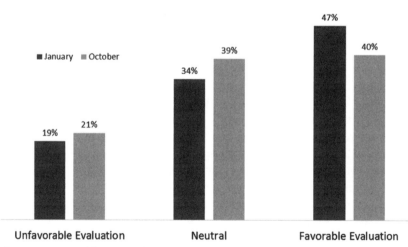

Figure 9.5.   Republicans' evaluation of Trump in January and October waves.

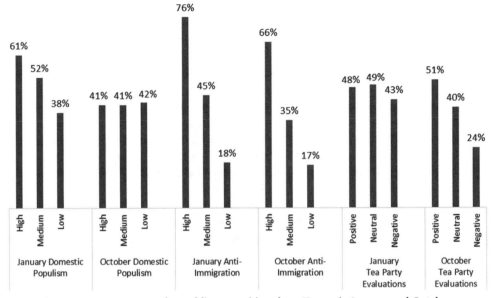

Figure 9.6.   Percentage of Republicans positive about Trump in January and October based on January attitudes. *Note:* "Positive" refers to a respondent rating Trump as "Outstanding" or "Well above Average."

We begin with the all-important question of how well Trump did winning over supporters of other candidates during the campaign, and how well he did keeping his high ratings among his nomination supporters over the same period. Trump did not do particularly well in either case. Among his January supporters, the percentage rating him favorably declined from 82 percent in January to 64 percent in October. Thus, although support for Trump remained high into the general election, there was a significant decline in favorability among Republicans who initially backed him for their party's nomination.

On the other hand, there was no significant increase in positivity (only from 24 percent to 25 percent) among Republicans who supported a different candidate for the GOP nomination, and Trump's favorability remained low even in the heat of the general election contest with Hillary Clinton. In fact, in October there were more non-Trump Republicans who rated him "well below average" or "poor" (33 percent) than gave him one of the two highest ratings (25 percent). Thus, there is every indication in our data that the divide within the Republican Party rank and file over Donald Trump persisted through Election Day.

When we shift to the connection between Trump support and immigration and domestic populism attitudes and attitudes toward the Tea Party, we find more significant changes since January.[3] Anti-immigrant sentiment and domestic populism were strong predictors of Trump support in the primaries. But as the campaign took shape, were these divisions reinforced or were they muted?

It turns out that as the immigration issue dominated the campaign more and more as issues of taxation, Social Security, and the minimum wage receded in our respondents' minds when evaluating Trump. Whereas in January, those most supportive of protecting Social Security, raising the minimum wage, and taxing high-income Americans were the most supportive of Trump's nomination, and rated him most favorably, by October, there was virtually no difference in Trump favorability by level of support for these programs. In fact, favorability varies only from 40 percent and 42 percent across all three categories, a two-point difference, as opposed to the 23 percent difference in January. Rather than being contrasted with other Republican nomination candidates who were more doctrinaire in their free market ideology (which moved domestic populists to support Trump) in the general election, his positions were contrasted with a traditional Democratic liberal, whose positions were far more populist on all three issues.

On the other hand, immigration attitudes remain strongly related to Trump favorability. There is a decline in Trump favorability across all levels of immigration sentiment, but the decline is uniform, still leaving a very clear pattern of support.

The final comparison we make is with evaluations of the Tea Party and the Republican Party. Tea Party favorability was slightly negatively related to Trump support in the January wave and not related at all to Trump favorability. But with Hillary Clinton instead of Ted Cruz as the chief adversary, Tea Party supporters warmed up to Trump. By October, those most favorable toward the Tea Party were significantly more favorable toward Trump than those less favorable. This results from a strong drop in Trump favorability among the anti-Tea Party group and a significant increase in favorability among the most pro-Tea Party group (the largest increase we find within any Republican subgroup). By October, we see a very clear pattern where twice as many of the most pro-Tea Party group view Trump favorably as the most anti-Tea Party contingent. Among those most favorable toward the Tea Party in October, 51 percent had a favorable view of Trump, while among those least favorable toward the Tea Party, only 24 percent did. The effect of Tea Party favorability on Trump evaluation is larger than any effect except for that of immigration.

As opposed to the large shifts between January and October in the effects of domestic populism and Tea Party favorability on Trump favorability, demographic factors show little change in their relationship to views of

Trump. In both waves, college graduates are significantly more likely to view Trump unfavorably, as are more frequent church goers and younger Republicans. In neither wave is there a significant relationship between either income or gender and Trump favorability.

TRUMP VERSUS CLINTON

Of course, evaluations of Trump do not tell us everything about the election or the campaign. Both Donald Trump and Hillary Clinton were polarizing figures. Figure 9.7 compares evaluations of the two major-party nominees in January and October. Given the high level of partisan polarization, we expect to find high levels of support for the party's nominee in our Republican sample. After all, according the 2016 exit polls, 88 percent of Republicans voted for Trump, so it should not be surprising that a large percentage of our Republican sample rated Trump more favorably than Clinton. In fact, while Trump was viewed as above average by 58 percent of Republicans, Clinton's positive ratings are miniscule. Only 7 percent of Republicans rated her above average, giving Trump a clear path to overwhelming support from Republicans in our sample. As a result, Trump was preferred by about 80 percent of the sample in both waves of our survey.

However, over the period between January and October, as figure 9.7 shows, it was Clinton who increased her support vis-à-vis Trump. The percentage of the sample which gave her a higher rating than Trump increased from 8 percent in January to 13 percent in October, while those viewing the two candidates as equal in evaluation dropped from 13 percent to 8 percent. Because the survey was done before the election, we do not know how these people actually voted, but the trend (albeit a small one) of lower favorability advantage for Trump over Clinton over the course of the campaign among our sample is in keeping with the decline in Trump favorability.

The first job of a party's candidate is to solidify support within his own party. So, the question is, to what degree did Trump win over his nomination opponents' supporters? Considering that Jeb Bush never endorsed Trump and that Ted Cruz and others were slow in doing so, we might expect less than unanimous support from opposing candidates' supporters.

That is exactly what we find. While almost all Trump supporters (96 percent) gave him a more positive evaluation than Clinton, almost a third (31 percent) of the supporters of other Republican nomination candidates did not, and almost one-in-five actually rated Clinton more highly than Trump.

There is also significant variation across Republican demographic groups in viewing Trump more favorably than Clinton in the October wave. As figure

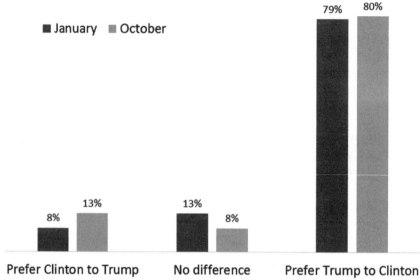

Figure 9.7. Comparative evaluations of Trump and Clinton by Republicans in January and October waves.

9.8 shows, women, younger voters, those with incomes under $30k, and college educated are markedly less likely to rate Trump more highly than Clinton, although in no case does more than 20 percent of the sample rate Clinton more favorably than Trump. For college-educated and younger voters, this mimics the weaker support for Trump's Republican nomination bid that they showed in January.

However, there are also differences in the effects of other demographics on support for Trump for the nomination versus preference for him over Clinton in the October wave. For example, in the nomination stage, less religious Republicans were significantly more supportive of Trump for the nomination than the more observant, but that pattern is far weaker when he is paired against Clinton. Trump did 12 percent worse in nomination support among those attending church once a week or more than among those attending less often, but these groups differ by only 3 percent in evaluating Trump more favorably than Clinton. This is not surprising given the attraction Cruz had in the nomination stage among evangelicals, and the rallying round Trump in the general election by Jerry Falwell Jr. and other evangelical leaders.

And not surprisingly we find a greater gender gap in the Clinton-Trump matchup than we did in the nomination stage where gender did not play a significant role.

When we turn to our issues indices, as figure 9.9 shows, we find large differences in effect for domestic populism but consistency in the effect of anti-immigration attitudes. Anti-immigration attitudes have an even stronger effect on the Trump-Clinton choice than they did in the primary phase. In fact, those highest on the anti-immigration scale (i.e., those most strongly favoring banning Muslims, deporting illegal immigrants, and building the wall) are almost unanimous in their preference for Trump over Clinton. On the other hand, only slightly more than half of those Republicans least supportive of these policies rate Trump higher than Clinton (the lowest percentage for any demographic or issue group). Trump did little to solidify his support among those who disagreed with his stance on immigration, and although this is only a minority of the party, it reinforces the rift within the party.

Those most supportive of domestic populist issues, a group which preferred Trump over his Republican opponents in the primary phase, shifted

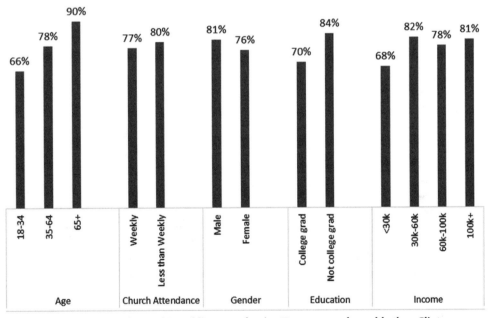

Figure 9.8.   Percentage of Republicans evaluating Trump more favorably than Clinton by demographics.

significantly to the Democratic candidate in the October wave. This is not surprising given the fact that Clinton was far more supportive of all three issues (raising the minimum wage, Social Security protection, and raising taxes on the wealthy) than Trump, who wavered on all three during the campaign. But the domestic populism results do show how differently issues can play in the two phases of the campaign.[4]

IMPLICATIONS

Donald Trump will face significant challenges as president. He was widely regarded by leaders of his own party as unprepared to be president and temperamentally unsuited to lead his party, to say nothing of the nation. As if that is not a sufficiently difficult perception to overcome, our analysis strongly suggests the headwinds facing many of his policy commitments may be strong. While his support on domestic populism issues did not mark his general election candidacy, there can be little doubt that his nomination-stage stands on these issues, which put him at odds with much of his party in Congress, played an important role in his support for the nomination. His Cabinet and top staff appointments during the transition suggest a president-elect who has all but forgotten his nomination constituency on these issues.

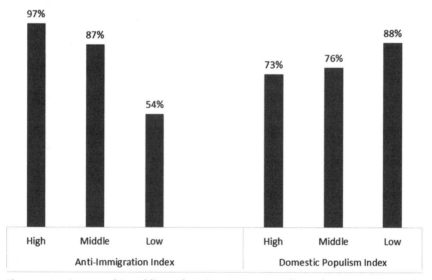

Figure 9.9.   Percent of Republicans favoring Trump over Clinton by immigration and domestic populism.

While his apparently conservative turn on taxes, the minimum wage, and entitlements may align him with most of his party in Congress, it also risks alienating important parts of his electoral constituency whose economic interests do not reflect the party consensus on Capitol Hill.

It is clear in our data that Trump's stands on immigration issues were of great importance to his Republican supporters in both the nomination and general election stages. To a significant degree, these issues too put him at odds with long-standing Republican policy commitments. These are issues that are probably of greater importance to Trump's ability to deliver on his campaign promises, but divisions within his party on trade, banning Muslims, immigration reform, and building a wall on the border may push at least a minority of Republicans into occasional alliances with Democrats, especially in the Senate. These issues are of deep symbolic importance to white working-class voters, and navigating the currents and shoals of Republican politics in Washington may test Trump's ability to persuade his supporters of his dedication to their interests.

These questions by no means exhaust the challenges Trump will face. Outsider candidates are susceptible to foot-dragging and outright opposition from within their own party as the last outsider president, Jimmy Carter, found out. Trump's shoot-from-the-hip style could play thin if it stimulates a crisis or unsettles the economy. Trump and several of his appointees will face rigorous questions about conflicts of interest that could bedevil his administration with scandal, real and perceived. While these and other tests will surely arise, our analysis suggests the basis of Trump's support among Republicans will be a mixed blessing as he faces challenges anticipated and unexpected, which may leave Republican majorities less able to govern than the heady days after the election led many to expect.

NOTES

1. "Growth & Opportunity Project," Republican National Committee, 2013, http://goproject.gop.com/RNC_Growth_Opportunity_Book_2013.pdf.

2. The survey was carried out by YouGov and surveyed a nationally representative sample of 763 Republican identifiers and leaners in late January-early February (referred to in this chapter as the January wave). In October YouGov reinterviewed 550 of these same Republicans.

3. For the remainder of this chapter, for comparability we use January measures of domestic populism, anti-immigration sentiment, and Tea Party evaluations in predicting both January and October attitudes.

4. Not surprisingly, in October Tea Party evaluations are as strongly related to rating Trump more favorably than Clinton as are immigration attitudes.

10

Polling in the 2016 Election

Ariel Edwards-Levy, Natalie Jackson, and Janie Velencia

Even before November's election results cast a harsh spotlight on pollsters, the industry was already undergoing a period of transition in the face of changing technology and steeply rising costs. Despite performing relatively well at the national level, polls missed the outcomes in enough key states to render Donald Trump's Electoral College win a surprise and create the impression that polling failed. This chapter looks at the changes that have affected polling in recent electoral cycles, what happened in 2016, and how to read election and nonelection policy polls moving forward.

CHALLENGES AND THE EVOLUTION
OF ELECTION POLLING

The state of the polling industry has shifted rapidly since the mid-1980s, when landline phones were ubiquitous and Americans were generally willing both to answer pollsters' calls and to cooperate in taking their surveys.

That changed as increased telemarketing made Americans more wary of unsolicited phone calls and as wider use of caller ID gave them the tools to avoid answering them. A 2012 Pew Research report found that response rates to its surveys had dropped by twenty-seven points in fifteen years, from 36 percent in 1997 to just 9 percent in 2012.[1]

Declining response rates aren't necessarily a threat to the accuracy of surveys if the people who still agree to take them hold similar opinions to those opting out—that is, if nonresponse is random across the sample. Data show that between 1999 and 2014, major national surveys showed little change in accuracy against U.S. Census Bureau data on a number of demographics.

"If four out of five people hang up on you, it doesn't make any difference compared to the olden days when only one out of five hung up on you, insofar as the people who hang up are fairly random to the people who don't hang up," David Dutwin, the executive vice president and chief methodologist for the survey firm SSRS, told the *Huffington Post* in February 2016. "And as shocking as it may seem, the research really shows that that's more true than false."[2]

Lower response rates make traditional telephone polling more expensive because pollsters have to call more people to get the desired number of responses. At the same time, Americans' increasing adoption of cell phones and, accordingly, their abandonment of traditional landlines pushes costs higher again. Using random digit dialing, the cost to complete an interview in a cell phone survey is generally at least twice as high as the cost to complete an interview in a landline survey, according to a 2010 study conducted by the American Association for Public Opinion Research, or AAPOR.[3] That is because cell phones must be dialed by hand according to Federal Communications Commission rules, but landlines can still be dialed using automated technology.

A 2016 study by the Centers for Disease Control found that 49 percent of all adults lived in "cell-phone only" households as of the first half of 2016, up from just 3 percent in 2003, and from 39 percent as recently as late 2013. Another 17 percent of adults had a landline, but nevertheless said they received "all or almost all" of their calls via mobile phones.[4]

The change is especially concerning for pollsters because the demographics of "cell-phone only" adults differ sharply from those in households with landlines, including more young adults, minorities, and low-income Americans. In order to get a representative sample of Americans by telephone, cell phones must be included.

MOVING POLLS TO THE INTERNET

In response to the rising costs and challenges in telephone surveys, pollsters are developing alternative ways to reach populations. The most fruitful thus far has been Internet polling, although that comes with a substantial change in how pollsters draw samples and recruit respondents. Traditional phone polling begins with the idea of a "probability sample," defined by AAPOR as a sample where "all persons in the target population have a known chance of being interviewed and, ideally, no one is left out."

In contrast, many online surveys, including those from widely used purveyors such as YouGov and SurveyMonkey, instead rely on respondents recruited from across the Internet, weighted to reflect the universe they're intended to represent. This departure from random sampling has been controversial in the field, but nonetheless Internet polling is here to stay.

The use of online polling expanded rapidly in 2016 throughout the primaries and the general election. An analysis of GOP presidential primary polls[5] conducted by the *Huffington Post* in May 2016 (two months prior to the Republican National Convention, but after Donald Trump had become the presumptive Republican nominee), found a 257 percent increase in Internet polls from the previous GOP primary cycle in 2012. The count went from 47 polls in 2012 to 168 polls in 2016. In 2012, Internet polls made up 18 percent of all national GOP presidential primary polls. In 2016, they made up 47 percent of the total. At the same time, live telephone polls declined by 15 percent. Polls conducted solely using an interactive voice response system (IVR polls, also known as automated polls) declined by 11 percent. There was also an increase in mixed mode polls, mostly among IVR pollsters, who are restricted to contacting landlines by Federal Communication Commission rules, began to conduct a portion of their polls (often 10 percent to 20 percent of the total sample) online as the cycle progressed.

Most of the new pollsters that emerged during the 2016 primary cycle were Internet polling companies. There were 17 new pollsters in the 2016 GOP primary cycle that had not polled in the 2012 primary. These pollsters made up 46 percent of all national presidential primary polls. Seventy-eight percent of the polls conducted by new pollsters were Internet polls.

These patterns continued in the general election. Among all national general election polls, Internet polling increased by 203 percent between 2012 and 2016 (from 105 polls to 319 polls).[6] Internet polls were the most dominant mode in 2016 national general election polls, making up 54 percent of all total polls conducted in the cycle. Live telephone polls came in second, making up 31 percent of all polls, followed by mixed-mode polls (10 percent) and IVR-only polls (5 percent). By contrast, Internet polls made up just 18 percent of all national general election polls in 2012. In that last cycle, live telephone polls were the most dominant force, making up 49 percent of polls, IVR polls made up 32 percent of the total, and 18 percent were Internet polls. Mixed-mode polls made up just 1 percent of the 2012 total.

The 2016 election also saw an influx of surveys from a small number of prolific pollsters. Out of the 49 pollsters who polled in 2016, 6—Morning Consult, Ipsos/Reuters, Rasmussen, NBC/SurveyMonkey, Lucid/*Times-*

Picayune and YouGov/*Economist*—were responsible for 41 percent of the total national polls. Rasmussen used a combination of automated phone calls and online responses, while the other pollsters in this group conducted their pools online.

STATE POLLS ALSO SHIFTED TO INTERNET

State-level polls in the 2016 general election also made a move toward the Internet in comparison to state polls in the 2012 cycle. There was a 408 percent increase in state-level Internet polls from the last presidential election, from 113 polls in 2012 to 574 polls in 2016. Internet polls made up 44 percent of all state polls. Live telephone polls came in second, making up 35 percent of all polls, followed by mixed-mode polls (18 percent) and IVR-only polls (2 percent). By contrast, Internet polls made up just 10 percent of all state-level polls in 2012. Telephone polls accounted for 81 percent, with live telephones and IVR polls making up 41 percent and 40 percent respectively.

POLL PERFORMANCE IN 2016

Assessing how close the polls were to the actual outcome is more complicated than a simple "they did well," or "they failed." National polls generally tended to reflect the outcome of the election reasonably well. Hillary Clinton won the popular vote by slightly more than two percentage points, and most national polls within the last week of the campaign showed her leading by one-to-five points. A few national polls showed a six-to-seven-point lead, which was clearly too high, but most fell within the margin of error of the popular vote outcome. At the state level, however, election results did not always line up with the polling averages in key states. Polls generally indicated that Clinton would win the states she needed in order to win the Electoral College, which resulted in all of the poll-based election forecasts predicting a Clinton win. Of course, the result was a surprise Trump win in the Electoral College.

The most efficient way to assess poll performance is to examine how the polling aggregates compared to the actual election results. For this purpose, we'll use the aggregate numbers produced by the *Huffington Post Pollster* (*HuffPost Pollster*), *FiveThirtyEight*, and *RealClearPolitics*. The modeling strategies and which polls are included are different for each outlet. *RealClearPolitics'* is the simplest, using an arithmetic mean of the last week of election polls in their database. They include most publicly released polls, but do not use some newer pollsters and methods. Notably, *RealClearPolitics* doesn't include a lot of online polls, with the exception of YouGov, Survey-Monkey, Ipsos, and GfK.[7]

HuffPost Pollster used a Bayesian Kalman Filter model to aggregate 2016 election polls, which is much more complex than a simple average. Briefly, Kalman filter models combine data that are known to be "noisy"—or not completely precise—into a single estimate of the underlying "signal"—that is, what's actually happening. For *HuffPost*, that means the model looks for trends in the polls and produces its best estimate of the polling average. More technically, what the model calculates is a *trend line* estimate, not an average as most people think of it. The reason is that a simple average would be very susceptible to the deviations of individual polls. One outlier poll could pull the average in a completely different direction than the rest of the polls indicate. Our algorithm resists this tendency by requiring a trend in the movement of multiple polls in order to change the direction of the aggregated estimate. However, if more data come in and indicate that the deviant results are actually part of a trend, the trend line adjusts to accommodate that new information. So the model doesn't ignore outlier polls; it just downplays them unless it becomes clear that they're actually the beginning of a trend.

The advantage of using a Kalman filter model is that it doesn't swing wildly in response to outlier polls. The disadvantage is that it's slower to react to real polling changes than a traditional average. The model used by *FiveThirtyEight* for their poll aggregations was more responsive to a single poll and thus swung around much more quickly than the *HuffPost Pollster* model.

Figure 10.1 shows the errors among the aggregators compared to the actual results. It uses the margin between Trump and Clinton for each state subtracted from the margin between Trump and Clinton in the actual results. Negative values mean that the aggregate poll estimate misestimated the margin between candidates in a way that underestimated Clinton, and positive values indicate the margin underestimated Trump. *RealClearPolitics* did not have aggregate values for all states, so for some the only comparisons are *Pollster* and *FiveThirtyEight*. The chart is sorted by the difference between *Pollster*'s estimates and the actual results, lowest to highest.

As expected, Clinton's vote share was most underestimated in the states in which she performed the best, and Trump's shares were most underestimated in his strongest states. That pattern is typical. Due to undecided proportions and fewer polls, poll aggregates generally underestimate candidates in their strongest states. All of the aggregates underestimated Clinton's win margin in California, and underestimated Trump's margin in Missouri and Indiana.

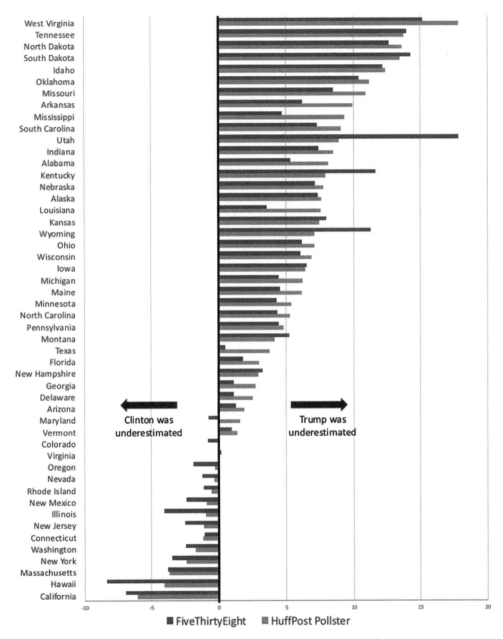

Figure 10.1. How much poll aggregations underestimated Trump vote by state.

Pollster and *FiveThirtyEight* both substantially underestimated Trump's strength in West Virginia, Tennessee, the Dakotas, Idaho, and Oklahoma. Both underestimated Clinton in Hawaii, Massachusetts, and New York.

Overall, though, Trump's margins were underestimated in many more states than Clinton's. *HuffPost Pollster*'s aggregations underestimated Clinton in ten states, got the margin almost exactly right (within half a percentage point) in four states, and underestimated Trump in the remaining thirty-six states. *FiveThirtyEight* underestimated Clinton in fourteen states, had one state within half a percentage point, and underestimated Trump in the remaining thirty-five states. Of the twenty-eight estimates that *RealClearPolitics* (not included Illinois in figure 10.1) had for the two-way Trump vs. Clinton race, the aggregate underestimated Clinton in nine states, was within half a percentage point in four states, and underestimated Trump in fifteen states. For their four-way race there were only estimates for twenty-four states, in which eight underestimated Clinton, three were within half a percentage point, and thirteen underestimated Trump.

Pollster's average error—in either direction—was 5.67 percentage points. *FiveThirtyEight*'s was nearly the same at 5.84 percentage points. *RealClearPolitics* didn't have aggregates for some of the states with the largest errors, so their averages were lower: 3.56 percentage points for the two-way aggregates and 4.10 percentage points for the four-way aggregates.

There are some interesting differences in errors by state, though, which makes the poll selection and modeling processes evident. *RealClearPolitics* had much larger error in its four-way New Mexico estimate and their two-way Maryland estimate than any other aggregate. In Massachusetts and Texas, *RealClearPolitics* underestimated the margin in the opposite direction than *Pollster* and *FiveThirtyEight*. *FiveThirtyEight*'s notable differences from other aggregates were in Hawaii, Utah, Kentucky, and Wyoming. *HuffPost Pollster* was a bit of an outlier in West Virginia, Mississippi, Arkansas, Louisiana, and Texas.

Interestingly enough, the three states which have been the focus of the election's surprise outcome—Pennsylvania, Michigan, and Wisconsin—are not very interesting on this chart. The errors were substantial: All aggregators underestimated the margin for Trump by three to five points in Pennsylvania, three to six points in Michigan, and by seven to eight points in Wisconsin. But these error ranges are in the middle of the pack compared to other states' errors. The lesson from that observation is that poll—and poll aggregate—errors were substantial in many states, not just in those that made the difference in the election. Errors that still call the outcome correctly, as most of these errors did, are still errors that need attention.

IMPLICATIONS FOR POLICY POLLING

The debate over what factors caused pollsters to err in 2016 is likely to continue for some time, as is the argument as to what extent the miss represents either a critical failure for the industry or simply a demonstration of overcertainty by pundits and forecasters. But regardless of the magnitude of the error, polling systematically overstated the likelihood of a Clinton win.

That's something pollsters will have to grapple with in the next election. It's also something that, as the country settles down to the business of governing, raises a more immediate question: how much can polls be trusted to measure the public's support for policies?

That question is more than academic. While horse-race surveys may command the bulk of attention, polls that gauge the national mood on issues of policy serve at least as important a role in the democratic process. Writing off their results as intrinsically unreliable would potentially leave much of the nation voiceless in the years between elections.

"Public opinion polls are an important form of accountability on our government. They are a kind of check and balance," Nick Gourevitch, a pollster for the Democratic firm Global Strategy Group, observed following the election. "Public opinion polls help prevent our elected officials from pursuing policies completely at odds with the public's desires."[8]

Fortunately, some of the major pitfalls faced by campaign polling are inherently less problematic for policy surveys. Likely voter models— pollsters' methods for determining which Americans will turn out in the election—were probably a significant source of inaccuracy.

"Because we can't know in advance who is actually going to vote, pollsters develop models predicting who is going to vote and what the electorate will look like on Election Day," analysts at Pew Research explained in a post-election essay. They observed,

> This is a notoriously difficult task, and small differences in assumptions can produce sizable differences in election predictions. We may find that the voters that pollsters were expecting, particularly in the Midwestern and Rust Belt states that so defied expectations, were not the ones that showed up. Because many traditional likely-voter models incorporate measures of enthusiasm into their calculus, 2016's distinctly unenthused electorate—at least on the Democratic side—may have also wreaked some havoc with this aspect of measurement.[9]

Pollsters have adopted a wide variety of metrics to assess respondents' likelihood of voting. Some, such as Gallup (which chose not to release presidential horse-race polling in 2016), rely on a battery of questions, including asking about a respondent's self-described past voting behavior and interest in the current election, while others simply ask people whether or not they plan to vote.[10] Another method involves matching survey data to voter files, which contain information on individuals' vote histories.

To underscore how much pollsters' decisions can affect their results, the *New York Times* gave raw polling data from Florida to four different pollsters in September 2016, and asked them to analyze it.[11] The participants diverged on how they adjusted their samples and identified likely voters, with results ranging from a one-point lead for Trump to a four-point lead for Clinton.

Issue polls, which generally seek to represent all Americans, rather than a given year's electorate, require less extrapolation. Pollsters still have to consider how to weight their sample to make it representative of the nation as a whole, and which demographic factors to consider when doing so. But while no one can know in advance who'll turn out to vote in an election, those trying to reflect the population of the United States can at least rely on census data as a target.

Another possible factor in the election polling miss that issue polls do not have to worry about is a late shift toward Trump in the few days between final poll releases and Election Night.[12] Such a shift would be unusual—past elections have tended to remain relatively stable in their final stages.[13]

But exit polling indicates that late-deciding voters in some key states, rather than breaking evenly between the candidates, split heavily for Trump. In Michigan, voters who said they'd made up their mind in the last week before the election went for Trump over Clinton by eleven points, compared to an even split among those who reported deciding earlier. In Pennsylvania, voters who decided in the final week went to Trump by a seventeen-point margin, versus a two-point edge among those who decided previously.[14]

In Wisconsin, where not a single pre-election poll showed Trump ahead, the difference was even more stark: the 14 percent of voters who said they'd decided in the last week before the election preferred Trump to Clinton by twenty-nine points, while those who decided earlier favored Clinton by a two-point margin.[15]

Not all pollsters saw evidence of such a swing. But regardless, such issues of timing present less of a problem for issue polling, which doesn't revolve around capturing Americans' opinions during such a narrowly defined time period as an election campaign. Although some surveys may be planned to coincide with specific dates, such as the State of the Union, in general, there's not a hard-and-fast deadline after which Americans' views on an issue stop mattering.

Finally, even polling errors large enough to put horse-race surveys at odds with the results of an election may have less meaningful consequences when it comes to interpreting public opinion. Differences of two points in election surveys can change the outcome, but a two-point difference in opinion on an issue isn't usually substantial.

HuffPost Pollster's final aggregate of national polls gave Clinton a 5.3-point lead over Trump.[16] The final tally as of early 2017 put Clinton up 2.1 points in the popular vote, an error of 3.2 points. In horse-race surveys, such a margin can mean the difference between winning and losing. In opinion polls, such a distinction may be far less politically meaningful.

To take one example, Barack Obama's net approval rating—+16.4 points at the end of his term, per *HuffPost Pollster*'s aggregate—means that he left office on a relative high note, in comparison both to his earlier second-term numbers and to his recent presidential predecessors.[17] That would remain broadly the case if his net approval rating were, instead, 3.2 percentage points lower at +13.2, or, indeed, if it were 3.2 percentage points higher at +19.6.

For another example, a post-election poll from Quinnipiac University found that Americans oppose building a wall along the border with Mexico, one of Donald Trump's signature policy proposals, by a 13-point margin, with 42 percent in support and 55 percent in opposition.[18] If Americans instead opposed such a project by a 9.8-point margin, it would remain reasonable to conclude that such a project would be relatively unpopular.

The very real possibility of such errors, however, serves as a reminder that such results *should* be treated by readers and pundits as virtually identical. The baseline margin of error of most polls stands around plus-or-minus 3 percentage points when accounting only for how much the numbers might change due to the random chance of who is selected to participate in the poll, let alone other potential sources for error.[19]

That is a good reason for caution against making too much of any purported shifts in public opinion that amount to just a point or two of variation, and which are just as likely to represent random noise as they are to amount to a notable change. It should also serve as a reminder to be wary of apparent differences in opinion between subgroups, whether it's Republicans and Democrats, millennials and baby boomers, or white and black Americans. Such groups, which make up only a part of each survey's population, accordingly carry even higher margins of error.

CHALLENGES FOR PUBLIC POLICY POLLS

While policy polling may be spared from some of the problems afflicting horse-race polls, they're also potentially subject to a number of serious issues whose presence should inform the way their results are interpreted.

Among them: elections force the public into making quantifiable decisions. In 2016, people chose to vote for Clinton, Trump, a third-party candidate, or not to vote at all. In comparison, many people never adopt strong positions on current events or policy issues, especially those that are complicated or receive limited news coverage. This leaves respondents malleable, making them more likely to support a bill if they're told it's endorsed by a politician in their party, or to reject it if told that it's backed by an opponent.

The 1975 Public Affairs Act, to take one classic example, doesn't exist. But Republicans are more likely to oppose repealing the fictitious bill when they're told that President Barack Obama wants to do so, while Democrats object when they're told it's a Republican proposal.[20]

"The lesson here is straightforward: Many poll respondents will offer opinions on issues they know little or nothing about, making it difficult to distinguish pre-existing opinions from reactions formed on the basis of the words of the question," pollsters Mark Blumenthal and Emily Swanson wrote in 2013. "Poll respondents will find it even easier to offer an opinion when informed where well-known political leaders stand on the issue. It is always best when interpreting survey results to consider how familiar Americans are with the issue, how many are reluctant to offer an opinion and how those who are closely following an issue differ from those who are not."[21]

Issue polling may also be deeply affected by how pollsters choose to word their questions. That problem is virtually nonexistent in horse-race polls, where wording generally reflects the questions people will see on their ballot, allowing for relatively uniform phrasing.

In policy issues, by contrast, there's often no clear template for wording, and small changes can carry outsized effects. Experiments that test reactions to changes in wording shed light on how malleable opinions can be, especially when tied to partisanship.

In one survey conducted by the *Huffington Post* and YouGov, for example, Republicans asked to compare their current financial situation to "when President Obama was first elected" were nineteen points likelier than those asked about "the year 2008" to say that their finances had gotten worse. Democrats who saw Obama's name mentioned, in contrast, were twenty points less likely than those who did not to admit that income inequality had risen during his tenure.[22]

Some surveys intentionally rely on such effects. Campaign pollsters often conduct polls with loaded language to test effective messaging, while interest groups may do so in order to shore up support for their positions. But even when public pollsters, such as media outlets, think tanks, or universities are simply trying to conduct a straightforward test of public opinion, there's still often little consensus on how a question should be framed, or how much detail about a current event should be provided.

Among Trump's first acts as president-elect was to announce a deal to keep several hundred jobs at an Indiana factory rather than moving all its production to Mexico. Two online surveys measuring public opinion on the deal chose both to describe it in varying ways and to ask fundamentally different questions about its effects. A Morning Consult survey found that the deal left 60 percent of voters feeling more favorably toward Trump, while an *Economist*/YouGov poll found that just 38 percent of Americans approved of the deal.[23]

Some of that difference likely comes down to how each of the questions was framed. The Morning Consult poll described the deal in broadly upbeat terms, telling voters that Carrier had "decided to keep roughly 1,000 manufacturing jobs in the state of Indiana rather than moving them to Mexico after forming an agreement with President-elect Donald Trump and Vice President-elect Mike Pence." The *Economist*/YouGov survey, in contrast, asked about "a deal Donald Trump negotiated with Carrier, an air conditioning equipment manufacturer, to reduce the number of jobs the company had planned to relocate from a plant in Indiana to Mexico."

More fundamentally, the Morning Consult survey also asked readers how the deal reflects on Trump, while the *Economist*/YouGov poll asked for opinions about the deal itself. But whether one survey did a better job of capturing the real effect of the announcement on public opinion is impossible to quantitatively measure.

Election surveys, for all their flaws, can be validated or invalidated by the results of the elections they seek to measure. In contrast, there's no such test that can tell us which pollster most accurately measures, say, Americans' "true" level of admiration for a president or support for a border wall—or whether pollsters are getting it right at all.

CONCLUSION

Pollsters have a difficult road ahead to regain public trust and re-establish a reputation for accuracy in the next election cycle. The American Association for Public Opinion Research created a task force to study the pre-election polls before the outcome of the election was known, and their conclusions will be especially helpful in shaping how the field reacts and works toward solving the problems that 2016 laid bare. Even though polls only missed the outcome in a few states, the aggregates make it clear that polls have considerable error, even right before the election. This should serve as a reminder that polls—especially election polls that try to guess who will vote and who won't—have more error than just what we measure with margins of sampling error. At the same time, we need polls to give us an idea of the pulse of the nation on a wide variety of topics, and despite the industry's problems, polls are the best way to provide insight into how large numbers of Americans think during elections and in between.

NOTES

1. "Assessing the Representativeness of Public Opinion Surveys," Pew Research Center for the People and the Press, May 15, 2012, http://www.people-press.org/2012/05/15/assessing-the-representativeness-of-public-opinion-surveys/.

2. Ariel Edwards-Levy and Natalie Jackson, "Do Polls Still Work If People Don't Answer Their Phones?" *Huffington Post*, February 4, 2016, http://www.huffingtonpost.com/entry/polling-when-people-dont-answer-phones_us_56b3b06ee4b04f9b57d8e014?m7zrrudi.

3. "New Considerations for Survey Researchers When Planning and Conducting RDD Telephone Surveys in the U.S. with Respondents Reached via Cell Phone Numbers," American Association for Public Opinion Research Cell Phone Task Force, 2010, 77–78, 95–108, https://www.aapor.org/AAPOR_Main/media/MainSiteFiles/2010AAPORCellPhoneTFReport.pdf.

4. Stephen J. Blumberg and Julian V. Luke, "Wireless Substitution: Early Release of Estimates from the National Health Interview Survey, January–June 2016," Centers for Disease Control and Prevention, December 2016, https://www.cdc.gov/nchs/data/nhis/earlyrelease/wireless201612.pdf; Stephen J. Blumberg and Julian V. Luke, "Wireless Substitution: Early Release of Estimates from the National Health Interview Survey, July–December 2013," Centers for Disease Control and Prevention, July 2014, http://www.cdc.gov/nchs/data/nhis/earlyrelease/wireless201407.pdf.

5. *HuffPost Pollster* only analyzed polls in the GOP primary for sake of equal comparison given that there was no Democratic primary in the 2012 race to adequately compare to.

6. *HuffPost Pollster* aggregates all publicly available polling data that meets set standards and transparency requirements and makes the data available publicly online and through an application programming interface (API). The 2016 analysis presented here includes all polls in that database, plus any polls that were rejected for transparency or methodological reasons, to create a complete dataset of polls that is comparable to the 2012 poll datasets of all publicly available polls.

7. GfK, unlike other online pollsters, uses a probability-based telephone recruitment method to build their panel and provides Internet access to those who don't have it. Because of this unique recruitment method, they are considered a probability-based Internet poll.

8. Nick Gourevitch, Twitter post, November 13, 2016, 11:10 a.m., https://twitter.com/nickgourevitch/status/797834080901623808; Nick Gourevitch, Twitter post, November 13, 2016, 11:12 a.m., https://twitter.com/nickgourevitch/status/797834408841670657.

9. Andrew Mercer, Claudia Deane, and Kyley McGeeney, "Why 2016 Election Polls Missed Their Mark," Pew Research Center, November 9, 2016, http://www.pewresearch.org/fact-tank/2016/11/09/why-2016-election-polls-missed-their-mark/.

10. Frank Newport and Colleen Sullivan, "How Does Gallup Define 'Likely Voters,' " *Gallup*, May 24, 2001, http://www.gallup.com/poll/3169/how-does-gallup-define-likely-voters.aspx.

11. Nate Cohn, "We Gave Four Good Pollsters the Same Raw Data. They Had Four Different Results." *New York Times*, September 20, 2016, http://www.nytimes.com/interactive/2016/09/20/upshot/the-error-the-polling-world-rarely-talks-about.html.

12. Kyle Kondik and Geoffrey Skelley, "In 2016's Game of Musical Chairs, the Music Stopped at the Wrong Time for Clinton," *Sabato's Crystal Ball*, November 30, 2016, http://www.centerforpolitics.org/crystalball/articles/in-2016s-game-of-musical-chairs-the-music-stopped-at-the-wrong-time-for-clinton/.

13. Harry Enten, "How Much Do 'October Surprises' Move the Polls?" *FiveThirty-Eight*, October 30, 2016, http://fivethirtyeight.com/features/how-much-do-october-surprises-move-the-polls/.

14. Exit Poll, "Michigan President," CNN, last updated November 9, 2016, http://www.cnn.com/election/results/exit-polls/michigan/president; Exit Poll, "Pennsylvania President," CNN, last updated November 9, 2016, http://www.cnn.com/election/results/exit-polls/pennsylvania/president.

15. Exit Poll, "Wisconsin President," CNN, last updated November 9, 2016, http://www.cnn.com/election/results/exit-polls/wisconsin/president.

16. "2016 General Election: Trump vs. Clinton," *HuffPost Pollster*, http://elections.huffingtonpost.com/pollster/2016-general-election-trump-vs-clinton.

17. "Obama Job Approval," *HuffPost Pollster*, as of January 3, 2017, http://elections.huffingtonpost.com/pollster/obama-job-approval; David Nield, "How Obama's Rising Approval Ratings Compare with Recent Presidents," *FiveThirtyEight*, August 16, 2016, http://fivethirtyeight.com/features/how-obamas-rising-approval-ratings-compare-with-recent-presidents/.

18. "American Voters Support Abortion, Oppose the Wall, Quinnipiac University National Poll Finds; Voters Differ with Trump on Guns, Taxes, Other Issues," Quinnipiac University Poll, November 23, 2016, https://poll.qu.edu/national/release-detail?ReleaseID = 2406.

19. Natalie Jackson, "Focusing on Error in Polls Isn't Sexy, but It's Necessary," *Huffington Post*, September 21, 2016, http://www.huffingtonpost.com/entry/poll-margin-of-error_us_57e1e985e4b08d73b82e4e33.

20. Ariel Edwards-Levy, "Republicans Like Obama's Ideas Better When They Think They're Donald Trump's," *Huffington Post*, September 21, 2015, http://www.huffingtonpost.com/entry/donald-trump-republicans-democrats-poll_us_55e5fbb8e4b0c818f6196a82.

21. Mark Blumenthal and Emily Swanson, "Beware: Survey Questions about Fictional Issues Still Get Answers," *Huffington Post*, April 11, 2013, http://www.huffingtonpost.com/2013/04/11/survey-questions-fiction _n_2994363.html.

22. Ariel Edwards-Levy, "Opinions on Barack Obama's Economic Legacy Don't Have Much to Do with the Economy," *Huffington Post*, May 10, 2016, http://www.huffingtonpost.com/entry/obama-economic-legacy_us_57325736e4b016f3789778f7.

23. Arthur Delaney, "Donald Trump Takes Victory Lap at Carrier Plant," *Huffington Post*, December 1, 2016, http://www.huffingtonpost.com/entry/trump-carrier-jobs_us_

58407507e4b017f37fe36cdb; Jon Reid, "Carrier Deal a Political Winner for Trump, Poll Shows," Morning Consult, December 6, 2016, https://morningconsult.com/2016/12/06/ carrier-deal-political-winner-trump-poll-shows/; *The Economist*/YouGov Poll, December 3–5, 2016, http://d25d2506sfb94s.cloudfront.net/cumulus_uploads/document/l9vhwrcgbo /econToplines.pdf.

11

Twitter Rants, Press Bashing, and Fake News

The Shameful Legacy of Media in the 2016 Election

Diana Owen

In many ways, media trends in the 2016 presidential campaign resembled well-established norms. Media messages were a blitz of negativity, controversy, scandal, and misinformation. The "feeding frenzy"[1] was on steroids, as the press thrived on relentless attacks and "gotcha" reporting. Campaign news, as has been the case since the 1980s, was far more bad than good. The media's disproportionate focus on polls and the horse race between the candidates continued unabated. The purveyors hailed from all manner of media—established print news sources, cable television, talk radio, online news sites, blogs, social media, and bogus news platforms. The quality and tone of election media varied greatly within and across platforms.

But there were new developments that pushed the boundaries of these already troubling trends. During the campaign, social media fed the cable news media beast and drowned out legacy news journalism. Social media became an unchecked mouthpiece for one candidate, his surrogates, and outside peddlers of misinformation. Cable news increasingly relied on social media as a main source of stories, and treated posts as if they were on par with investigative reporting. Journalists for the *New York Times*, *Los Angeles Times*, *Washington Post*, and other legacy news organizations provided a steady stream of well-researched, carefully-sourced investigative reports throughout the campaign. These stories were largely obscured by incessant

167

coverage of incendiary tweets, rumors, quarrels, and campaign intrigue that overtook the news agenda. This development is significant as a majority of Americans relied on cable news for their campaign news.[2]

The barrage of information during the campaign was so undisciplined and devoid of core journalistic standards that fake news stories established a foothold alongside reporting by legitimate organizations. Reporters often were as concerned with building their brand by grabbing attention via social media[3] as they were with getting the facts straight, and did little to counterpunch this trend. As Thomas Patterson observed, "Civility and sound proposals are no longer the stuff of headlines, which instead give voice to those who are skilled in the art of destruction. The car wreck that was the 2016 election had many drivers. Journalists were not alone in the car, but their fingerprints were all over the wheel."[4]

NEWS MEDIA COVERAGE

Americans were very attentive to the presidential campaign. According to the Pew Research Center, over 90 percent of the electorate accessed news about the election in a given week. Voters were more likely to learn about the election from television news than other media, although their reliance on digital sources was higher than in any prior election. About four-fifths of voters followed the election on television, with 54 percent watching the events unfold on cable news. Nearly half of the public used news websites or apps, and 36 percent read a print newspaper. Forty-four percent of the public got election news from radio.[5]

The ongoing issues plaguing news organizations in the digital era seriously influenced news coverage of the election. Newsrooms that were already operating with depleted resources experienced further cuts, limiting their ability to engage in investigative reporting and accompany the candidates on the campaign trail.[6] In 2015, newsrooms lost 10.4 percent of journalist positions, or 3,800 jobs in one year.[7] Many reporters covered the campaign from a desk chair and computer, relying on secondhand information from other journalists, polling organizations, citizens' eyewitness accounts, and videos from campaign sites and archives. The symbiotic relationship between the established press and social media tightened, as journalists combed posts and tweets for story lines.

Still, journalists from legacy news organizations produced stories using textbook investigative reporting techniques. Both presidential candidates had complicated financial entanglements with businesses and foundations. Journalists probed these relationships, and exposed how they would come into play for the winning candidate. Breaking with precedent, Republican candidate Donald Trump refused to release his tax returns. The *New York Times* obtained documents from the early 1990s indicating that Trump paid no federal taxes for years. The stories detailed how Trump had used tax loopholes to stave off financial ruin from failing businesses.[8] Trump responded by saying that "he was smart," and blaming Hillary Clinton for not closing the loopholes when she was in office. He also threatened to sue the *New York Times* for reporting the story.[9] The major issue that dogged Democratic nominee Hillary Clinton throughout the campaign was her use of a private email server when she was secretary of state. In early July 2016, the FBI announced that its investigation of the emails revealed no justification for criminal charges. Journalists examined the email situation from multiple perspectives ranging from the ethics of setting up a private server, the risks posed to national security, and the content of the emails. Poring over thousands of Clinton's emails, they raised concerns that access to Clinton and high-ranking State Department officials had been granted to big donors to the Clinton Foundation.[10] The email story resurfaced as the campaign was coming to a close when a new batch of emails was discovered.

Much of cable networks' campaign coverage revolved around regular panels of partisan commentators who argued ad nauseam over the meaning of a 140-character tweet. Fact-checking on cable news entailed having panelists engage in a dispute over an information fragment, typically ending without resolution. In-depth reporting was supplanted by a steady flow of sensational factoids, many of which were derived from candidates' and their surrogates' communications. To suit their format, cable news organizations repackaged legacy journalists' detailed analyses as superficial "breaking news" snippets devoid of context or factual nuances.

The horse race, which has dominated election news coverage since the 1970s, remained the most prevalent news story line. A Harvard Shorenstein Center/Media Tenor study found that 42 percent of coverage in 2016 was of the horse race. More than one hundred polls, often telling conflicting stories, were reported during the general election. After the horse race, the major focus of stories was on scandals and controversies (17 percent), such as Clinton's email server and Trump's treatment of women. Only 10 percent of election stories mentioned policy issues. A small percentage of coverage dealt with candidates' personal qualities (4 percent) and leadership experience (3 percent).[11] As per usual, other stories dealt with the game aspect of the election—candidates' organizations, staff, and strategies—as well as fund raising and the role of money in the campaign.

The conventional wisdom that bad press coverage can be a death knell for a candidate did not hold during the 2016 campaign. The preponderance of press coverage during the general election for both Clinton and Trump was unrelentingly negative. As Thomas Patterson observes, press bias is not rooted in party or ideology, but rather in the propensity to highlight what's wrong with politics and ignore what is right.[12] The Harvard Shorenstein Center/Media Tenor study revealed that Clinton received bad press 64 percent of the time. The situation was even more extreme for Trump, with 77 percent negative coverage. Eighty-four percent of coverage of issues criticized the candidates' positions, such as Trump's views about banning Muslims from entering the country and Clinton's ties to Wall Street bankers. Media coverage of Trump was more positive during the nominating campaign, while the tone of Clinton stories remained about the same throughout the entire election cycle. The amount of positive coverage for the presidential candidates is largely attributable to horse-race stories conveying favorable poll results rather than good reports about their character, leadership potential, or issue positions.

The adage that publicity—even bad publicity—is better for politicians than being ignored gained some credence in the 2016 contest. The amount of press attention may have mattered more for the outcomes of the nominating and the general election campaigns than the tone of coverage. The volume of press coverage of the candidates was extremely lopsided throughout the election cycle. During the Republican nominating campaign, Trump received 63 percent of the coverage, despite the presence of a large field of candidates. Clinton garnered the lion's share of reporting on the Democratic side. A NiemanLab analysis disclosed a strong correlation between the number of times a candidate was mentioned in the top twenty-five online news sources and the percentage of the primary vote s/he earned. Trump and Clinton both outpaced their adversaries in mentions and percentage of votes by wide margins.[13]

During the general election, Trump received 15 percent more coverage than Clinton, and more often was able to use his own words to make his case.[14] Cable news stations regularly would provide countdowns to Trump's appearances at rallies and interrupt regular programming to go live in anticipation of the drama to unfold. They were rewarded when Trump would make an incendiary proclamation, call out a crying baby, or have an attendee physically removed from the hall. Live broadcasts of Hillary Clinton's more sedate stump speeches were far less frequent. She gained more attention when she went on the offensive and criticized Trump's lack of qualifications for office than when she was outlining her policy proposals. Trump's surrogates, such as campaign manager Kellyanne Conway or spokeswoman Katrina Pierson, were fixtures on the cable news circuit. After being fired as Trump's campaign manager, Corey Lewandowski was hired on as a commentator for

CNN. Clinton's campaign manager Robby Mook and communications director Jennifer Palmieri were barely visible on air. As a result, Trump had more opportunities than Clinton to gain publicity and set the news agenda. His slogan, "Make America Great Again," was in play far more often than Clinton's "Stronger Together."

BULLYING THE MEDIA

Donald Trump took aggressive action against the negative coverage he was receiving during the campaign. He sought to discredit the press on the stump and through Twitter rants. Trump bullied journalists whom he felt covered him unfairly, such as Fox News' Megyn Kelly, and made fun of a *New York Times* reporter with a disability. He banned certain media organizations from his events, including the *Washington Post*, whose coverage was undeterred by the move. Reporters had little direct access to Trump on the campaign trail. He granted interviews sparingly, mostly as rewards to friendly reporters, and demanded the questions in advance. Trump defiantly refused journalists' requests for information, especially his tax returns. He threatened to sue publications for stories about his finances and issues with women. At a rally in Scranton, Pennsylvania on the final day of the campaign, Trump launched into a diatribe against the *New York Times* that was characteristic of his treatment of the press throughout the election. "They are so dishonest, folks. You can't even read articles in certain papers anymore. *New York Times* is a total lie. You can't, I mean, you can't—it is so false. Nothing to do with me. I'm just telling you, such lies. Such lies, such fabrications, such made-up stories. Now the *Times* is going out of business pretty soon. That's the good news."[15]

It is puzzling that the press reported regularly on Trump's attacks on their profession, amplifying his message designed to undermine the media's credibility with the electorate. By delegitimizing the formal press, Trump established an alternative media universe among his supporters where he could say and do what he wanted without being held accountable. He promoted his Twitter account as a viable alternative to the established media. Trump's strategy deflected negative information and legitimate concerns raised about his candidacy. It contributed to an environment where fake news could masquerade as valid journalism. Importantly, his actions challenged the valued principle of a free press acting as a check on political actors and institutions.

SOCIAL MEDIA

Social media have become a staple of U.S. elections since their advent in the 2008 presidential contest. The visibility and influence of social media in campaigns have increased dramatically with each election cycle along with the number of users. Over 200 million Americans use Facebook each month,[16] and 40 percent of them regularly get their news from the platform.[17] According to the Pew Research Center, the number of voters who tracked election news through social media (28 percent) and followed candidates (16 percent) during the 2014 midterm campaigns more than doubled from the 2010 elections. This trend marked a notable increase over the 17 percent of voters who used social media in any way during the 2012 presidential contest where voter interest was significantly higher.[18] More voters in 2016 got campaign information through social media than in the past. Sixty-five percent of the electorate accessed election news through digital sources. Forty-four percent of the public learned about the election through social networking sites, especially Facebook and Twitter, and 23 percent of voters were active on issue-based group websites. While use of social media is growing across age groups, younger people are the most inclined to consider social media to be a useful and trustworthy source of campaign information.[19]

Users accessed election-related social media content intentionally, and they also came across it incidentally through their networks. More people posted political content to their Facebook feeds and Twitter accounts than in prior presidential contests. A study of Facebook found strong evidence of political polarization online. Users have five politically like-minded friends versus one who differs from them ideologically. Thus, the content that users encounter online tends to reinforce their existing beliefs rather than expose them to opposing viewpoints.[20]

There has been a substantial climb in the number of people who follow candidates' social media feeds. In 2016, 20 percent of voters regularly learned about the campaign from candidate or campaign groups' websites, apps, or emails.[21] Over 16 million people followed Donald Trump's official Twitter feed, compared to 11 million who followed Hillary Clinton. Voters think that social media allows them to get campaign information faster than through mainstream media and that it comes directly from the source rather than a press filter. Social media also make voters feel more personally connected to candidates.[22] Importantly, users trust social media content. They see it as an alternative to the mainstream media, even though much of the content originates with the mainstream press and political organizations. The public increasingly shares political material, such as memes and videos, within their networks, thus proliferating campaign messages. These factors worked in favor of Donald Trump establishing social media as a powerful alternative to the mainstream press among his followers.

Social media platforms promote political content targeted at voters based on user profiles. Targeted candidate ads pop up unsolicited when voters access their social media accounts. Political news and advocacy pages made specifically for Facebook and other social media are designed to reach audiences within the digital sphere exclusively. Some online political groups have more than two million followers.[23] Targeted ads placed by Google and other vendors set video content in front of specific voters that captured "micromoments" in the campaign that they may have missed in the glut of election information. The Clinton campaign created ads about immigration and other policy issues that appeared on voters' social media accounts in states where they were most relevant.

The playbook for candidates using social media in campaigns involves a two-pronged strategy. Social media are a pillar of the inside game to solidify the candidate's base. However, social media's most powerful function is to stoke the fires of the established press through an outside strategy that markets messages expressing big ideas that have broad appeal. The two campaigns managed their social media in vastly different ways. Trump's heavy use of outside tactics eclipsed Clinton's inside baseball, rendering her social media campaign mute in the larger media sphere.

The Clinton campaign's social media strategy was aimed at solidifying her base rather than promoting slogans and attracting a larger audience. Messages targeted specific groups considered to be critical for the campaign's success, including women, minority group members, and young people. Social media appeals asked voters to declare, "I'm with her." Attempts at mobilizing supporters to act were modest. At times the Clinton team failed to take advantage of technological affordances that would have allowed them to simulcast popular campaign events featuring celebrities, like Beyonce, Jay Z, Lady Gaga, and Katy Perry. Under normal circumstances, a conservative social media strategy would have been prudent, as it allows the candidate to control the message and avoid gaffes. However, the 2016 electoral environment rendered Clinton's social media presence nearly invisible, especially when faced with an opponent who made Twitter his personal megaphone.

Early on, Trump discovered that by firing off offensive tweets making unsubstantiated, outrageous claims, he could dominate the news cycle. The *New York Times* compiled a list of "the people, places, and things Donald Trump has insulted on Twitter," which in December 2016 stood at 289.[24] He repeatedly launched ad hominem attacks against his primary opponents and "crooked" Hillary. People who challenged or questioned him were labeled "stupid," "bad," "crazy," "horrible," "dumb," "overrated," and worse. He used Twitter to reinforce his catch phrases, such as "Build the Wall" and "Lock Her Up." To illustrate Trump's poor treatment of women during the first presidential debate, Clinton recounted how Trump had denigrated former Miss Universe Alicia Machado for gaining weight by calling her "Miss

Piggy" and "Miss Housekeeping." Trump took to Twitter, and accused Clinton of helping the Venezuelan-born actress become a U.S. citizen in order to use her as a prop in the debate. He called Machado "disgusting" and "a con," and told people to check out her nonexistent sex tapes.

The Clinton and Trump campaigns sought to manage the input of voters to augment their messages. Trump regularly would retweet laudatory posts from supporters, at times appearing ignorant of their affiliations with discredited groups, including white supremacists.[25] A *Saturday Night Live* skit featured actor Alec Baldwin as Trump retweeting a high school student named Seth. The skit was based on Trump's actual retweeting of sixteen-year-old Seth's attack on CNN. A Pew Research Center study concluded that candidates' social media were greatly controlled, "leaving fewer ways overall for most voters to engage and take part."[26] Campaigns "flooded the social media zone" with their own content, eclipsing the ability of voter-generated material to gain traction.

VIDEO AS A NEWS SOURCE

News organizations and social media platforms have come to rely heavily on professional, amateur, and archival video in their campaign coverage. Videos are now a vital aspect of legacy news organizations' campaign coverage as well as their documentation of the historical record. The *New York Times* and the *Washington Post* created extensive video archives of the 2016 campaign, and videos regularly accompanied their written stories. Cable news organizations filled many hours of airtime with video content. In an era of armchair reporting, video provides a sense of authenticity to campaign reports. Video evidence allows journalists to furnish background material on candidates, check the consistency of their positions over time, and scrutinize their command of facts. Videos add drama to election reporting, and can incite journalists to engage in "gotcha journalism" by catching candidates behaving badly. In addition, the audience for video has been increasing with each election cycle, as platforms have improved and streaming services have become less costly. An April 2016 study by Google and Ipsos Connect found that one quarter of the electorate relied heavily on digital video to find out about the candidates and issues. Almost half of the voters who regularly viewed election videos were millennials who prefer to consume information visually. Between April 2015 and March 2016, viewers had watched more than 110 million hours of election-related video on YouTube.[27]

Archival footage of Clinton and Trump was readily available, as both candidates had been public figures for much of their adult lives. Clinton was on video record as a public servant and Trump as a celebrity. Video reports gain the most attention when they support a consistent narrative about a candidate. A widely-publicized clip of Hillary Clinton at a fund-raising event with supporters depicted her stating that half of Donald Trump's supporters fell into a "basket of deplorables," indicating that they were racist, sexist, and homophobic. The statement played into the narrative that Clinton could not relate to—and even looked down upon—white, less-educated, lower socio-economic status voters. While Clinton attempted to claw back the statement while it was dominating the headlines, Trump supporters rallied around the moniker as a badge of honor, even sporting the slogan on T-shirts and caps.

A prominent media frame characterized thrice-married Donald Trump, who once owned the Miss Universe beauty pageant, as a misogynist. During a Republican primary debate, moderator Megyn Kelly of Fox News asked Trump to address the fact that he has "called women you don't like fat pigs, dogs, slobs, and disgusting animals." Trump responded by feuding with Kelly on Twitter. Video of his stump speeches on cable news reinforced the misogynist frame by depicting Trump referring to Kelly as a "bimbo" and worse. The video drama escalated as Trump and Kelly played "cat and mouse" throughout the campaign.

Perhaps the most damaging video of the campaign relayed a 2005 conversation between Donald Trump and *Access Hollywood* correspondent Billy Bush that was captured before Trump participated in a segment about his cameo on a soap opera. In it Trump brags about how his celebrity status allows him to do what he pleases with women. The video dominated news coverage for days, and was raised in the second presidential debate. Trump dismissed the statements as "locker room talk," a premise that offended some high-profile athletes. Numerous women came forward alleging that Trump had sexually harassed or assaulted them, countering Trump's denials.

HALF-TRUTHS, OUTRIGHT LIES, AND THE METEORIC RISE OF FAKE NEWS

The amount of misinformation, misleading stories, and boldface lies that were propagated is an unfortunate hallmark of the 2016 campaign. Susan Glasser argues that journalism has come to reflect the realities of reporting in post-truth America, a period where objective facts are subordinate to emotional appeals and personal beliefs in shaping public opinion.[28] Donald Trump made a habit of using his Twitter feed to blast out statements that could not be verified or which were complete untruths. Try as they might to fact-check and hold Trump accountable, journalists were unable to stem the tide of disinformation.

Surrogates defended Trump's blatant disregard for the truth. Post-election, campaign manager Kellyanne Conway and former campaign manager Corey Lewandowski argued that Trump's misleading statements were not meant to be taken literally, and blamed the press for reporting on them. Questioned about the veracity of Trump's tweets during a *60 Minutes* interview, House Speaker Paul Ryan responded, "It doesn't matter to me. He won the election. The way I see the tweets you're talking about, he's basically giving voice to a lot of people who have felt that they were voiceless." Vice presidential nominee Mike Pence said that he found Trump's tweets to be "refreshing."[29]

Trumps misleading tweets coincided with the rise of fake news during the campaign. The term "fake news," which formerly had been used to describe parody news programs, like the *Daily Show* and *The Colbert Report*, took on a new, more sinister meaning during the 2016 presidential contest. Fabricated, sensational stories made to appear as if they were real news articles proliferated on websites, such as *Infowars*, *The Rightest*, *The Denver Guardian*, and *National Report*. These sites were designed to look like legitimate news platforms or political blogs, although the quality of the sites varied greatly. Fake news authors, some of whom were paid thousands of dollars during the campaign, created political fiction that played into voters' ideological biases. Outlandish stories fed preexisting beliefs about parties and candidates, making them appear credible to insular audiences. While some stories were outright fabrications and hyperpartisan screeds, hybrid forms contained elements of truth that lent to their credibility. Conspiracy theories, hoaxes, and lies were spread efficiently through Facebook, Snapchat, and other social media. Fake news reached millions of people during the campaign, some of whom were more willing to believe an anonymous Facebook post than an attributed article in the *New York Times*.[30]

While false stories have proliferated on social media for years, fake news was barely part of the lexicon until October when the campaign headed into the home stretch. There were reports that Pope Francis had endorsed Donald Trump, Hillary Clinton had sold weapons to ISIS, and an FBI agent was found dead after leaking Clinton emails. A fake site made to resemble *ABC News* posted an erroneous story that a protester at a Trump rally was paid $3,500 by the Clinton campaign. The tale prompted Trump's son Eric to tweet, "Finally, the truth comes out"—a message he deleted after it was widely circulated. Fake news engines went into overdrive on Election Day, circulating rumors of massive voter fraud in certain states.[31]

Fake news can have serious consequences for innocent people, as illustrated by the "Pizzagate" story that coalesced around an unlikely set of circumstances. As the presidential campaign was coming to a close, FBI Director James Comey reopened the investigation into Hillary Clinton's use of a private email server during her time as Secretary of State. The new investigation was based on messages found on a computer used by former New York congressman Anthony Weiner, the estranged husband of Clinton aide Huma Abedin. Weiner was under investigation for allegedly sending inappropriate text messages to an underage girl. A rumor claiming that the new emails "point to a pedophilia ring" with Hillary Clinton at the center was retweeted thousands of times. The accusations quickly spread across social media platforms and prompted blog postings and articles on fake news sites. They were further propagated through talk radio, where Alt-Right host Alex Jones alleged that Clinton and her campaign chairman, John Podesta, engaged in satanic rituals. A YouTube video by Jones proclaiming that Clinton had "personally murdered and chopped up and raped" children was viewed almost a half a million times. The plot thickened further when Wiki-Leaks released personal emails from Podesta's account indicating that he occasionally enjoyed eating at a pizza restaurant in northwest Washington, D.C. The Twitter hashtag #pizzagate soon began trending, with many of the tweets originating in the Czech Republic, Cyprus, and Vietnam, and were being spread by bots, not humans. The rumors soon morphed into allegations that the pizza restaurant's owner was running a child sex ring and hiding the victims in underground tunnels, accusations that soon encompassed other businesses in the area. The businesses were threatened by menacing phone calls and social media posts, and lost patrons. Sparked by the rumors, a man drove from North Carolina to liberate the purported child sex slaves. He fired an assault rifle inside the pizza restaurant as staff and patrons fled into the street.[32]

CONCLUSION

The 2016 presidential election demarcates the era of post-truth news. It is a treacherous time for journalists and responsible news organizations. The press's legitimacy is being challenged by an alternative media universe where Twitter rants and fake news hijack the political agenda obscuring the important issues of the day. As Susan Glasser laments, "The election of 2016 showed us that Americans are increasingly choosing to live in a cloud of like-minded spin, surrounded by the partisan political hackery and fake news that poisons their Facebook feeds."[33]

Backlash against publicizing misleading information and fake news has come from various quarters. Hillary Clinton publicly condemned false news as an epidemic that puts lives at risk, and called for bipartisan efforts to confront it.[34] Pope Francis equated spreading disinformation with sin. He stated that it is "probably the greatest damage that the media can do" because "it directs opinion in only one direction and omits the other part of the truth."[35]

The bleak financial realities of the news business that have forced layoffs and limited resources for reporting have created a dilemma for a press seeking to fulfill its responsibilities to be a watchdog for the public interest. The news industry's bottom line benefitted from coverage of the 2016 campaign. As Jim Rutenberg observes, "to the news media have gone the spoils. With Mr. Trump providing must-see TV theatrics, cable news has drawn record audiences. Newspapers have reached online readership highs that would have been unimaginable just a few years ago."[36]

The post-truth trends that evolved during the election have continued unchecked in its aftermath. Curbing the tide of false information will be difficult. Raising awareness of the issue is a first step in dealing with the post-truth news problem. Newsrooms need to take the lead in reclaiming their position in the media ecosystem. The resources available for newsgathering in the digital age should position the press to do its best work, even as media organizations rework their business models to remain viable. The media must rediscover and firmly assert their foundational practices of fact-checking and proper sourcing. Left unaddressed, the potential effects of the post-truth media on the requirement of an informed citizenry and democratic governance are chilling to contemplate.

NOTES

1. Larry J. Sabato, *Feeding Frenzy* (New York: Free Press, 1991).

2. Jeffrey Gottfried, Michael Barthel, Elisa Shearer, and Amy Mitchell, "The 2016 Presidential Campaign—a News Event That's Hard to Miss." Research Report. Washington, D.C.: Pew Research Center for the People and the Press, February 4, 2016. http://www.journalism.org/2016/02/04/the-2016-presidential-campaign-a-news-event-thats-hard-to-miss/.

3. Sridhar Poppu, "Millennial Reports Grab Campaign-Trail Spotlight," *New York Times*, March 5, 2016, http://www.nytimes.com/2016/03/06/style/election-2016-millennial-reporters.html.

4. Thomas E. Patterson, *News Coverage of the 2016 General Election: How the Press Failed the Voters*. Research Report. Shorenstein Center on Media, Politics and Public Policy in conjunction with Media Tenor, December 2016.

5. Jeffrey Gottfried, et al., February 4, 2016.

6. Jim Rutenberg, "Media's Next Challenge: Overcoming the Threat of Fake News," *New York Times*, November 6, 2016. http://www.nytimes.com/2016/11/07/business/media/medias-next-challenge-overcoming-the-threat-of-fake-news.html.

7. Ken Doctor, "Newsonomics: The Halving of America's Daily Newsrooms," *NiemanLab*, July 28, 2015, http://www.niemanlab.org/2015/07/newsonomics-the-halving-of -americas-daily-newsrooms/.

8. David Barstow, Mike McIntire, Patricia Cohen, Susanne Craig, and Russ Buettner, "Donald Trump Used Legally Dubious Method to Avoid Paying Taxes," *New York Times*, October 31, 2016, http://www.nytimes.com/2016/11/01/us/politics/donald-trump-tax .html?_r = 0.

9. Adam Liptak, "Donald Trump Would Have Trouble Winning a Suit over the Times's Tax Article," *New York Times*, October 4, 2016, http://www.nytimes.com/2016/ 10/05/us/politics/donald-trump-taxes-legal-case-new-york-times.html.

10. Rosalind S. Helderman, Spencer S. Hsu, and Tom Hamburger, "Emails Reveal How Foundational Donors Got Access to Clinton and Her Close Aides at State Dept.," *Washington Post*, August 22, 2016, https://www.washingtonpost.com/politics/emails-reveal -how-foundation-donors-got-access-to-clinton-and-her-close-aides-at-state-dept/2016/08/ 22/345b5200-6882-11e6-8225-fbb8a6fc65bc_story.html?utm_term = .896fb9c6b1a7.

11. Thomas E. Patterson, December, 2016.

12. Thomas E. Patterson, December, 2016.

13. Jonathan Stray, "How Much Influence Does the Media Really Have over Elections? Digging into the Data," *NiemanLab*, January 11, 2016, http://www.niemanlab.org/ 2016/01/how-much-influence-does-the-media-really-have-over-elections-digging-into -the-data/.

14. Thomas E. Patterson, December, 2016.

15. Callum Borchers, "The Single Minute That Perfectly Illustrates Donald Trump's Anti-media Campaign," *Washington Post*, November 8, 2016, https://www.washington post.com/news/the-fix/wp/2016/11/08/the-single-minute-that-perfectly-illustrate-donald -trumps-anti-media-campaign/?utm_term = .a379e7d84962.

16. John Herrman, "Inside Facebook's (Totally Insane, Unintentionally Gigantic, Hyperpartisan) Political-Media Machine," *The New York Times Magazine*, August 24, 2016, http://www.nytimes.com/2016/08/28/magazine/inside-facebooks-totally-insane -unintentionally-gigantic-hyperpartisan-political-media-machine.html.

17. Jeffrey Gottfried, et al., February 4, 2016.

18. *Cell Phones, Social Media and Campaign 2014,* Pew Research Center, November 3, 2014.

19. Jeffrey Gottfried, et al,, February 4, 2016.

20. Eytan Bakshy, Solomon Messing, and Lada Adamic, "Exposure to Ideologically Diverse News and Opinion on Facebook," *Science*, May 7, 2015, http://science.sci encemag.org/content/early/2015/05/08/science.aaa1160.full.

21. Jeffrey Gottfried, et al., February 4, 2016.

22. Marissa Lang, "2016 Election Circus: Is Social Media the Cause?" *San Francisco Chronicle*, April 5, 2016, http://www.govtech.com/social/2016-Presidential-Election -Circus-Is-Social-Media-the-Cause.html.

23. John Hermann, August 25, 2016.

24. Jasmine C. Lee and Kevin Quealy, "The 289 People, Places, and Things Donald Trump Has Insulted: The Complete List," *New York Times*, December 6, 2016, http://www .nytimes.com/interactive/2016/01/28/upshot/donald-trump-twitter-insults.html?_r = 0.

25. Nolan D. McCaskill, "Trump Retweets Another White Supremacist," *Politico*, February 27, 2016, http://www.politico.com/blogs/2016-gop-primary-live-updates-and-re sults/2016/02/donald-trump-white-supremacist-retweet-219915.

26. *Election 2016: Campaigns as a Direct Source of News*, Pew Research Center, July 18, 2016.

27. Kate Stanford, "How Political Ads and Video Content Influence Voter Opinion," *Google Newsletter*, March 2015, https://www.thinkwithgoogle.com/articles/political-ads -video-content-influence-voter-opinion.html.

28. Susan B. Glasser, "Covering Politics in a 'Post-Truth' America," *Brookings Essay*, December 2, 2016, https://www.brookings.edu/essay/covering-politics-in-a-post-truth -america/?utm_campaign = brookings-comm&utm_source = hs_email&utm_medium = email&utm_content = 38712889.

29. Dahlia Lithwick and Robert L. Tsai, "Actually, Paul Ryan, the President's Words Do Matter," *Slate*, December 5, 2016, http://www.slate.com/articles/news_and_politics/ jurisprudence/2016/12/paul_ryan_says_it_doesn_t_matter_when_trump_lies_on_twitter _that_s_garbage.html.

30. Will Oremus, "Stop Calling Everything 'Fake News,'" *Slate*, December 6, 2016, http://www.slate.com/articles/technology/technology/2016/12/stop_calling_everything _fake_news.html.

31. Katie Rogers and Jonah Engel Bromwich, "The Hoaxes, Fake News, and Misinformation We Saw on Election Day," *New York Times*, November 8, 2016, http://www.ny times.com/2016/11/09/us/politics/debunk-fake-news-election-day.html?_r = 0.

32. Mark Fisher, John Woodrow Cox, and Peter Hermann, "Pizzagate: From Rumor, to Hashtag, to Gunfire in D.C.," *Washington Post*, December 6, 2016, https://www.wash ingtonpost.com/local/pizzagate-from-rumor-to-hashtag-to-gunfire-in-dc/2016/12/06/4c7 def50-bbd4-11e6-94ac-3d324840106c_story.html?utm_term = .7d37c847c11e.

33. Susan B. Glasser, December 2, 2016.

34. Noam Scheiber, Maggie Haberman, and Emmarie Huetteman, "Trump Is Still Not Very Popular, and His Problem with Women Could Return," *New York Times*, December 8, 2016, http://www.nytimes.com/2016/12/08/us/politics/trump-picks-twitter-fight-with -union-local-chief-in-indiana.html?rref = collection%2Fnewseventcollection%2Felection -2016&action = click&contentCollection = politics&region = stream&module = stream_ unit&version = latest&contentPlacement = 1&pgtype = collection.

35. Jessie Hellmann, "Pope Francis: It's a Sin to Spread Fake News," *The Hill*, December 7, 2016, http://thehill.com/blogs/blog-briefing-room/news/309179-pope-francis-its-a -sin-to-spread-fake-news-focus-on-scandals.

36. Jim Rutenberg, November 6, 2016.

12

The $7 Billion Election

Emerging Campaign Finance Trends and Their Impact on the 2016 Presidential Race and Beyond

Michael E. Toner and Karen E. Trainer

Donald J. Trump's election as the forty-fifth president of the United States was as improbable and historic as any election in the modern era, and Trump and his presidential campaign likewise made history in the campaign finance arena as well—namely, by becoming the first candidate to be elected president in decades while being substantially outspent by his opponent, Hillary Rodham Clinton. In so doing, Trump and his campaign committee shattered many long-standing assumptions about the American campaign finance system and what candidates and campaigns must do to win the presidency. The Clinton campaign and its allies collectively raised and spent twice as much money during the 2016 presidential race as did the Trump campaign and its allies.[1] Yet despite facing a significant campaign resource disadvantage, Trump, relying on a shrewd earned and social media strategy, won a comfortable Electoral College majority and may have helped pave a new way for candidates to pursue the Oval Office in the future.

With the dust still settling on the 2016 election, total spending on the election is estimated at nearly $7 billion, which made the 2016 presidential race the most expensive in American history.[2] To put that spending tally in context, a total of $6 billion was expended on the 2012 election, which was an unprecedented amount at that time.[3] The record amounts of money expended on the 2016 election were fueled primarily by a significant increase in spending by Super PACs and other outside groups, which collectively spent 32 percent more funds than they did during the 2012 election.[4] However, political party expenditures declined in 2016 and constituted a smaller share of total electoral spending, which is a trend that has emerged during the last ten to fifteen years. Increasingly, we are witnessing a tale of two fund-raising stories—a robust story for Super PACs and other outside groups, which can accept unlimited contributions and which comprise an ever-larger share of total campaign spending, and a more challenging story for political parties and many candidates, which labor under strict contribution limits and prohibitions. The result is an increasingly fragmented and less politically accountable campaign finance system which, absent new legislation or judicial action, could become even more pronounced in the future.

MAJOR PRESIDENTIAL PARTY NOMINEE FUND-RAISING DROPPED IN 2016 FOR THE FIRST TIME IN MANY YEARS

To properly understand contemporary presidential campaign fund-raising trends, it is necessary to briefly discuss the creation of the presidential public financing system in the 1970s and the gradual abandonment of that system by leading presidential candidates during the last two decades.

The presidential public financing system was established after the Watergate scandal and first went into effect for the 1976 presidential election. Under the system, presidential candidates have the option of accepting public funds for their primary election or general election campaigns, or both. For the primaries, presidential candidates can receive matching funds from the government of up to $250 for each individual contribution they receive. For the 2016 primaries, each presidential candidate could receive a maximum of approximately $48 million in matching funds.[5] However, candidates electing to receive matching funds for the 2016 presidential race were subject to a nationwide spending limit during the primaries of approximately $48 million, as well as state-by-state spending limits based upon the population of each state. Under the federal election laws, the primary season runs from the time a person legally becomes a presidential candidate through the national nominating conventions, which can last eighteen months or even longer. The national and state-by-state spending limits apply throughout this period of time. By contrast, candidates who decline to take matching funds are not subject to any spending limits for the primaries and are free to raise as much money as they can, subject to the contribution limits.[6] For the general election, presidential candidates have the option of accepting a public grant to finance all of their political activities and be subject to a nationwide spending limit, or candidates can turn down public funds and raise private contributions subject to the contribution limits and operate without any spending restriction. The public grant for the general election in 2016 was approximately $96 million.[7]

The presidential public financing system gradually became obsolete during the last twenty years as more and more presidential candidates operated their campaigns outside of the system in order to free themselves of the spending limits that come with the acceptance of public funds. In the 2000 presidential race, George W. Bush raised $100 million for his primary campaign and became the first candidate to turn down matching funds for the primaries and be elected president when he defeated Al Gore. In 2004, both major party nominees for the first time turned down matching funds for the primaries, as George W. Bush raised $270 million and John Kerry raised $235 million for the primary season. Significantly, both Bush and Kerry in 2004 accepted the $75 million public grant for the general election and joined every major party nominee since 1976 in doing so. However, the historical practice of accepting public funds for the general election was shattered in 2008 when President Obama became the first presidential candidate to be elected president who turned down public funds for both the primaries and the general election, which helped clear the way for Obama to raise an astounding $750 million for his campaign, including $414 million for the primaries alone. By contrast, Senator John McCain in 2008 raised $221 million for the primaries but opted to accept the $85 million public grant for the general election, which provided McCain with a total of only $306 million for his entire campaign, which was barely 40 percent of the total funds that the Obama campaign had at its disposal.[8] In 2012, both Obama and Mitt Romney opted out of the public financing system for both the primaries and the general. In total, their campaigns raised $1.22 billion, a 16 percent increase over the $1.05 billion raised by the major party nominees in 2008.[9]

As table 12.1 indicates below, fund-raising by major party nominees for president generally increased during each election cycle since the 2000 Bush-Gore election. However, in 2016 total fund-raising by the major party nominees (including contributions and loans from Trump to his campaign) totaled only 73 percent of the total amount raised by the major party nominees in 2012. Senator Bernie Sanders' campaign, which raised approximately $232 million for the 2016 primary, far outraised and outspent the Trump campaign during the same time period.[10] The $499 million raised by the Clinton and Sanders campaigns collectively for the 2016 primary did not come close to

Table 12.1.   Summary of Major Party Nominee Fund-raising Totals (2000–2016)

Candidate	Primary Fund-raising Total	General Fund-raising Total	Total Campaign Funds
2016			
Trump	$89 million	$240 million	$329 million*
Clinton	$267 million	$302 million	$569 million
2012			
Obama	$442 million	$296 million	$738 million
Romney	$253 million	$230 million	$483 million
2008			
Obama	$414 million	$336 million	$750 million
McCain	$221 million	$85 million**	$306 million
2004			
Bush	$270 million	$80 million**	$350 million
Kerry	$235 million	$80 million**	$315 million
2000			
Bush	$100 million	$75 million**	$175 million
Gore	$50 million**	$75 million**	$125 million

Source: Federal Election Commission data. 2016 primary and general totals are estimates based on total fund-raising as of June 30, 2016.
Notes: *$66 million of this amount represents contributions or loans made by Trump to his campaign. **Candidate Accepted Public Funds.

matching the record-breaking $651 million raised by the Clinton and Obama campaigns combined for the 2008 primary.[11]

Neither the Trump nor the Clinton campaign came close to breaking Obama's record-setting 2008 fund-raising total of $750 million for his campaign. Trump won the presidency in 2016 with $329 million raised, which was only half of what Obama had raised eight years earlier and was less than what the winning presidential candidates raised in 2004, 2008, and 2012.[12] Trump was also the first candidate this century to raise and spend less campaign funds than his general election opponent and go on to win the election.

As table 12.1 shows, the Clinton campaign raised over 70 percent more than the Trump campaign during the course of the 2016 presidential race. In total, the Clinton campaign and other political committees supporting her (including the DNC) raised $1.2 billion, twice the amount raised by Trump's campaign and other political committees supporting him (including the RNC).[13] The Trump campaign, however, had a significant advantage in earned media—including news media coverage and communications disseminated for free on social media platforms such as Twitter and Facebook—that helped make up for its fund-raising deficit. As of March 2016, studies estimate that earned media referencing Trump had a value of nearly $2 billion, compared to only $746 million for Clinton, and Trump enjoyed $400 million of earned media in February 2016 alone.[14] By the day after the election, Trump's earned media for the election cycle had increased to about $5 billion in value, which was double the amount for Clinton.[15]

The Trump campaign also spent significantly less than the Clinton campaign. Studies estimate that the Trump campaign spent less than $5 per vote in total, while the Clinton campaign spent double that amount.[16] By contrast, in six battleground states, paid advertisements supporting Clinton outnumbered commercials supporting Trump by three to one. However, despite a clear campaign resource advantage, Clinton ended up losing five of those six states.[17]

OUTSIDE GROUP EXPENDITURES BROKE RECORDS IN 2016, FUELED PRIMARILY BY INCREASED SUPER PAC SPENDING

The passage of the McCain-Feingold campaign finance law, combined with court decisions permitting unlimited corporate, union, and individual contributions to finance independent expenditures sponsored by outside organizations such as Super PACs and 501(c) organizations, has led to a proliferation of outside groups in recent years that are having a growing impact on federal elections. These outside groups, which have flourished on both the right and the left, are increasingly engaged in political activities that were once the province of political parties, such as voter registration drives, absentee ballot programs, GOTV, voter identification, and political advertising and issue advocacy efforts.

The McCain-Feingold law, which took effect during the 2004 presidential election cycle, prohibits the RNC and the DNC and the other national political party committees from raising or spending soft-money funds for any purpose. "Soft money" is defined as funds raised outside of the prohibitions and limitations of federal law, including corporate and labor union general treasury funds and individual contributions in excess of federal limits. Funds raised in accordance with federal law come from individuals and from federally registered PACs and are harder to raise; hence, these funds are commonly referred to in campaign finance parlance as "hard money." Prior to McCain-Feingold, the national political parties were legally permitted to accept unlimited corporate, union and individual soft-money contributions and could use these funds to help underwrite a wide variety of political and electoral activities, including voter registration efforts, absentee ballot drives, GOTV activities, slate cards, and similar ticket-wide political activities. The national political parties prior to McCain-Feingold were also able to use soft-money contributions to help finance issue advertisements supporting and opposing federal candidates. "Issue advertisements" are public communications that frequently attack or promote federal candidates and their records, but which refrain from expressly advocating the election or defeat of any candidate (which is referred to as "express advocacy").

In *Citizens United v. FEC*, the U.S. Supreme Court in 2010 struck down the long-standing prohibition on corporate independent expenditures in connection with federal elections. That same year, in *SpeechNow v. FEC*, a federal appeals court invalidated limits on contributions from individuals to political committees that fund only independent expenditures for or against federal candidates. In advisory opinions issued after the *SpeechNow* decision, the FEC concluded that political committees formed strictly to make independent expenditures supporting or opposing federal candidates could accept unlimited contributions from individuals, corporations, and labor organizations.[18] These new kinds of political committees, which are prohibited from making contributions to federal candidates and to other federal political committees, are commonly referred to as "Super PACs."

501(c) entities are organized and operate under Section 501(c) of the Internal Revenue Code and include social welfare organizations established under Section 501(c)(4) and trade associations and business leagues organized under Section 501(c)(6). Section 501(c)(4) and 501(c)(6) entities are permitted to accept unlimited corporate, union, and individual contributions and may engage in partisan political activities, provided such political activities are not their primary purpose. By contrast, Super PACs, as political committees registered with the FEC, are by definition partisan entities and may spend all of their funds on partisan political activities. Super PACs are required to publicly disclose their donors, whereas 501(c) organizations are generally not.

Super PACs and 501(c) organizations spent approximately $1.5 billion in connection with the 2016 election. As figure 12.1 illustrates, this amount outstrips the $1 billion spent by such outside groups in connection with the 2012 election and is over four times more than the $338 million spent by outside groups in connection with the 2008 election. Super PAC and 501(c) entity spending in connection with the 2016 presidential race heavily favored Clinton, as outside groups spent nearly three times more in support of Clinton than they did in support of Trump.[19]

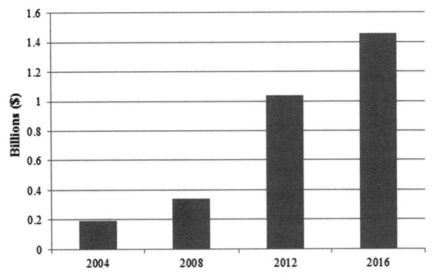

Figure 12.1. Outside spending by election cycle (excluding political party committees). *Source*: Center for Responsive Politics, https://www.opensecrets.org/outsidespending/cycle_tots.php?cycle = 2016&view = A&chart = N. Figure created by Michael E. Toner and Karen E. Trainer.

The largest Super PAC of the 2016 election cycle, Priorities USA Action, spent over $130 million in support of Clinton. This amount comprised 76 percent of outside spending in support of Clinton during the election cycle.[20] Priorities USA Action aired 77,000 advertisements during the general election period, nearly as many as the Trump campaign's 85,000.[21] Table 12.2 lists the largest nonparty outside spenders for the 2016 election cycle, almost all of which are Super PACs.

2016 also saw the proliferation of Super PACs geared toward electing a particular presidential candidate. Single-candidate Super PACs funded most outside group advertising during the primary phase of the presidential race.[22] A total of 188 single-candidate Super PACs registered with the FEC for the 2015–2016 election cycle, compared with only 103 during the 2011–2012 cycle. The 2016 presidential single-candidate Super PACs also raised and spent well over double the amount raised and spent by single-candidate Super PACs in the 2012 cycle.[23] Interestingly, the largest single-candidate Super PACs in the 2012, 2014, and 2016 cycles all supported candidates that ultimately lost.[24]

Campaigns are legally prohibited from coordinating their activities with Super PACs, but a number of candidates engaged in activities that neverthe-

Table 12.2.   Largest Nonparty Outside Spenders (2016 Election Cycle)

Name	Entity Type	2015–2016 Disclosed Spending
Priorities USA Action (Pro-Clinton)	Super PAC	$132,438,801
Right to Rise USA (Pro-Jeb Bush)	Super PAC	$86,817,138
Senate Leadership Fund	Super PAC	$85,096,402
Senate Majority PAC	Super PAC	$79,593,191
Conservative Solutions PAC (Pro-Marco Rubio)	Super PAC	$55,443,483
National Rifle Assn	PAC/501C	$52,906,796
Get Our Jobs Back	Super PAC	$50,010,166
Congressional Leadership Fund	Super PAC	$39,071,249
Women Vote!	Super PAC	$33,574,994

Source: Center for Responsive Politics, https://www.opensecrets.org/outsidespending/summ.php?disp = O.

less benefited the Super PACs supporting them. Some presidential candidates adopted a strategy of working with a single-candidate Super PAC before formally entering the race. In some cases, a candidate's campaign committee provided public information or video footage that was later used by a Super PAC supporting that same candidate.[25] For example, after Marco Rubio's campaign tweeted a link to a website criticizing Senator Ted Cruz's tax plan, Rubio's Super PAC aired an advertisement making similar criticisms.[26] In total, the Super PACs supporting Jeb Bush, Rand Paul, Lindsey Graham, Mike Huckabee, George Pataki, Rick Perry, and Scott Walker raised $181 million in 2015.[27] However, some of these candidates struggled to raise funds for their own campaigns and were forced to exit the race before the first presidential primaries and caucuses were even held.

Single-candidate Super PACs have become increasingly common in downballot races as well. For example, the largest single-candidate Super PAC in 2016 for a U.S. Senate race, Granite State Solutions, spent $21 million in support of New Hampshire Senator Kelly Ayotte. The largest single-candidate Super PAC at the U.S. House level, Maryland USA, spent $3.2 million to support Amie Hoeber in the Sixth Congressional District of Maryland.[28] On the whole, outside groups spent $282 million on ten top Senate races, which amounted to 51 percent of total spending in connection with those races.[29]

Contributions to Super PACs in the 2015–2016 election cycle were made primarily by wealthy individuals. Despite concerns by some campaign finance observers about the potential for corporately funded Super PACs to emerge in the wake of the *Citizens United* ruling, corporate contributions to Super PACs during the 2016 election cycle comprised only 8 percent of total Super PAC donations (through July 31, 2016) and labor union contributions to Super PACs comprised less than 2 percent of the total.[30]

Remarkably, contributions from sixty of the largest donors accounted for 57 percent of overall Super PAC spending on the presidential race through the middle of October 2016.[31] Contributions to Super PACs by donors contributing over $500,000 totaled over $1 billion as of a week before the 2016 election, and this figure constituted nearly 15 percent of the total amount of money spent on the election.[32] Table 12.3 identifies the top ten Super PAC donors of the 2016 election cycle, several of which were individuals.

Labor unions also spent a significant amount of funds on the 2016 election. As of late August 2016, labor union spending in connection with the election (including contributions to Super PACs) totaled $108 million, an increase of 38 percent compared to spending for the same time frame during the 2012 election.[33] By Election Day, the total increased to $167 million. Although this amount represented record spending by labor unions, it paled in comparison to election-related contributions and expenditures made by individuals

Table 12.3. Top Super PAC Donors, 2015–2016 Election Cycle

Donor Name	Total Amount	Ideology
Thomas Steyer	$66,044,744	100% Dem
Sheldon and Miriam Adelson	$52,700,000	100% Rep
S. Donald Sussman	$36,645,000	100% Dem
Fred Eychaner	$32,000,000	100% Dem
National Education Assn	$26,300,299	100% Dem
Carpenters & Joiners Union	$23,548,194	98% Dem
Robert Mercer	$22,451,000	100% Rep
Paul Singer	$21,506,464	100% Rep
Michael R. Bloomberg	$21,090,864	100% Dem
James & Marilyn Simons	$18,025,000	100% Dem

Source: Center for Responsive Politics, https://www.opensecrets.org/outsidespending/summ.php?cycle = 2016 &disp = D&type = V&superonly = S, https://www.opensecrets.org/outsidespending/summ.php?cycle = 2016&disp = D&type = O&superonly = S. Super PACs that made significant contributions to other Super PACs are excluded from the list.

Table 12.4. Largest Traditional PACs by Total Contributions Made (2016 Election Cycle)

PAC Name	2015–2016 Total Contributions
National Assn of Realtors PAC	$3,912,000
National Beer Wholesalers Assn PAC	$3,515,700
AT&T Inc PAC	$3,100,750
Honeywell International PAC	$2,785,864
National Auto Dealers Assn PAC	$2,747,250
Lockheed Martin PAC	$2,600,750
Blue Cross/Blue Shield PAC	$2,585,898
American Bankers Assn PAC	$2,524,507
Credit Union National Assn PAC	$2,462,350
Intl Brotherhood of Electrical Workers PAC	$2,413,200
National Assn of Insurance & Financial Advisors PAC	$2,312,400

Source: Center for Responsive Politics, https://www.opensecrets.org/pacs/.

and was less than the total amount contributed by the top five Super PAC donors noted above.[34]

Despite the increase in labor union spending, 501(c) entities as a whole spent significantly less on the 2016 election than they did on the 2012 election. In 2016, 501(c) groups spent approximately $181 million, compared to over $308 million in 2012.[35] The number of 501(c) groups active in the election also decreased in 2016 as compared to 2012. In 2012, 266 501(c) groups spent funds in connection with the election as compared to only 87 in 2016.[36]

Because Super PACs and 501(c) organizations may not make contributions to federal campaign committees, traditional PACs—which can only accept hard-dollar contributions subject to federal contribution limits and source prohibitions—remain an important vehicle for supporting federal candidates.[37] Table 12.4 lists the ten largest PACs based upon the total amounts contributed to candidates during the 2016 election cycle. Each of these PACs are "connected" PACs associated with corporations, trade associations, labor organizations, and membership organizations. A number of connected PACs also sponsored advertisements supporting or opposing federal candidates in addition to making direct contributions to candidates.

POLITICAL PARTY FUND-RAISING DECLINED IN 2016 AND PARTY EXPENDITURES REPRESENTED A SMALLER SHARE OF TOTAL SPENDING ON THE ELECTION

There are growing indications that national political party committees are becoming less relevant in federal elections as spending increasingly shifts to

Super PACs and other outside groups that are not subject to the hard-dollar fund-raising requirements that apply to the national political party committees.

In late 2014, Congress passed an appropriations bill that included provisions allowing national political party committees to establish separate subaccounts with additional contribution limits. Contributions made to these accounts may be used to pay for office building expenditures, expenses incurred in recounts and other legal proceedings, and national convention expenses. Individuals and PACs may make contributions to these separate subaccounts in addition to making contributions to a national political party's main political account. For example, an individual may contribute up to $33,400 per year to the DNC's main political account, plus up to $33,400 per year to each of the DNC's office building, recount, and convention subaccounts. Accordingly, an individual may contribute up to $133,600 per year to the DNC or RNC. Between January 1, 2015, and June 30, 2016, national political party committees raised a total of $86.7 million into these new subaccounts.[38]

Despite the ability to raise funds into newly established national party subaccounts, fund-raising totals for the RNC and DNC continued to decline in 2016 as compared with previous election cycles. In fact, when fund-raising figures are adjusted for inflation, the RNC and DNC raised less money collectively during the 2016 election cycle than they did in any previous election cycle dating back to 2004. Figure 12.2 lists fund-raising totals (adjusted for

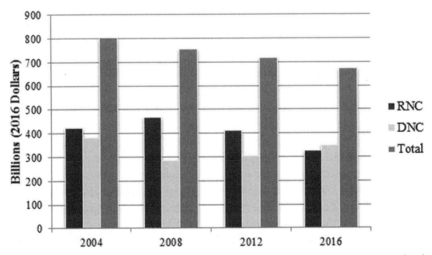

Figure 12.2.   Political party fund-raising in presidential election cycles. *Source*: Federal Election Commission data.

inflation to 2016 dollars) for the RNC and DNC in presidential election cycles since 2004.

On the spending side, the RNC and DNC each spent far less during the 2016 election than in previous election cycles on independent expenditures in support of their presidential nominees. As of mid-October 2016, the RNC had spent $321,000 on advertisements opposing Clinton, and none on advertisements supporting Trump. By comparison, the RNC spent $18.2 million on independent expenditures in support of Bush in 2004, $53.5 million on independent expenditures in support of McCain in 2008, and $42.4 million on independent expenditures supporting Romney or opposing Obama in 2012.[39] The DNC spent over $120 million on independent expenditures in connection with the 2004 presidential election, but only $1.1 million on independent expenditures in connection with the 2008 presidential election. Revealingly, the DNC did not make any independent expenditures in connection with any races in the 2012 or 2016 election cycles.[40]

Because outside groups do not labor under the hard-dollar fund-raising restrictions that apply to the national political parties, outside groups can raise large amounts of money from a small group of donors in a very short period of time. As a result, Super PACs, 501(c) organizations, and other types of outside groups are now spending more on independent expenditures and other election-related communications than are political party committees. Outside spending, particularly by Super PACs, continued to grow in 2016. Spending by Super PACs comprised 47 percent of outside spending in the 2012 election, compared to 65 percent during the 2016 election cycle.[41] Overall outside spending jumped from $1.3 billion in 2012 to $1.7 billion in 2016, with Super PAC spending comprising $1.1 billion of that total.[42]

Spending by political parties comprised only 15 percent of total outside group spending in connection with the 2016 election, compared to 20 percent for the 2012 election cycle. Figure 12.3 illustrates the breakdown of spending between different types of entities during the 2012 and 2016 election cycles.

Given the fund-raising advantages that outside groups currently enjoy over national political party committees, this spending imbalance may become even more pronounced in the future unless the campaign finance laws are changed to allow the national political parties to raise and spend the same kinds of funds as outside groups are legally able to do.

Political party committees continued to engage in extensive joint fund-raising activities in 2016. Under FEC regulations, candidates and political parties may simultaneously raise hard-dollar funds through joint fund-raising committees ("JFCs,") which permit candidates and political parties to combine the per-recipient contribution limits and thereby solicit greater amounts of money from donors at any one time.[43]

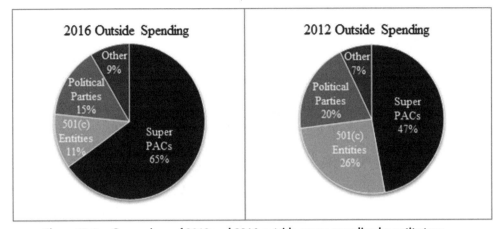

Figure 12.3.   Comparison of 2012 and 2016 outside group spending by entity type.
Source: Center for Responsive Politics, https://www.opensecrets.org/outsidespending/
fes_summ.php, https://www.opensecrets.org/outsidespending/fes_summ.php?cycle=
2012. Figures created by Michael E. Toner and Karen E. Trainer.

The Hillary Victory Committee, which was comprised of the Clinton campaign committee, the DNC, and forty state Democratic Party committees, raised $529.5 million and was the largest JFC of the 2016 election cycle.[44] By comparison, the Trump Victory Committee, which was comprised of the Trump campaign committee, the RNC, and twenty-one state Republican Party committees, raised $108.2 million.[45]

The Hillary Victory Committee engaged in aggressive general political advertising, which is unusual for a JFC. Through the end of June 2016, the Hillary Victory Committee paid $38 million to advertising and marketing vendors,[46] which covered the cost of disseminating advertisements that closely resembled commercials aired by the Clinton campaign, but which included a fund-raising appeal for the Hillary Victory Committee at the end of the advertisement.[47] However, since the advertisements were paid for by the Hillary Victory Committee, the advertising cost was ultimately shared among multiple entities rather than being paid for entirely by the Clinton campaign. Some campaign finance critics voiced concern over this advertising activity since the Hillary Victory Committee operated with a much higher contribution limit than the Clinton campaign.[48] As of this writing, it remains to be seen whether the FEC will take any adverse action against the Hillary Victory Committee or the Clinton campaign as a result of this novel political activity.

In April 2014, the Supreme Court in *McCutcheon v. FEC* invalidated the individual biennial aggregate limit on federal campaign contributions as unconstitutional under the First Amendment. Prior to *McCutcheon*, federal law had capped the total amount of money that individuals could contribute to federal candidates and other federal political committees collectively during each two-year election cycle. Before the biennial aggregate contribution limit was struck down, individuals were prohibited from contributing more than $123,200 to all federal candidates and political committees combined during the 2014 election cycle. The aggregate contribution limit existed in addition to the per-recipient "base limit" that applies to particular campaign committees, political party committees, and other federal political committees.[49] With the aggregate contribution limit gone, individual donors now only need to adhere to the base contribution limits and are free to contribute to an unlimited number of candidate committees and other political committees.

As of mid-October 2016, 1,174 individuals had contributed amounts to political committees other than Super PACs for the 2016 election in excess of the $123,200 aggregate limit that existed prior to the *McCutcheon* ruling.[50] On average, each of these individuals contributed a total of $281,568 to federal campaigns, PACs, and political party committees.[51] Moreover, many of these individuals also contributed to Super PACs and other outside groups.[52] By contrast, during the 2014 election cycle, only 727 individuals exceeded the pre-existing aggregate contribution limit.[53]

THE TRUMP CAMPAIGN MADE EXTENSIVE USE OF ONLINE ADVERTISING AND SOCIAL MEDIA

The Internet came of age politically in 2008 as then-Senator Barack Obama's campaign developed an unprecedented web-based strategy that involved millions of Americans in the presidential race through sophisticated and cutting-edge online technologies. During the 2012 and 2016 presidential elections, candidates, PACs, and outside interest groups once again developed and implemented new Internet technologies to disseminate political information in real time to millions of voters and raised increasing amounts of campaign funds online.

One key factor that has contributed to the rapid growth of the Internet in American politics during the last decade has been the FEC's deregulatory approach to online activities. In 2006, the FEC adopted regulations, which remain in place today, concerning use of the Internet in federal elections. The FEC's regulations exempt the Internet from the various prohibitions and restrictions of the McCain-Feingold law with only one exception: paid advertising placed on another person's website.[54] The practical effect of the FEC's regulations has been that individuals, volunteers, and anyone else with access to a computer can conduct a wide range of Internet activities on behalf of federal candidates—such as setting up and maintaining websites, blogging, tweeting, emailing, linking, and posting videos on YouTube—without fear that the FEC will monitor or restrict their activities. Although it is difficult to measure or gauge precisely, there is no question that the FEC's hands-off regulatory approach to online political activities has helped the Internet play a growing and vital role in American politics in the last decade.

The Obama campaign had a significant online advantage over the McCain campaign during the 2008 presidential race.[55] In somewhat of a surprise, Republican candidates made major strides during the 2010 midterm election in using the Internet to advance their candidacies, and some Republican candidates even surpassed their Democratic opponents in several important online metrics.[56] Given the Internet gains that some prominent Republican candidates achieved in 2010, it was unclear at the outset of the 2012 presidential race whether the Obama campaign would have as pronounced an online advantage over the Republican nominee as was the case in 2008. However, by any plausible metric, the Obama campaign dominated the Romney campaign online in 2012, and this may have contributed to the Obama campaign's voter turnout advantage in the battleground states on Election Day.[57]

During the final months of the 2016 presidential race, the Trump campaign's spending focused on online advertising rather than on more traditional types of advertising. In August 2016, the Trump campaign's largest vendor was a digital advertising firm, which was paid $11.1 million.[58] The digital advertising firm was also the Trump campaign's largest vendor in July 2016, receiving $8.4 million, which was nearly half of the campaign's total fund-raising for the month.[59] In August, the Trump campaign funded five online advertisements for every three online advertisements funded by the Clinton campaign.[60] The Clinton campaign, on the other hand, spent approximately $200 million on TV advertisements in the final months of the election, more than twice the amount spent by the Trump campaign.[61]

The Trump campaign also relied heavily on social media throughout the campaign. During the Republican National Convention, the Trump campaign paid for the "promoted hashtag of the day" on Twitter.[62] Overall online interest in Trump, measured by Google searches and mentions on Twitter and Facebook, among other social media platforms, was three times higher than online interest in Clinton.[63]

Table 12.5 compares social media metrics for the Trump and Clinton campaigns and illustrates Trump's sizeable advantage in a number of key areas.

The Trump campaign credited Facebook with helping the campaign raise $250 million online during the 2016 race, and there is no question that

Table 12.5.   Comparison of Campaign Online Activity

Metric	Trump	Clinton
Number of Twitter Followers	10.7 Million	8.1 Million
Number of Facebook Page Likes	10.2 Million	5.4 Million
Number of "People Talking About This" on Facebook	3.1 Million	3.3 Million
*Number of YouTube Videos	14.9 Million	10.6 Million
Instagram Followers	2.2 Million	1.8 Million

Source: William Arruda, "Donald Trump vs. Hillary Clinton—The Social Media Report," *Forbes*, August 7, 2016, http://www.forbes.com/sites/williamarruda/2016/08/07/donald-trump-vs-hillary-clinton-the-social-media-report /2/#2fc58d27160a. Data as of August 5, 2016.
Note: *Neither candidate had an official YouTube channel. These numbers represent the number of videos on YouTube referencing the candidate.

Trump's adroit use of social media was a key factor in his winning the presidency.[64]

LOOKING AHEAD TO 2020

Donald Trump's remarkable win in the 2016 presidential election will be studied by political scientists and campaign operatives alike for many years. Trump's path to victory also must be assessed by campaign finance scholars because Trump won the White House while being significantly outspent by multiple candidates in the Republican primary and by Hillary Clinton in the general election. No candidate in the modern era has ever overcome such a campaign resource disadvantage and been elected president, but then again no candidate in recent memory was as adept as Trump in communicating directly with voters, mastering social media, and attracting copious amounts of earned media. In many ways, Trump's election calls into question the continued vitality of many assumptions in campaign finance literature that a presidential candidate can never raise enough money and that those candidates who can afford to pay for huge campaign staffs and paid advertising programs have an overwhelming advantage in capturing the White House.

Assuming Trump seeks reelection in 2020, it is hard to imagine that any viable Republican primary challenger could emerge with all the strengths of incumbency in modern presidential politics. On the Democratic side, assuming Joseph Biden, the outgoing vice president, and 2016 vice presidential nominee Tim Kaine decline to run, all the ingredients will exist for a wide-open primary with a large number of next-generation candidates. Although there may not be a clear frontrunner for the 2020 presidential race, Bernie Sanders' ability to come out of nowhere in the 2016 race and raise over $200 million for what was seen as a long-shot primary battle against Clinton is powerful evidence that multiple Democratic presidential candidates will likely be able to amass substantial campaign war chests for the primaries and the general election alike. The stage will then be set for the 2020 presidential contest to be as highly competitive as 2016 and feature unexpected campaign finance innovations and developments.

NOTES

1. The Clinton campaign and its allies (including the Democratic National Committee ["DNC"] and Super PACs supporting Clinton) collectively spent approximately $1.2 billion on the 2016 election while the Trump campaign and its allies (including the Republican National Committee ["RNC"] and supportive Super PACs) collectively spent approximately $600 million. Isaac Arnsdorf, "Trump Won with Half as Much Money as Clinton Raised," *Politico,* December 8, 2016, http://www.politico.com/story/2016/12/trump-clinton-campaign-fundraising-totals-232400.

2. Ashley Balcerzak, "UPDATE: Federal Elections to Cost Just under $7 Billion, CRP Predicts," November 2, 2016, https://www.opensecrets.org/news/2016/11/update-federal-elections-to-cost-just-under-7-billion-crp-forecasts/.

3. Ibid.

4. "Outside Spending," OpenSecrets.org, https://www.opensecrets.org/outsidespending/index.php?type = Y.

5. Federal Election Commission, "Federal Election Commission Certifies Federal Matching Funds for Stein," August 2, 2016, http://fec.gov/press/press2016/news_releases/20160802_2release.shtml.

6. Individuals could contribute up to $2,700 per election to presidential candidates for the 2016 election and federal multicandidate PACs could contribute up to $5,000 per election, with the primary and general elections considered separate elections. The individual contribution limits are adjusted for inflation each election cycle.

7. The public grant for the general election and the corresponding national spending limit are adjusted for inflation each election cycle. See Federal Election Commission Brochure, "Presidential Spending Limits for 2016," http://www.fec.gov/pages/brochures/pubfund_limits_2016.shtml.

8. The Obama campaign had a remarkable resource advantage over the McCain campaign in 2008, including a nearly 4-to-1 edge during the general election phase of the campaign. The Obama campaign's broad resource advantage was particularly pronounced in the final weeks of the 2008 campaign. In September 2008 alone the Obama campaign raised over $150 million, and between October 15 and November 24 the Obama campaign raised an additional $104 million and spent $136 million. To put these Obama campaign fund-raising and spending figures in perspective, the McCain campaign received only $85 million of public funds to finance all of its political activities during the entire general election campaign.

9. Federal Election Commission data.

10. Ibid.

11. Ibid.

12. As of May 30, 2016, days after clinching the Republican nomination, the Trump campaign had only raised a total of $63 million to date. Of this amount, $46 million was loaned or contributed by Trump himself, while only $17 million came from other donors. The last time a major party candidate raised and spent so little to become the party's nominee was in 2000, when Gore spent $50 million in connection with the Democratic primary. However, Gore accepted public funds for the 2000 race, while Trump did not. Christopher Good, "Donald Trump on Pace to Raise Less Money Than Almost Any Other Presidential Candidate in Modern Era." ABC News, June 21, 2016, http://abcnews.go .com/Politics/donald-trump-pace-raise-money-presidential-candidate-modern/story?id = 40007132.

13. Arnsdorf, "Trump Won with Half as Much Money as Clinton Raised."

14. Nicholas Confessore and Karen Yourish, "$2 Billion Worth of Free Media for Donald Trump," *New York Times,* March 15, 2016, http://www.nytimes.com/2016/03/16/ upshot/measuring-donald-trumps-mammoth-advantage-in-free-media.html.

15. Ginger Gibson and Grant Smith, "At Under $5 Each, Trump's Votes Came Cheap," *Reuters,* November 9, 2016, http://www.reuters.com/article/us-usa-election-spending-id USKBN1341JR.

16. Ibid.

17. These states were Florida, Ohio, North Carolina, Pennsylvania, Nevada, and Iowa. Scott Blackburn, "Money Doesn't Buy Elections: 2016 Presidential Election Edition," Center for Competitive Politics, November 9, 2016, http://www.campaignfreedom.org/ 2016/11/09/money-doesnt-buy-elections-2016-presidential-election-edition/.

18. FEC Advisory Opinions 2010–09 and 2010–11.

19. Blackburn, "Money Doesn't Buy Elections: 2016 Presidential Election Edition."

20. Soo Rin Kim, "Mine, All Mine: Single Candidate Super PACs, Creeping Down-Ballot," Center for Responsive Politics, November 10, 2016, https://www.opensecrets.org/ news/2016/11/mine-all-mine-single-candidate-super-pacs-creeping-down-ballot/.

21. Michael Beckel, "Team Clinton Sponsored 75 Percent of TV Ads in 2016 Presidential Race," Center for Public Integrity, November 8, 2016, https://www.publicintegrity .org/2016/11/08/20452/team-clinton-sponsored-75-percent-tv-ads-2016-presidential-race.

22. Wesleyan Media Project, "Clinton and Sanders Even in Ad War, Cruz and Rubio Gain on Bush in S. Carolina," February 18, 2016, http://mediaproject.wesleyan.edu/wp -content/uploads/2016/02/2016Release2_FINAL-3.pdf.

23. Center for Responsive Politics, "2016 Outside Spending by Single-Candidate Super PACs," https://www.opensecrets.org/outsidespending/summ.php?cycle = 2016&chrt = V &disp = O&type = C.

24. Center for Responsive Politics, "2012 Outside Spending by Single-Candidate Super PACs," http://opensecrets.org/outsidespending/summ.php?cycle = 2012&chrt = V&disp = O&type = C. The largest single-candidate Super PAC in 2012, Restore our Future, supported Romney in the presidential race. The largest single-candidate Super PAC in 2014, Put Alaska First PAC, supported Senator Mark Begich's re-election in Alaska. The largest single-candidate Super PAC in 2016, Priorities USA Action, supported Clinton's presidential campaign.

25. Under FEC regulations, information that campaigns publicly disseminate that is subsequently used by a Super PAC or other entity generally cannot result in unlawful coordination.

26. Matea Gold, "The Rubio Campaign Tweets—and the Super PAC Airs an Ad," *Washington Post*, February 4, 2016, https://www.washingtonpost.com/politics/rubio -super-pac-ads-follow-playbook-of-campaigns-rapid-response-site/2016/02/04/448a8120 -cb5a-11e5-a7b2-5a2f824b02c9_story.html.

27. Kenneth P. Vogel and Isaac Arnsdorf, "The Politico 100: Billionaires Dominate 2016," *Politico*, February 8, 2016.

28. Kim, "Mine, All Mine: Single Candidate Super PACs, Creeping Down-Ballot."

29. Kenneth P. Doyle, "Outside Groups Dominate Spending in Key Senate Races," *Bloomberg BNA Money & Politics Report*, November 2, 2016.

30. Theo Francis, "Despite Citizens United, Corporate Super PAC Contributions Trail Individuals, Study Finds," *The Wall Street Journal*, November 2, 2016, http://www.wsj .com/articles/despite-citizens-united-corporate-super-pac-contributions-trail-individuals -study-finds-1478059201.

31. Rebecca Ballhaus, "Wealthy Donors Played Outsize Role This Election," *The Wall Street Journal*, November 7, 2016, http://www.wsj.com/articles/wealthy-donors-played -outsize-role-this-election-1478561726.

32. Paul Blumenthal, "Super PAC Mega-Donors Expand Election Influence with Record $1 Billion in Contributions," *Huffington Post*, November 1, 2016, http://www.huf fingtonpost.com/entry/super-pac-donors_us_5817b30be4b0390e69d21648.

33. Brody Mullins, Rebecca Ballhaus, and Michelle Hackman, "Labor Unions Step Up Presidential-Election Spending," *The Wall Street Journal*, October 18, 2016, http:// www.wsj.com/articles/big-labor-unions-step-up-presidential-election-spending-147678 3002.

34. Dave Jamieson, "Labor Unions Spent a Record Amount on the Elections," *Huffington Post*, November 8, 2016, http://www.huffingtonpost.com/entry/labor-union-election -2016_us_58223b92e4b0e80b02cd7259.

35. Robert Maguire, "$1.4 Billion and Counting in Spending by Super PACs, Dark Money Groups," Center for Responsive Politics, November 9, 2016, https://www.open secrets.org/news/2016/11/1-4-billion-and-counting-in-spending-by-super-pacs-dark-money -groups/.

36. Soo Rin Kim, "Super PAC Spending Hits $500 Million, While 501(c)s Hit the Brakes," Center for Responsive Politics, September 1, 2016, https://www.opensecrets.org/ news/2016/09/super-pac-spending-reaches-500m/.

37. Traditional PACs, unlike Super PACs, may make contributions to federal candidates and other federal political committees. Traditional PACs are prohibited from accepting corporate and labor union contributions and may accept contributions from individuals up to $5,000 per calendar year. Traditional PACs are referred to herein as "PACs."

38. Federal Election Commission, Contributions to Accounts of National Party Committees, September 9, 2016, http://www.fec.gov/press/summaries/2016/tables/party/ Prty10_2016_18m.pdf.

39. Kenneth P. Vogel and Alex Isenstadt, "RNC TV Ad Spending for Trump: $0," *Politico*, October 13, 2016, http://www.politico.com/story/2016/10/rnc-donald-trump-ad -spending-229711.

40. Federal Election Commission data.

41. "Outside Spending," OpenSecrets.org, https://www.opensecrets.org/outsidespend ing/fes_summ.php? These figures include party spending.

42. Ibid.

43. For example, if a JFC included a presidential campaign, a national political party committee, and two state political party committees, individual donors could contribute up to $48,400 to the JFC—up to $5,400 to the presidential campaign ($2,700 for the primary and $2,700 for the general election), $33,400 to the national political party, and $10,000 each to the two state political parties. Any prior contributions that individual donors made to any of the entities participating in the JFC would count against what could be contributed to the JFC.

44. "Joint Fundraising Committees," OpenSecrets.org, http://opensecrets.org/jfc/index.php.

45. Federal Election Commission data.

46. Kenneth P. Vogel and Isaac Arnsdorf, "DNC Sought to Hide Details of Clinton Funding Deal," *Politico*, July 26, 2016, http://www.politico.com/story/2016/07/dnc-leak-clinton-team-deflected-state-cash-concerns-226191.

47. Michael Beckel, "Clinton's Super-Sized Fundraising Machine Pushes Legal Boundaries," Center for Public Integrity, November 7, 2016, https://www.public integrity.org/2016/11/07/20437/clinton-s-super-sized-fundraising-machine-pushes-legal-boundaries.

48. Individuals could contribute up to $436,100 to the Hillary Victory Committee, but only $5,400 ($2,700 for the primary and $2,700 for the general) to the Clinton campaign.

49. These "base limits" include a $2,700 per election limit on individual contributions to federal campaign committees and a $5,000 annual limit on individual contributions to PACs.

50. Jack Noland, "In First Post-McCutcheon Presidential Election, More Big Donors, Giving More," Center for Responsive Politics, November 10, 2016, https://www.open secrets.org/news/2016/11/in-first-post-mccutcheon-presidential-election-more-big-donors-giving-more/.

51. Ibid.

52. Ibid.

53. Ibid.

54. For example, if an individual spends money to take out an advertisement for a federal candidate that appears on the home page of CNN.com or as a sponsored result in a Google search, the transaction will be subject to regulation in a fashion similar to television, radio, and other mass-media advertising. However, messages that individuals create on their own websites or post without charge on other websites such as Twitter, Facebook, or YouTube are not subject to FEC regulation.

55. The Obama campaign far surpassed the McCain campaign in a number of key online indicators in 2008, particularly in the volume of Obama political activity that occurred on popular social networking websites such as Facebook, YouTube, and Twitter. For example, the Obama campaign had nearly 2.4 million Facebook friends, while the McCain campaign had under 625,000. Andres Rasiehj and Micah Sifry, "The Web: 2008's Winning Ticket," *Politico*, November 12, 2008, http://www.politico.com/story/2008/11/the-web-2008s-winning-ticket-015520. Similarly, the Obama campaign had more than 125,000 Twitter followers as compared with only 5,319 for the McCain campaign, and the Obama campaign posted more than 1,800 videos on YouTube, whereas the McCain campaign posted only 330 such videos; Ibid.

56. See HeadCount, "GOP Winning Social Media battle by Wide Margin," http://www.headcount.org/wp-content/uploads/2010/09/VIEW-REPORT1.pdf.

57. For example, as of November 6, 2012, Obama had 21.8 million followers on Twitter compared to 1.7 million followers for Romney. The Obama campaign posted 931 YouTube videos between January 1, 2011 and November 6, 2012, compared to 320 videos posted by the Romney campaign. CampaignPop Social Analytics for the 2012 Campaign, http://www.campaignpop.com.

58. Matea Gold and Anu Narayanswamy, "Donald Trump Finally Ramped Up Campaign Spending. So Where Did the Money Go?" *Washington Post*, September 21, 2016, https://www.washingtonpost.com/news/post-politics/wp/2016/09/21/donald-trump-finally-ramped-up-his-campaign-spending-so-where-did-the-money-go/.

59. Melissa Yeager, "Internet Blind Spot Highlighted in Trump's 8.4 Million Digital Expenditure," Sunlight Foundation, August 23, 2016, http://sunlightfoundation.com/2016/08/23/internet-blind-spot-highlighted-in-trumps-8-4-million-digital-expenditure/.

60. Philip Bump, "Hillary Clinton Owns the TV airwaves, but Donald Trump May Be Winning Online," *The Washington Post,* September 21, 2016, https://www.washingtonpost.com/news/the-fix/wp/2016/09/21/hillary-clinton-owns-the-tv-airwaves-but-donald-trump-may-be-winning-online/.

61. Issie Lapowsky, "Here's How Facebook Actually Won Trump the Presidency," *Wired*, November 15, 2016, https://www.wired.com/2016/11/facebook-won-trump-election-not-just-fake-news/.

62. Natalie Andrews, "On Social Media, Hillary Clinton and Donald Trump Have Different Styles," *The Wall Street Journal*, July 28, 2016, http://blogs.wsj.com/washwire/2016/07/28/on-social-media-hillary-clinton-and-donald-trump-take-different-approaches-to-connect-with-voters/.

63. Laeeq Khan, "Trump Won Thanks to Social Media," *The Hill*, November 15, 2016, http://thehill.com/blogs/pundits-blog/technology/306175-trump-won-thanks-to-social-media.

64. Lapowsky, "Here's How Facebook Actually Won Trump the Presidency."

13

It Wasn't the Economy, Stupid

Racial Polarization, White Racial Resentment, and the Rise of Trump

Alan I. Abramowitz

While Donald Trump's victory in the 2016 presidential election was one of the most shocking upsets in modern political history, it can be seen as the natural outgrowth of the racial realignment that has transformed the American electorate since the 1970s. For decades before Trump came on the political scene, Republican elected officials and candidates sought to lure racially conservative white Democrats in the South and elsewhere into the GOP camp with racially tinged messages about the dangers posed to whites by African-American crime, forced busing of schoolchildren and affirmative action, and by emphasizing the complicity of Democratic politicians in these threats. Those efforts clearly paid electoral dividends, helping to elect Republican presidents from Richard Nixon to George W. Bush and to transform the South from the most Democratic region of the nation into a Republican stronghold.

Between 1992 and 2012, the nonwhite share of voters in presidential elections more than doubled, going from 13 percent to 28 percent. But growing racial and ethnic diversity had very different effects on the two major parties. The nonwhite share of Republican voters increased modestly between 1992 and 2004, going from 4 percent to 12 percent, mainly due to the ability of Republican candidates to attract a sizable chunk of the growing Hispanic vote. After 2004, however, the nonwhite share of Republican voters fell slightly to 10 percent in both 2008 and 2012. Meanwhile, the nonwhite share of Democratic voters increased steadily—going from 21 percent in 1992 to 45 percent in 2012. This trend reflected the attraction of the party and its presidential candidates to nonwhite voters but also the continued drift of white voters to the GOP, especially in the South. In 2012, Barack Obama lost the white vote by an astonishing margin of 20 percentage points according to the national exit poll—by far the largest deficit among white voters of any successful Democratic presidential candidate. Yet he won the national popular vote by nearly four percentage points due to an overwhelming 82 percent to 16 percent margin of victory among nonwhite voters.

There were two major components to the racial realignment of the U.S. party system between 1992 and 2012—the overwhelming preference of a growing nonwhite voting bloc for the Democratic Party and the continued movement of white voters from the Democratic Party to the Republican Party, especially in the South. By 2012, according to data from the American National Election Study, the GOP enjoyed a record 55 percent to 39 percent advantage in leaned party identification among white voters nationwide and an astonishing 66 percent to 29 percent advantage among white voters in the South.

There were several factors that helped to drive white voters into the Republican camp during the years between 1992 and 2012—economic issues such as government spending and taxation and cultural issues such as abortion and same-sex marriage clearly played a role in this shift. But there is little doubt that issues surrounding race played a major role in the realignment of the white electorate. As the nation's population and its electorate were becoming more diverse, there is clear evidence that a growing number of white voters felt threatened by the loss of their previously dominant status in American society and American politics. This can be seen in data from American National Election Study surveys on the level of racial resentment among white voters.

The concept of racial resentment, as used by social scientists, refers to subtle feelings of hostility toward African Americans. It is different, in that sense, from old-fashioned racism, which involves beliefs about the inherent superiority and right to dominance of the white race. In the data from the American National Election Studies, the racial resentment scale is constructed from how strongly respondents agreed or disagreed with the following assertions: (1) Irish, Italian, Jewish, and many other minorities overcame prejudice and worked their way up. Blacks should do the same without any special favors. (2) Generations of slavery and discrimination have created conditions that make it difficult for blacks to work their way out of the lower class. (3) Over the past few years, blacks have gotten less than they deserve.

(4) It's really a matter of some people not trying hard enough; if blacks would only try harder, they could be just as well off as whites. While these questions focus directly on attitudes toward African Americans, scores on the racial resentment scale also correlate highly with feelings toward other racial minorities and out-groups.[1]

The data displayed in table 13.1 show that between the Ronald Reagan-George H. W. Bush era and the Obama era, there was a marked increase in the level of racial resentment among white voters in the United States. Over these three decades, the proportion of white voters scoring at the high end of the racial resentment scale rose from 42 percent to 51 percent. But this increase in white racial resentment was not uniform. As the data displayed in figure 13.1 show, the increase was limited to Republicans. There was actually a modest decline in racial resentment among white Democrats between the Reagan-G.H.W. Bush era and the Obama era. Among white Republicans, however, racial resentment increased dramatically. The proportion of white Republicans scoring at the high end of the racial resentment scale rose from 44 percent during the Reagan-G.H.W. Bush years to 64 percent during the Obama years.

As recently as the late 1980s, there was little difference between white Democrats and Republicans when it came to racial resentment. By 2008, however, there was a yawning gap between white Democrats and Republicans on this scale. That gap would grow even wider by 2016. But it is important to note that the increase in racial resentment among white Republicans did not occur suddenly after Obama's emergence on the national political scene in 2008. Instead, racial resentment rose steadily over this entire time period. It was not Obama who sparked the rise in racial resentment among white Republicans; rather, it was the growing visibility and influence of African Americans and other nonwhites within the Democratic Party along with ongoing efforts by Republican candidates and strategists to win over racially conservative white voters by portraying Democrats as soft on crime and favoring policies benefitting minorities at the expense of whites such as welfare and affirmative action.

Table 13.1.   Racial Resentment among White Voters from Reagan to Obama

| Presidential Era | Racial Resentment Level | | | Total | (n of cases) |
	Low	Moderate	High		
Reagan-G.H.W. Bush	27%	31%	42%	100%	(1781)
Clinton	24%	32%	44%	100%	(2113)
G. W. Bush	23%	28%	49%	100%	(1419)
Obama	22%	27%	51%	100%	(1228)

Source: American National Election Studies Cumulative File.

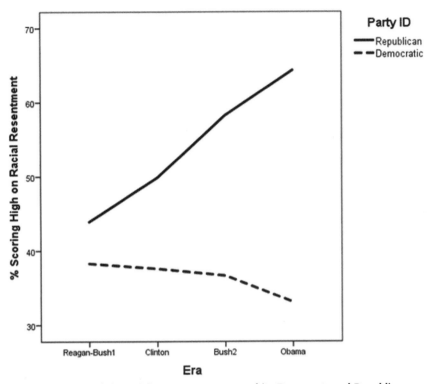

Figure 13.1. Trends in racial resentment among white Democrats and Republicans from Reagan to Obama. *Notes*: Leaning independents included with party identifiers. In the x axis, "Bush1" refers to George H. W. Bush, "Bush2" refers to George W. Bush. *Source*: American National Election Studies Cumulative File.

There is no way of knowing from these data whether the growing divide between white Democrats and Republicans was the result of racially motivated party switching—voters choosing a party based on their racial attitudes—or partisan persuasion—party supporters adopting liberal or conservative racial attitudes in response to cues from party leaders. In all likelihood, both of these forces were at work over this time period. Regardless of the direction of influence, however, the end result was a much closer alignment between racial and partisan attitudes among white voters.

RACIAL RESENTMENT, THE WHITE WORKING CLASS, AND THE 2016 PRESIDENTIAL ELECTION

By the end of the Obama years, the Republican electorate was characterized by very high levels of racial resentment—a situation that would make it much easier for a candidate with a message focused on white racial resentment to enjoy success in a Republican primary contest and to unite GOP voters behind his candidacy after winning the nomination. But unifying the Republican base was not enough to allow Donald Trump to win the general election against Hillary Clinton. To do that, Trump had to expand his appeal to white working-class voters who were unhappy about the direction of the nation during the Obama years—voters who made up a large share of the electorate in the swing states of the Northeast and Midwest.

In seeking to explain Donald Trump's surprising victory, a number of political commentators have focused on the role of rising economic discontent among white working-class voters adversely affected by the Great Recession and globalization and frustrated with the failure of mainstream Republican leaders to address their concerns. According to this economic discontent theory, Trump's opposition to free trade agreements and promise to bring back lost manufacturing jobs resulted in strong support from less-educated white voters.[2] Indeed, Trump himself famously bragged about his support from "the poorly educated" following one of his primary victories.[3]

An alternative explanation of support for Trump among white working-class voters focuses on a different part of his message, a part the candidate himself emphasized from the beginning of his presidential campaign—appeals to white racial fear and resentment.[4] Trump's characterization of Mexican-American immigrants as criminals and rapists, his frequently repeated promise to build a wall along the Mexican border and make Mexico pay for it, his proposal to deport 11 million undocumented immigrants, his false allegation that thousands of Muslims in New Jersey had celebrated when the World Trade Center towers came down on September 11, 2001, and his call for a ban on foreign Muslims entering the country were, in many ways, the centerpiece of his campaign.[5]

Throughout his primary campaign, Trump regularly used his Twitter feed to promote messages originating with white supremacists, including the false claim that the large majority of white homicide victims in the United States. in recent years were killed by blacks. He claimed, implausibly, not to know anything about former Ku Klux Klan leader David Duke when asked about Duke's support for his candidacy.[6] Moreover, Donald Trump's use of messages designed to appeal to racial resentment and fear among white voters did not begin with his 2016 presidential campaign. Trump made his first big splash in presidential politics in 2011 as the most prominent promoter of the conspiracy theory that became known as birtherism—the patently false claim that Barack Obama, the nation's first African-American president, was born not in Hawaii but in Africa and was therefore ineligible to serve as president.[7]

At a time when he was considering a run for the presidency in 2012, Trump's advocacy of birtherism was clearly designed to appeal to a large segment of white voters who were upset about the presence of a black man in the White House. Even though he ultimately decided to forego a run for the GOP nomination in 2012, the issue of birtherism clearly worked for Trump. He received enormous media coverage for this outlandish claim, and polling data showed that a large proportion of Republican voters came to question Obama's citizenship and his legitimacy as president.[8] Not surprisingly, given the success of his initial venture into birtherism, Trump continued to promote this racist conspiracy theory for years, even suggesting that the long-form birth certificate released by the White House in 2011 may have been fraudulent.[9]

It is clear that stoking racial fear and resentment was a central element of Donald Trump's strategy in 2016. Trump's campaign slogan, "Make America Great Again," clearly implied much more than bringing back lost manufacturing jobs. The slogan also signaled voters that a President Trump would turn back the clock to a time when white people enjoyed a dominant position in American society. In case anyone thought that Trump would change his message after securing the GOP nomination, his decision to give *Breitbart News* executive Steven Bannon, one of the leading figures in the white nationalist Alt-Right movement, a major role in the campaign made it clear that appeals to racial fear and resentment would continue even as the candidate "pivoted" to the general election.[10]

Data from the 2016 American National Election Study Pilot Survey, an online survey of 1,200 American adults conducted in late January 2016, show a sharp divide between white Democrats and Republicans on the racial resentment scale. Among Democratic identifiers and leaners, 55 percent scored at the low end of the scale while 17 percent scored at the high end of the scale. In contrast, among Republican identifiers and leaners, 11 percent scored at the low end of the scale while 49 percent scored at the high end of the scale. However, among white Democrats, there was a substantial difference between college graduates and those without college degrees: 79 percent of white Democrats with college degrees scored at the low end of the racial resentment scale compared with only 45 percent of white Democrats without a college degree, and 22 percent of white Democrats without a college degree scored at the high end of the scale compared with only 3 percent of white Democrats with a college degree.

These results suggest that Trump's explicit appeal to white racial resentment had the potential to peel away a segment of the Democratic electorate. Evidence from the ANES Pilot Study provides further support for this possibility. Although the Pilot Study was conducted more than nine months before the November election, the results indicated that Donald Trump already held a substantial lead over Hillary Clinton among white voters based on the relative ratings of the two candidates on the feeling thermometer scale: 57 percent of white voters rated Trump more favorably than Hillary Clinton while 40 percent rated Clinton more favorably than Trump. White Republicans preferred Trump to Clinton by a margin of 87 percent to 10 percent while white Democrats preferred Clinton to Trump by margin of 83 percent to 15 percent.

Racial resentment was a powerful predictor of relative ratings of Trump and Clinton on the feeling thermometer scale. While white voters who scored low on the racial resentment scale preferred Clinton to Trump by a margin of 73 percent to 22 percent, white voters who scored high on the racial resentment scale preferred Trump to Clinton by a margin of 85 percent to 12 percent. Moreover, the effect of racial resentment on candidate preference holds up even after controlling for party identification. White Democrats who scored low on racial resentment preferred Clinton to Trump by a margin of 91 percent to 6 percent. In contrast, among white Democrats who scored high on racial resentment, Clinton and Trump were tied at 48 percent each. Similarly, white Republicans who scored high on racial resentment preferred Trump to Clinton by 97 percent to 1 percent while the small group of white Republicans who scored low on racial resentment preferred Trump to Clinton by only 51 percent to 36 percent.

In a multivariate analysis, racial resentment was the strongest predictor of relative ratings of Trump and Clinton on the feeling thermometer scale after party identification. The effect of racial resentment on relative ratings of Trump and Clinton was substantially greater than the effects of attitudes toward trade agreements and economic opportunity. Once racial resentment was taken into account, neither education nor family income had any effect on relative ratings of Trump and Clinton. These findings support the conclusion that Donald Trump's special appeal to white working-class voters was based largely, if not entirely, on racial resentment.

CONCLUSIONS

Despite losing the national popular vote by two percentage points, Donald Trump was able to win a clear majority in the Electoral College by eking out narrow victories in three crucial swing states—Michigan, Pennsylvania, and Wisconsin. The key to those victories was Trump's huge margins among white working-class voters, and racial resentment was clearly a major factor in this group's support for the New York real estate mogul.

To a much greater degree than any previous Republican presidential candidate, Donald Trump utilized explicit appeals to white fear and resentment of racial and ethnic minorities including African Americans, Mexican Americans, and Muslims. He made his initial mark in presidential politics in 2011 by becoming the most visible proponent of the "birther" myth—repeatedly suggesting that Barack Obama had not been born in the United States and was therefore not legally eligible to service as president. He continued to raise this issue during his 2016 campaign, supplementing it with dubious claims of widespread voter fraud in minority communities, retweets of messages from white supremacist individuals and organizations, and attacks on Mexican immigrants and Muslims. These appeals clearly played a major role in his successful campaign for the Republican presidential nomination and, based on the evidence presented in this chapter, they were probably critical to his success in peeling away enough traditional Democratic voters in a few crucial swing states to win a majority of electoral votes.

NOTES

1. See Edward G. Carmines, Paul M. Sniderman, and Beth C. Easter, "On the Meaning, Measurement and Implications of Racial Resentment," *Annals of the American Academy of Political and Social Science* 634 (2011): 98–116.

2. See Jack Rasmus, "Trump, Trade and Working Class Discontent," *Counterpunch*, July 22, 2016, http://www.counterpunch.org/2016/07/22/trump-trade-and-working-class-discontent/. See also, Jon Hilsenrath and Bob Davis, "The Great Unraveling: Election 2016 Is Propelled by American Economy's Failed Promises," *Wall Street Journal*, July 7, 2016, http://www.wsj.com/articles/election-2016-is-propelled-by-the-american-economys-failed-promises-1467909580; and Torstein Bell, "The Invisible Economic Catastrophe that Donald Trump Spotted," *New Statesman*, November 10, 2016, http://www.newstatesman.com/politics/staggers/2016/11/invisible-economic-catastrophe-donald-trump-spotted.

3. Peter W. Stevenson, "Donald Trump Loves the 'Poorly Educated'—And Just about Everyone Else in Nevada," *Washington Post*, February 24, 2016, https://www.washingtonpost.com/news/the-fix/wp/2016/02/24/donald-trump-loves-the-poorly-educated-and-just-about-everyone-else-in-nevada/.

4. Christopher Ingraham, "Two New Studies Find Racial Anxiety Is the Biggest Driver of Support for Trump," *Washington Post*, June 6, 2016, https://www.washingtonpost.com/news/wonk/wp/2016/06/06/racial-anxiety-is-a-huge-driver-of-support-for-donald-trump-two-new-studies-find/?utm_term = .484b5ac8ea3d. See also Matthew Yglesias, "Why I Don't Think It Makes Sense to Attribute Trump's Support to Economic Anxiety," *Vox*, August 15, 2016, http://www.vox.com/2016/8/15/12462760/trump-resentment-economic-anxiety.

5. Ronald B. Rapoport, Alan I. Abramowitz, and Walter J. Stone, "Why Trump Was Inevitable," *New York Review of Books*, June 23, 2016, http://www.nybooks.com/articles/

2016/06/23/why-trump-was-inevitable/; see also Molly Ball, "Donald Trump and the Politics of Fear," *The Atlantic*, September 2, 2016, http://www.theatlantic.com/politics/archive/2016/09/donald-trump-and-the-politics-of-fear/498116/.

6. Eric Bradner, "Donald Trump Stumbles on David Duke, KKK," CNN, February 29, 2016, http://www.cnn.com/2016/02/28/politics/donald-trump-white-supremacists/.

7. Michael Barbaro, "Donald Trump Clung to 'Birther' Lie for Years, and Still Isn't Apologetic," *New York Times*, September 16, 2016, http://www.nytimes.com/2016/09/17/us/politics/donald-trump-obama-birther.html.

8. See Josh Clinton and Carrie Roush, "Poll: Persistent Partisan Divide over 'Birther' Question," NBC News, August 10, 2016, http://www.nbcnews.com/politics/2016-election/poll-persistent-partisan-divide-over-birther-question-n627446.

9. Andrew Kaczynski, "Trump Questioned Obama Birth Certificate in 2014, Despite Campaign Statement," *BuzzFeed*, September 16, 2016, https://www.buzzfeed.com/andrewkaczynski/trump-questioned-obama-birth-certificate-in-2014-despite-cam.

10. See Jonathan Martin, Jim Rutenberg, and Maggie Haberman, "Trump Appoints Media Firebrand to Run Campaign," *New York Times*, August 17, 2016, http://www.nytimes.com/2016/08/18/us/politics/donald-trump-stephen-bannon-paul-manafort.html. See also Michael D. Shear, Maggie Haberman, and Michael S. Schmidt, "Critics See Stephen Bannon, Trump's Pick for Strategist, as Voice of Racism," *New York Times*, November 14, 2016, http://www.nytimes.com/2016/11/15/us/politics/donald-trump-presidency.html.

14

The "Emerging Democratic Majority" Fails to Emerge

Sean Trende

After the 2008 elections, many thought we'd reached the end of political history. Riding a rising demographic electorate, the story went, Democrats were the ascendant party. To use the verbiage popular in realignment literature, there might be "deviating" elections where the Republicans could pull out a win, due to recession, war, or scandal,[1] but overall we should expect elections to favor the Democrats in the near future. *Time* magazine went further, declaring Republicans "an endangered species."[2]

This sort of talk should have set off alarm bells among elections analysts, because these sorts of predictions are made all the time and rarely turn out well. For example, in 1976, in the immediate aftermath of those elections, Everett Carll Ladd, one of the leading psephologists in the country, wrote, "[t]he Republican party cannot find, outside of the performance of its presidential nominee, a single encouraging indicator of a general sort from its 1976 electoral performance. . . . What we see manifested here is a secular deterioration of the GOP position. The Democrats have emerged almost everywhere outside the presidential arena as the 'everyone party.'"[3] This, of course, was written immediately before Republicans began to *emerge* from the depths of irrelevance, winning the presidency in 1980, the House and Senate in 1994, and wresting full control of Washington from the Democrats for the first time in almost fifty years in 2000.

So it should not come as any sort of surprise that 2009 represented a nadir for the Republican Party, rather than an extinction event. These sorts of predictions almost *always* fail. So it was this time. In 2010, 2014, and 2016, Republicans swelled their numbers in Washington and throughout the country, to the point where, according to a metric of overall party strength I created with my *RealClearPolitics* colleague David Byler, the Republican Party now finds itself in the strongest position it has been in since the 1920s.[4]

By now, I think it is plain that the "demographics-is-destiny argument" case against the Republican Party, as exemplified by the cautious book *The Emerging Democratic Majority* by John Judis and Ruy Teixeira and in multiple less-cautious books that followed, is badly flawed, if not finally put to bed.[5] It's ultimately difficult to pin down supporters of the theory on exactly what the book predicts—which makes it somewhat nonfalsifiable—but I am fairly certain that it did not predict that Republicans would win four of the seven elections after *The Emerging Democratic Majority* was published.

Nor did it predict (I am fairly certain) that Republicans would pick up over sixty House seats and eleven Senate seats over the course of this decade, virtually wiping out Democrats in the nonurban South. The demographics-as-destiny theory did not predict that Republicans would pick up eleven governorships, reducing Democrats to their weakest position since 1920 (before that, you have to go back to the Reconstruction period to find Democrats in a similar position). It didn't predict Republicans would gain control of fifteen state senates and sixteen state legislatures over the course of 2010–2016, pick up over two hundred state senate seats and seven hundred state house seats, and take control of all three branches of government in twenty-five states, all while reducing Democrats to just six "trifectas" (in California, Oregon, Hawaii, Delaware, Connecticut, and Rhode Island).[6]

The demographics-as-destiny theory, whatever else may be said for it, did not envision the rise of Donald Trump. It simply should not be possible, twenty-four years into the Emerging Democratic Majority, for the Republicans to run a white, male septuagenarian who had never run for office and whose policy agenda was almost completely at odds with that of the "rising electorate." He certainly should not have been able to win—and this is often overlooked—after a presidency marked by economic growth, relative peace, and few major scandals. Put simply, under the theory, Donald Trump shouldn't have been able to win in an otherwise-neutral environment.

So where did the theory go wrong? Perhaps the best way to approach this is by breaking the theory down into constituent parts, and analyzing the groups that were supposed to make up this majority (and a few that weren't).

AFRICAN AMERICANS

The African American electorate has been heavily Democratic since 1936; the last Republican presidential candidate to carry their vote was Herbert Hoover in 1932.[7] Since the 1960s, Democrats have typically been able to count on receiving between 80 percent to 90 percent of the black vote.

Because of this, the most important demographic question for 2016—What will happen to the African American vote?—was overlooked. It was assumed, reasonably, that Democrats would perform very well with black voters. People nevertheless missed how much just small changes could make, and the importance of that vote to President Obama's victory in 2008 and 2016.

Figure 14.1 shows the African American share of the presidential electorate according to exit polls, from 1980 to 2016:

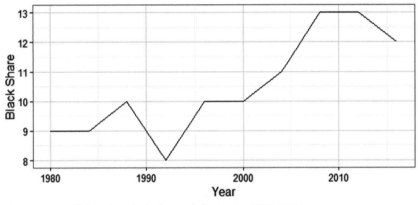

Figure 14.1. African American share of electorate, 1980–2016.

Figure 14.2 shows the Republican share of the African American share of the presidential electorate from 1980 to 2016:

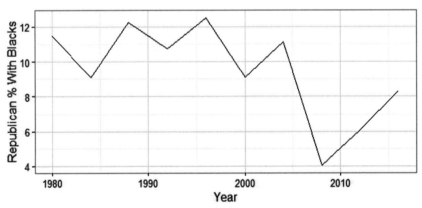

Figure 14.2. African American vote for Republicans, 1980–2016

The African American share of the modern electorate has typically been range-bound, floating somewhere between 8 percent of the electorate and 11 percent. Republicans could count on winning about 10 percent of that vote (note: unless otherwise indicated, vote shares in this chapter are taken from the "two-party vote"—i.e., third parties are removed).

This changed in 2008. The African American share of the electorate jumped to 13 percent in 2008 and surprised many (myself included) by staying that high in 2012. The Republican share of the African American vote likewise declined to 4 percent in 2008, before improving to 6 percent in 2012.

Many people underestimated just how important this outsized showing was to the Democratic Party's interests in 2008 and 2012. Had Barack Obama's showing among African Americans resembled John Kerry's showing, his victory margin in 2008 would have been reduced by 3.5 points. Had it reverted to mean in 2012, his victory margin would have been less than a point.

There's a ham-handed, somewhat racist argument that blacks voted for Obama at this rate because he is black. That is nonsense. African American Republicans don't perform particularly well with African Americans, the opposite of what we'd expect if this were all about race. African Americans vote Democratic because the vast majority of African Americans have seen Democratic Party candidates as best suited to advance their interests.

But I also don't think there was much denying that Obama probably turned out a fair number of African Americans who had never or rarely voted before 2008, who were hoping to "make history." Analysts should have taken more seriously the possibility that when the opportunity to make history disappeared, and the charismatic young candidate of color was replaced by an elderly white woman, that there would be at least some degree of a reversion to mean.

In addition, the midterm electorates, in hindsight, should have been a warning sign. According to the Voting and Registration Supplement of the Current Population Survey, conducted by the Census Bureau after every election, African American participation has typically lagged non-Hispanic White turnout by about six points. This was true in every election from 2000 to 2014 with two glaring exceptions: 2008 and 2012. In those elections, African American participation actually *exceeded* white participation.

So it isn't entirely surprising that in 2016, even with a controversial Republican candidate who had been the face of "birtherism" for many years, the African American share of the electorate fell further, and Republicans enjoyed a bit of a reversion to mean in their vote share here.

This was consequential. Had Clinton managed to perform as well among African Americans as President Obama in 2012, she would have added almost two full points to her national vote share, enough to replicate President

Obama's margin. She would have won Pennsylvania by two points, rather than losing by one.

Regardless, the African American vote is a good reminder that demographic history is not a one-way ratchet.

HISPANICS

While some analysts did foresee the potential that the African American share of the electorate might decline in 2012, the ready answer was that she would make this up among Hispanic voters, another pillar of the Emerging Democratic Majority theory. This was reasonable. Unlike African Americans, Hispanics are a fast-growing share of the electorate, and they too lean Democratic, although they are "swingier" than Democrats.

More importantly, Trump seemed to almost revel in provoking the Hispanic population. His bid for the presidency was announced with a promise to deport illegal immigrants, and with a claim that "When Mexico sends its people, they're not sending their best. They're not sending you. They're not sending you. They're sending people that have lots of problems, and they're bringing those problems with us. They're bringing drugs. They're bringing crime. They're rapists. And some, I assume, are good people."[8] Analysts seeing this and examining the early voting data confidently predicted that "this time, there really is a Hispanic surge."[9]

But this was not to be either. Figure 14.3 shows the complete trend line for Hispanic voter share of the electorate:

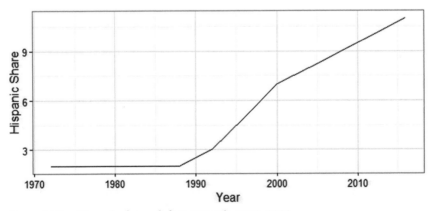

Figure 14.3.   Hispanic share of electorate (%), 1972–2016.

This looks like shocking growth until you realize the scale. In truth, the Hispanic share of the electorate has been increasing at a glacial pace. From 2004 to 2016, the Hispanic share of the electorate increased just three percentage points, from 8 percent to 11 percent. If you take the CPS numbers, the Hispanic share of the electorate is even smaller. In the end, 2016 was no exception to the trend; the Hispanic share increased from 10 percent to 11 percent.

Moreover, and perhaps surprisingly, Trump won 31 percent of the Hispanic vote, third parties excluded. In other words, Trump received a larger share of the Hispanic vote for the presidency than Mitt Romney, Bob Dole, George H. W. Bush (twice), and Gerald Ford.

But unlike African Americans, Hispanic voters are "swingy." In other words, they vote considerably more Republican in good Republican years nationally than they do in bad Republican years. Given this, it isn't surprising that Ronald Reagan in 1984 did better with Hispanics than Trump; he was winning nationally by about twenty points.

To put this in sharper relief, I've normalized the Hispanic vote share by the national Democratic performance. In other words, I've subtracted the Democratic national vote share from the Hispanic vote share. This statistic tells us how much more Democratic Hispanics are than the country as a whole in any given year. So, looking at figure 14.4, in 2016, Hispanics were eighteen points more Democratic than the country as a whole, as opposed to 2012, when they were twenty points more Democratic than the country as a whole.

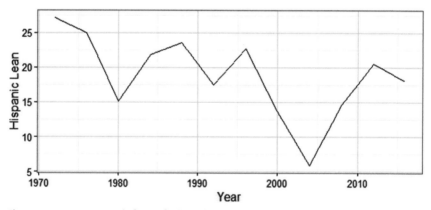

Figure 14.4.   Democratic lean of Hispanics, normalized, 1972–2016.

Looked at this way, Donald Trump's performance among Hispanics was better than Mitt Romney's, Bob Dole's, George H. W. Bush's in 1988 (the year after comprehensive immigration reform was last passed), Ronald Reagan's in 1984, Gerald Ford's in 1976, and Richard Nixon's in 1972.

What this is all a wind-up for is shown in figure 14.5:

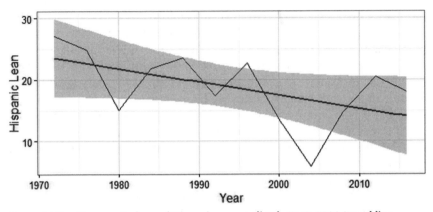

Figure 14.5.   Democratic lean of Hispanics, normalized, 1972–2016 (trend line included).

This adds a trend line to the data, which shows that while the Hispanic vote has been growing, it has also been gradually trending toward Republicans.

Before getting into why this might be the case, it is worth acknowledging that some deny that Trump performed this well among Hispanics. In truth, every time Republicans perform well among a minority group, interest groups insist that the exit polls are off.[10] The problem with these claims is that they are exceedingly difficult to sort out. We can try utilizing independent phone polls, but those have error margins and may not accurately reflect who actually turns out to vote. We can try to use ecological inference, but this doesn't work if Hispanics in diverse precincts vote differently than Hispanics in heavily Hispanics precincts.

For a contrary take, you should look at Harry Enten of *FiveThirtyEight*'s take, looking at heavily Hispanic precincts and finding a trend toward Donald Trump there.[11] In the end, exit polls are sort of like meat loaf: they aren't anyone's favorite, but they're what's for dinner. Sometimes they will be off (the 2004 data probably do overstate Bush's vote share with Hispanics), but over time they should be okay. More importantly, you can't explain away change with a constant; if the exits understated Clinton's vote share with Hispanics for structural reasons, then they probably understated Obama's shares as well, and the swing would remain.

So how could Trump have done better with Hispanics? First, there is probably a real floor for Republicans with Hispanics, somewhere in the neighborhood of 25 percent. Exit poll after exit poll suggests there's a substantial minority that favors a "hardline" approach to immigration. A 2013 Pew poll, for example, which has some reasonably favorable question wordings for the pro-reform side, found that around a third of Hispanics supported a "control the border first" approach.[12] My own research found that about a third of Hispanics backed three California ballot initiatives from the 1990s that many perceived as being hostile to Hispanics.[13] Jan Brewer, Sharron Angle, and a host of other Republican hard liners did surprisingly well with Hispanics. Simply put, Hispanics are a lot more complex than many analysts credited.

More importantly, the evidence that Hispanic voters are overwhelmingly motivated by the immigration issue is simply missing. In 2008, the exit polls asked a question about immigration reform. A majority of Hispanic voters indicated that immigration was either unimportant to them, or was important to them but they voted Republican anyway. We see the same thing in public opinion polls, which perennially show issues like the economy, healthcare, terrorism, and education topping immigration as important issues.[14]

This is also suggested by the exit poll data above. Remember, George H. W. Bush was a part of an administration that supported, then signed, comprehensive immigration reform in 1986. He lost the Hispanic vote by thirty-nine points, for a worse showing in absolute and relative terms than Donald Trump in 2016.

So why might George W. Bush have performed so well among Hispanic voters? In 2013 I listed a number of possible reasons aside from immigration reform:

- Bush was a governor of a state with a large Hispanic population, and had a history of interacting well with the state's Hispanic community;
- Bush speaks Spanish reasonably well;
- Bush supported big government programs, and Hispanics tend to be more economically liberal than whites;
- Bush was a wartime president, and Hispanic voters tend to be relatively hawkish;
- Bush's overall native appeal to downscale voters was greater than, say, Mitt Romney's;
- Bush didn't say things suggesting that he would make life so miserable for illegal immigrants that they would "self-deport";
- Bush was running against a boring, stiff, white candidate who lacked Barack Obama's innate appeal to young voters, and Hispanics are disproportionately young.[15]

Obviously on some of these metrics, Trump represented little improvement over Romney. But on others, he was substantially better. This probably explains at least some of his improvement.

One other point seems important. Unlike African Americans, the Hispanic share of the electorate becomes substantially more Republican as it becomes wealthier; in 2000 and 2008 the difference between the richest Hispanics and the poorest Hispanics was about twenty points. This is a larger gap than we see with non-Hispanic whites.

This has important implications for the future. Immigration from Latin America has now leveled off, so much of the increase in the Hispanic vote is going to come from those "Born in the U.S.A." As these voters climb the economic ladder, experience suggests, they will become more Republican. At a certain point, they will likely lose their identity as Hispanics to a large degree, just like the Irish and Italians before them.[16]

This explains, most likely, the gradual trend toward Republicans among Hispanics over the past fifty years, as Hispanic voters moved from border communities to the suburbs. It also could explain why ecological regression approaches, where heavily Hispanic precincts exert a lot of leverage, show Republicans performing worse among Hispanics than the exit polls.

NON-HISPANIC WHITES

But the biggest problem for the Emerging Democratic Majority theory came from the group that demographics-as-destiny advocates often ignore: non-Hispanic whites. It was foolish to pay little attention to this group not because whites are special, or frankly for any of the reasons set forth by the Alt-Right. Instead, the reasons are much more practical.

First, whites are 70 percent of the electorate. That is still a lot of votes. While that share is decreasing, the decline is gradual; about two points every election. At that rate, non-Hispanic whites will remain a majority of the electorate until 2056.

Second, and especially importantly for this election, the white vote is very well distributed. As I noted in the previous edition of this series, Hispanics are 17 percent of the national population, but they exceed 17 percent of the population of just nine states, only three of which are swing states (Colorado, Florida, and Nevada). African Americans represent 14 percent of the national population, but exceed 14 percent of the population of just sixteen states, only a handful of which (Florida, North Carolina, Virginia, and Michigan) are swing states.

By contrast, the white share of the population exceeds the national average in thirty-seven states, including almost every swing state. In other words, a candidate who performs well among non-Hispanic whites will do disproportionately well in the Electoral College, which is exactly what we saw in 2016.

Moreover, the non-Hispanic white vote has been trending toward Republicans for quite some time. Consider figure 14.6, which shows the Republican share of the white vote for president:

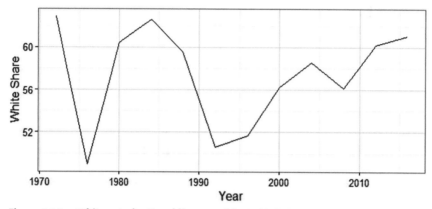

Figure 14.6.   White vote for Republican president, 1972–2016.

The third best vote-getter among whites in the past forty-four years? Donald Trump. His 61 percent share of the two-party white vote brushes against Ronald Reagan's and Richard Nixon's 63 percent in 1984 and 1972, respectively. As you can see, the Republican share has been on a steady uptick since 1992.

But sometimes Republicans run in worse environments than others. Ronald Reagan ran with roughly 7 percent growth at his back, as opposed to Trump, who ran while an incumbent president oversaw an economy with 2 percent to 3 percent growth.

So we can normalize for national vote share, which responds to these factors. The outlook for Democrats (figure 14.7) is even more stark:

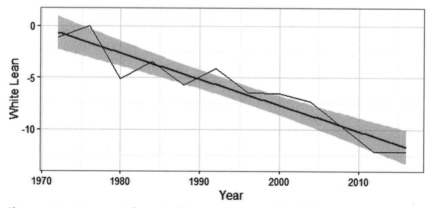

Figure 14.7.   Democratic lean of whites, normalized, 1972–2016.

We can be more rigorous, though. As I suggested in 2013, if we take data back to 1948 and run a regression analysis that controls for the economy, incumbency, and presidential job approval, the Republican share of the white vote has been ticking gradually rightward, to the tune of about a point per cycle.[17]

But this has been an uneven trend within whites. Democrats have advanced among whites with college degrees, which is exactly what Judis and Teixeira suggested. Figure 14.8 shows the trendline since 1976, the first year where we have such a breakdown from the exits:

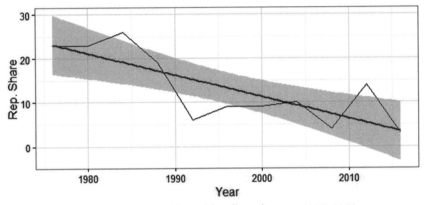

Figure 14.8.   Republican share, whites with college degrees, 1976–2016.

Of course, the Republican vote share overall has been much smaller the past few cycles than it was in 1972, 1980, or 1984. Figure 14.9 shows the trend line normalized for national vote share:

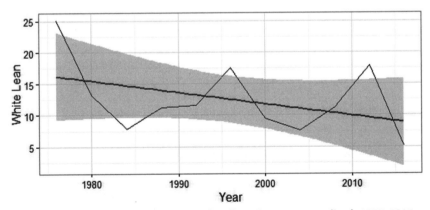

Figure 14.9.   Republican lean, whites with college degrees, normalized, 1976–2016.

Here the overall trend is less dramatic and is actually close to nonexistent if you eliminate 1976. Regardless, using either metric, Trump performs worse among whites with college degrees than any Republican in recent memory. This is consistent with the Emerging Democratic Majority thesis.

The problem is that the Emerging Democratic Majority theorists assumed that Democrats would at least hold their own among whites without college degrees. That . . . did not happen. Figure 14.10 shows the trend line among whites without college degrees.

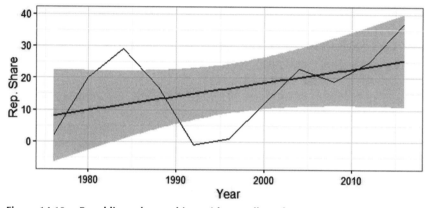

Figure 14.10.   Republican share, whites without college degrees, 1976–2016.

Figure 14.11 shows that trend line, normalized for national vote share:

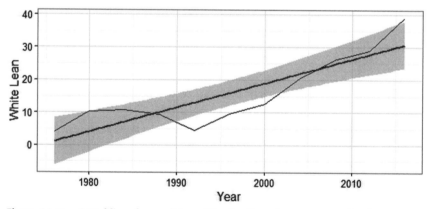

Figure 14.11.   Republican lean, whites without college degrees, normalized, 1976–2016.

It really is quite stunning, given that this group was the bedrock of the Democratic Party for much of its existence. Trump's thirty-seven-point margin among whites without college degrees is wider than any Republican in recent history, besting Reagan's twenty-nine-point margin from 1984. Normalized for national vote share, the margin is over ten points wider than the nearest competitor (2012). As one observer noted, it is as if the white working class decided to vote like Hispanics. The problem for Democrats is that, at least for now, there are three times as many working-class whites as there are Hispanics in the electorate.

This represents something of an opportunity for Republicans. If Trump were able to hold on to his share among whites without college degrees while winning back Romney's share of whites with college degrees, his margin among whites would balloon to twenty-six points, eclipsing Reagan's twenty-five-point margin from 1984. Of course, if he governs poorly, the opposite would be likely to happen in 2020, and he'd be headed for an ignominious defeat.

One final group deserves special attention: white evangelicals. In 2004, white evangelicals were 23 percent of the electorate, and cast 78 percent of their vote for George W. Bush. In 2012, they were 26 percent of the electorate, and gave Romney 78 percent of the vote. In 2016, they were again 26 percent of the electorate, and gave Trump 80 percent of their vote. Trump received more votes from white evangelicals than Clinton received from African Americans and Hispanics combined. They almost canceled the Democrats' advantage among nonwhites completely.

Obviously Donald Trump's vote share here is eye-popping, but it is worth noting one other thing: this group's share of the electorate has been increasing. Perhaps it is because of increased participation, but it may have something to do with a difference in fecundity between conservative whites and liberal whites. Jonathan Last hints at this in his book *What to Expect When No One's Expecting*, but it could certainly use closer study.[18]

A FEW OTHER POINTS

Two other divisions deserve mention, though I believe they can be dealt with quickly. The first is the division by gender. Judis and Teixeira made women the center of their new majority. Indeed, 2016 saw the largest gender gap on record, with men favoring Trump by eleven points and women favoring Clinton by thirteen. In the House it was almost as pronounced, with men favoring Republicans by twelve points and women favoring Democrats by ten.

It is true that Democrats won the popular vote (on which, more later), but that is beside the point here. The point is that Clinton won women by the second-largest margin of any candidate in the history of the exit polls, and still lost. This gets to the nut of the problem with the Emerging Democratic Majority thesis: it ignores counterreactions. Yes, women may have flocked to Clinton in record numbers, but the same factors that drove this trend may also have contributed to Trump's strong showing among men (which, normalized for national vote share, is the largest margin in history).

Second, millennials. There is little doubt that young voters are a boost for Democrats—indeed they are keeping Democrats in the game. But are they in the bag for Democrats? It is too soon to tell. In 2004, John Kerry won eighteen- to twenty-nine-year-olds by nine points. Barack Obama won these voters by a staggering thirty-four points in 2004. This margin shrank to twenty-four points in 2012. With Clinton, it was twenty-one points. One way of looking at this is that Clinton's margins among young voters are closer to Kerry's in 2004 than Obama's in 2008.

Of course, at a certain point, this generation will pose a big problem for Republicans if voting patterns don't change. Republicans' hope has to be that these voters will be like Boomers, who almost went for George McGovern in 1972 and put Jimmy Carter in the White House in 1976, but who are among the most conservative voters in the country today. If not, we might actually see a majority of the sort Judis and Teixeira described, albeit twenty years later.

THE POPULAR VOTE

In response to all of this, one might object that Clinton won the popular vote by two points. It is a credible response, but not, I think, a convincing one. For one thing, the Democrats' vote share has now declined in two consecutive elections. This occurred as the electorate became more diverse. This is not exactly what the demographic predictions would suggest.

Second, while I don't think that a race for the popular vote would have brought out enough voters in California to swing it to Trump, it really is difficult to say what would have happened in a head-to-head popular vote race. If one looks at the exits, Trump's vote share actually improved in a head-to-head question; he tied Clinton. In states like Texas, his vote share improved dramatically in the head-to-head question. Did Republicans in safely red states vote third party, or even for Clinton, knowing that their votes were ultimately meaningless? Is this why the Dallas and Atlanta suburbs swung so heavily toward Clinton, while suburbs around Milwaukee saw less movement?

Ultimately, though, pointing to Clinton's popular vote win is a little bit like pointing out that the Cleveland Indians scored as many runs as the Chicago Cubs, and that the 2016 World Series was therefore a tie. It's an interesting statistic, but unfortunately the World Series cares about the distribution of runs across games, and teams adjust their strategies accordingly.

CONCLUSION

The real problem with the Emerging Democratic Majority theory is foundational. It was always tricky to suggest that Democrats would be able to hold together a coalition of urban white liberals, suburbanites, working-class whites, blacks, and Hispanics. This is because governing is *hard*. Governing parties must make choices, and those choices will inevitably make some parties feel excluding. The shift among working-class whites is almost certainly a result of the Democrats' shift in emphasis from class issues to issues of racial and sexual identity. As I've said before, coalitions are like water balloons: if you press down on one side, another side pops up.

But this problem is the Republicans' problem now. Can they really keep enough blacks and Hispanics in the fold to win, while satisfying the often-competing desires of whites with and without college degrees? With a little luck, sure. But luck seems to be in short supply these days, the foreign affairs situation is fraught, and a recession in the next few years seems likely. The safer bet may be that in four years, we will be talking about the Republicans' Lost Majority as well.

NOTES

1. See, for example, Arthur Paulson, *Electoral Realignment and the Outlook for Democracy*, (Lebanon, New Hampshire: Northeastern University Press, 2007), 3.

2. See the May 18, 2009, cover of *Time*, http://content.time.com/time/covers/0,16 641,20090518,00.html.

3. Everett Carll Ladd, Jr., with Charles D. Hadley, *Transformations of the American Party System: Political Coalitions from the New Deal to the 1970s* (New York: W.W. Norton and Co., 1975), 293.

4. Sean Trende and David Byler, "Republican Party the Strongest It's Been in 80 Years," *RealClearPolitics*, November 17, 2016, http://www.realclearpolitics.com/articles/2016/11/17/republican_party_the_strongest_its_been_in_80_years.html.

5. For example, Dylan Loewe, *Permanently Blue: How Democrats Can End the Republican Party and Rule the Next Generation* (New York: Three Rivers Press, 2010).

6. "State government trifectas," *Ballotpedia*, https://ballotpedia.org/State_government _trifectas.

7. Nancy J. Weiss, *Farewell to the Party of Lincoln: Black Politics in the Age of F.D.R.* (Princeton: Princeton University Press, 1983).

8. "Full text: Donald Trump announces a presidential bid," *Washington Post*, June 16, 2015, https://www.washingtonpost.com/news/post-politics/wp/2015/06/16/full-text -donald-trump-announces-a-presidential-bid/?utm_term = .7e9bc79dbbb3.

9. Nate Cohn, "This Time, There Really Is a Hispanic Voter Surge," *New York Times*, Nov. 7, 2016, http://www.nytimes.com/2016/11/08/upshot/this-time-there-really-is-a-his panic-voter-surge.html.

10. See, for example, https://www.washingtonpost.com/news/monkey-cage/wp/2014/ 11/10/did-asian-americans-switch-parties-overnight-no/ (Asian Americans in 2014); http://www.latinodecisions.com/blog/2010/11/04/how-the-national-exit-poll-badly-mis sed-the-latino-vote-in-2010/ (Hispanics in 2010); http://www.thedemocraticstrategist.org/ donkeyrising/2004/11/bushs_hispanic_support_headed.html (Hispanics in 2004).

11. Harry Enten, "Trump Probably Did Better with Latino Voters Than Romney Did," *FiveThirtyEight*, Nov. 18, 2016, http://fivethirtyeight.com/features/trump-probably-did -better-with-latino-voters-than-romney-did/.

12. "'Borders First' a Dividing Line in Immigration Debate," Pew Research Center, June 23, 2013, http://www.people-press.org/files/legacy-pdf/6-23-13%20Immigration% 20Release%20Final.pdf.

13. Sean Trende, "The Politics of Arizona's Immigration Law," *RealClearPolitics*, July 8, 2010, http://www.realclearpolitics.com/articles/2010/07/08/the_politics_of_arizonas _immigration_law_106221.html.

14. See, for example, http://www.pewresearch.org/fact-tank/2016/07/15/the-economy -is-a-top-issue-for-latinos-and-theyre-more-upbeat-about-it/; http://www.foxnews.com/ politics/2016/05/20/hispanic-voters-most-concerned-about-jobs-economy-fox-news-la tino-poll-finds.html; http://www.pewresearch.org/fact-tank/2014/06/02/top-issue-for-his panics-hint-its-not-immigration/.

15. Sean Trende, "The GOP and Hispanics: What the Future Holds," *RealClearPoli-tics*, June 28, 2013, http://www.realclearpolitics.com/articles/2013/06/28/the_gop_and _hispanics_what_the_future_holds_119011.html.

16. Reihan Salam, "The future of Hispanic identity," *Reuters*, May 6, 2013, http:// blogs.reuters.com/reihan-salam/2013/05/06/the-future-of-hispanic-identity/.

17. Sean Trende, "The Democrats' Problem with White Voters," *Sabato's Crystal Ball*, July 18, 2013, http://www.centerforpolitics.org/crystalball/articles/the-democrats%E2% 80%99-problem-with-white-voters/.

18. Jonathan V. Last, *What to Expect When No One's Expecting* (New York and London: Encounter Books, 2013).

15

Ten Takeaways from Campaign 2016 and a Look Forward

Susan A. MacManus and Anthony A. Cilluffo

Whatever your feelings about Trump (excitement, vindication, horror, nausea . . .), his election is a reminder of the unpredictability of democracy. And it is worth keeping in mind that, while fixating on the process is all well and good, there will inevitably be occasions when the outcome fills you with shock and awe.

—Michelle Cottle
The Atlantic, November 22, 2016[1]

Every election is different in its nominees, context and electorate. How the new president performs, and how the two parties react to future events, will determine which party will grow and which will shrink. But ignoring the nation's demographic changes is not the recipe for future successes.

—Stuart Rothenberg
The Washington Post, November 22, 2016[2]

Donald J. Trump pulled off the political upset of the century when he won the 2016 presidential election. A political novice running against veteran politician Hillary Clinton, he faced strong headwinds from the media and his own party. From the beginning, the contrasts between the two were sharp—in virtually everything from personality to language and policy.

Clinton's supporters cast her as a trailblazer. She would become the first woman president, just as Barack Obama had become the first black president.

She would win by replicating (even expanding) Obama's winning coalition of minorities, millennials, and single women. But in supporting his policy positions, she would be seen as an insider and part of the establishment.

In contrast, Trump promoted himself as an outsider, an anti-establishment figure promising to turn Washington, D.C., on its head and reverse virtually every action taken by the Obama administration.

Two candidates with opposite views of the country's condition, neither well-liked, gave voters a choice in 2016: four more years of the same or something different? The election took so many twists and turns that it took voters a long time to decide, with many voting *against* the opposing party's candidate more than *for* their own party's nominee. Others voted for a third-party candidate or skipped the presidential race altogether. In the end, the clincher for many voters was change, and Trump embodied that change.

TEN TAKEAWAYS FROM 2016

After the dust settles in every election, there are takeaways, or lessons learned. Here are ten.

When long-simmering disappointments with the federal government among a key constituency (the middle class) reach a boiling point, voters revolt and reject the status quo in favor of drastic change.

For the past four years, surveys have consistently shown that nearly two-thirds of Americans believe the country is headed in the wrong direction. An even higher proportion gives Congress unfavorable ratings. Nearly seven in ten voters were dissatisfied with the federal government's performance, lending support to Trump's pledge to "drain the swamp." Other surveys have shown that many Americans believe the federal government has done little to help the shrinking middle class.

In the national exit poll, 68 percent of voters reported that their financial status has either stayed the same or worsened over the past four years. Many of these voters backed Trump. When asked what was the most important quality they look for in a candidate, 39 percent said the ability to "bring change"; 82 percent voted for Trump. Only 22 percent identified having the "right experience"; 90 percent of these voters sided with Clinton.

Post-election parallels have been drawn between the U.S election and the Brexit vote in the United Kingdom in summer 2016. In both elections (each seen as a stunning upset), previously disaffected voters re-engaged in the political process with hope that politicians would finally listen to them. For these voters, the election "wasn't about race or gender or Hillary Clinton's emails," wrote *The Wall Street Journal*. "It was about reclaiming a voice in how their country is governed."[3]

Micro-targeting strategies that ignore key portions of a party's traditional base can lead to defeat.

The Clinton campaign continued what Obama had done in 2008 and 2012—focusing on attracting racial and ethnic minorities and millennials, many of whom are concentrated in urban areas. Between 2012 and 2016, demographic studies reported substantial growth in minority populations and the rise of the millennial generation (those ages eighteen to thirty-four, now America's largest generation). The Clinton campaign aimed not just at replicating the Obama coalition, but *expanding* it. In the process, the campaign took for granted continued support from blue-collar white voters (including union members) living in suburban and rural areas. Nowhere was this strategy costlier to Clinton than in the Rust Belt ("Blue Wall") states (Wisconsin, Michigan, Ohio, and Pennsylvania).

The perception of Clinton's overemphasis on racial identity politics led some white Democrats, particularly blue-collar workers, to defect from the party that they now believed was more concerned about minorities than economic growth, wages, and trade.[4] Indeed, this election saw a larger partisan divide between "racially sympathetic" and "racially resentful" white voters than in either 2008 or 2012.[5]

But from the Clinton campaign's perspective, Trump's appeals to largely white crowds at rallies contained a strong racist element. In a post-election forum at Harvard University, Jennifer Palmieri, Clinton's communications director, condemned Trump adviser Stephen K. Bannon, executive chairman of *Breitbart*, for providing a "platform for white supremacists" (the "Alt-Right"—a Web-centric white-nationalist movement[6]) and proclaimed, "I would rather lose than win the way you guys did."[7]

The partisan differences among the three geographies of politics—cities, suburbs, and rural areas—were particularly stark. Clinton won large margins among the young, women, and minority voters that tend to live in cities. Trump, meanwhile, drove up turnout in suburban and rural areas.

Demographics are destiny—but their impacts are often incremental rather than immediate. Population statistics do not quickly turn into registered voter stats. Republicans may have dodged a bullet in 2016, but an autopsy of Mitt Romney's 2012 loss to Obama warned that unless the party focuses on outreach in minority communities, Republicans "will lose future elections."[8] Population demographics are dynamic, not static.

Projections of cohesiveness among key demographic groups
are often overly optimistic. Voting cues can differ even within
a gender, racial, or generational group.

Women: When Clinton lost the nomination to Obama in 2008, she faced criticism for failing to highlight the historic nature of her candidacy. Determined to avoid that mistake, she made her path-breaking potential a central part of messaging at various points of her campaign.[9] The prospect of the first female president, however, failed to generate the same excitement as the first black president, especially among younger voters. In an electorate desperately looking for change, "breaking glass ceilings doesn't feed families."[10] For others, gender issues just did not measure up to more pressing issues related to the economy and immigration.[11]

Clinton's candidacy as the first female nominee of a major party, combined with scandals and gaffes surrounding Trump's treatment of women, had led to predictions of a huge gender gap that would propel Clinton to the White House. These projections were undone, in part, by Trump's unexpectedly strong support from white women, particularly white college-educated women. Nationally, Clinton won the women's vote by a comfortable margin (13 percent over Trump) but split the white college-educated women's vote, winning by only a 7 percent margin. This smaller margin shows that women are influenced, not by gender alone, but also by their education, geography, income, and race/ethnicity.

Blacks: The electorate was more diverse in 2016 than in 2012, when Obama won all minority racial/ethnic groups by large margins. But in 2016, black voters did not deliver the same huge margins to Clinton, nor did they turn out at the same rate. (One estimate of black turnout showed it dropped more than 11 percent compared to 2012.[12]) All along, the Clinton campaign worried that Obama's support from blacks was due more to his persona and the historical significance of his candidacy, rather than to the Democratic Party's issue stances, especially among black millennials. Others attributed the fall-off to more restrictive voting practices, such as voter ID laws, in fourteen states,[13] while younger blacks pointed to economic reasons:

> The unfortunate reality is that, for a growing number of underserved blacks in this country, [they] have lost the American Dream under Obama [with rising minority youth unemployment rates and steep increases in Obamacare premiums]. Backing Obama's economic policies did Hillary Clinton no favors with millennials and working class blacks when it came to jobs and the economy.[14]

Latinos: Trump's incendiary remarks about immigration and a judge of Mexican descent who presided over a fraud case involving Trump University were expected to deliver unprecedented Hispanic margins to Clinton. Although Latinos turned out in record numbers, their lack of cohesion and an increase in white turnout dimmed Clinton's prospects.[15] She got 66 percent of the Latino vote, less than the 71 percent Obama got in 2012.[16] A nationally syndicated Hispanic columnist suggested six reasons why many Hispanics supported Trump:

> (1) They didn't trust Hillary Clinton, and they couldn't relate to her in any way. (2) They were just as fed up with the establishment as other Americans, and just as easily seduced by an outsider like Trump. (3) They were sick of politicians who don't offend anyone because they don't say or do anything consequential. (4) They agreed with many of Trump's ideas and policy proposals, and they were willing to overlook the wacky ones. (5) When Trump portrayed Mexican immigrants as violent criminals, they weren't bothered because they just assumed he wasn't talking about them. (6) Many are ambivalent about undocumented immigrants anyway, and, in fact, some look fondly on concrete walls, tighter borders, and more deportations.[17]

Millennials: After fractious party primaries where millennial choices on both sides (Bernie Sanders among Democrats and Marco Rubio among Republicans) lost to other candidates, many millennials had trouble uniting behind their party's nominee. On the left in particular, many of Sanders' supporters never united behind Clinton, whom they saw as ingrained in the "establishment" wing of the party, too cozy with Wall Street and big business, and too aggressive on foreign policy.[18] While some did vote for her as the lesser of two evils, many decided to stay home or switched to minor party or independent candidates.

When both parties' nominees are seen as flawed, candidate qualities and likability are less predictive of a voter's choice. Voters then turn to other rationales for their pick.

Conventional wisdom says the candidate with the highest favorability ratings will win the election. But in 2016, Trump was the most unpopular nominee in the recorded history of polling, and Clinton the second most unpopular.

What led Republicans and independents in key swing states to look beyond their unfavorable opinions of Trump? For some Republicans, the big motivator was recapturing the White House. For others, it was the looming appointment of a Supreme Court justice and the chance to influence the court's ideological balance for a generation (given the ages of current justices).

Constitutional conservatives believed Trump would likely nominate a strict constructionist like the late Justice Antonin Scalia. These voters were upset by rulings that circumvented democratic processes on issues such as gay marriage and Obamacare. Religious conservatives feared Clinton would appoint liberal justices that would rule counter to their faith. Trump won 56 percent of voters for whom the Supreme Court was "the most important factor"—21 percent of all voters.

Why would Christian voters, especially white evangelicals, even think of voting for Trump, given his marital history and his demeaning language of so many different groups?[19] To them, the choice came down to "corrupt vs. crude." While they disliked Trump's crass behavior, they could not accept Clinton's actions, which they saw as corrupt.[20]

In addition, voters rejected Clinton's values more than they resented Trump remarks. As Trump's campaign manager explained: Voters "voted the way voters have always voted: on things that affect them, not just things that offend them."[21]

Strong distrust of the media's campaign coverage, combined with changing media habits, diminish voter reliance on traditional news sources and lead them to seek alternative sources with no guarantees of accuracy.

A Gallup survey in September 2016 found that trust in the mass media had fallen to its lowest point since 1972, with only one-third of Americans saying they have a "great deal" or "fair amount" of trust that the media report news fully, accurately, and fairly.[22] While the number of news outlets with fact-checking divisions increased in 2016, voters regarded them as merely extensions of an outlet's ideological leanings. (One survey found that just 29 percent trust fact checkers to accurately assess candidate comments.[23])

High-level staffers from both campaigns complained about press bias. Clinton's aides repeatedly criticized the press for holding her to a different standard. One example was a relentless focus on her emails, compared to little scrutiny of Trump's tax returns.[24] They even criticized the media for promoting Clinton's victory as a "foregone conclusion,"[25] which they claimed lowered turnout. Trump's aides complained that the media continued to link him with a white supremacist group (even after he publicly denounced it) and described his language at rallies as ramping up racist sentiment (dog whistles sent out to the crowds).[26] Cable networks drew sharp criticism from a wide range of candidates during the primary season—Democrat Sanders for "anointing Hillary" and Republicans challenging Trump's massively uneven free media coverage. Trump's victory prompted Clinton supporters to blame Democratic friendly networks (MSNBC and CNN): "You built Trump up (while you were making millions), then you couldn't take him down."

For many voters, the widespread belief in traditional media bias pushed them toward social media for news. While both candidates made a similar number of social media posts, Trump's tweets received far more *interactions* than Clinton's; they were retweeted twice as often and "favorited" three times as often.[27] This reflected the fact that Trump's followers were much more hostile toward the traditional media than were Clinton's supporters.

Unlike traditional media, social media lacks any truth filter on content, enabling wildly false stories, or fake news, to go viral.[28] This makes it difficult for traditional media and their fact checkers to effectively sound the alarm about online falsehoods. It also raises constitutional questions about freedoms of speech and press and how to draw the line between outright false and misleading news. Yet the pressure is on to find a solution in light of a Stanford University study showing that 82 percent of preteens and teens cannot distinguish between sponsored content and a real news story on a website.[29] This problem is not limited to teenagers, making the problem more urgent. As the former managing editor of *Time* magazine has said: "How do we protect the essential resource of democracy—the truth—from the toxin of lies that surrounds it?"[30]

An overreliance on data and analytics at the expense of listening to knowledgeable field operatives can be a mistake, especially in diverse key swing states. So, too, can overreliance on national horse-race polls rather than state polls.

From the outset, Clinton sought to emulate Obama's winning tactics, notably by using big data analytics and campaign satellite offices led by a central campaign staffer. However, post-election critiques revealed that a number of campaign operatives in field offices had only cursory knowledge of local demographics, pressing issues, and respected community activists. (This was certainly the case in Florida in some key areas.) In contrast, the Trump campaign relied more heavily on local party organizations for virtually all registration and GOTV responsibilities in key swing states like Florida.

The disconnect between localized and centralized staff in Rust Belt states cost Clinton the White House. High-ranking Democrats with strong connections to the area (including former President Bill Clinton, Michigan Congresswoman Debbie Dingell, and U.S. Agriculture Commissioner Tom Vilsack of Iowa) said they had warned Clinton staffers about possibly losing blue-collar Democrats living in suburban and rural areas, to no avail. The campaign also neglected to conduct meaningful state polls or send Clinton to important areas in "Blue Wall" states.

The 2016 election highlighted the pitfalls of too much media coverage of national horse-race polls. These polls reflected the direction of the popular vote, which Clinton won, but not the Electoral College vote. The Trump campaign used state polls to great advantage. After the election, pollster Kellyanne Conway, who became Trump's campaign manager in August, acknowledged that when she came on board, the campaign decided to "stop looking at national polls and instead focus on state polls, particularly in swing states." [31] They won by "looking at . . . the electoral map of 270, because that's how you win the presidency."[32] Their internal poll results were the reason Trump campaigned in Wisconsin on relevant issues there. Clinton never visited Wisconsin during the general election campaign.

The disproportionate focus on *who* is winning polls rather than *why* contributes to erroneous predictions because they do not indicate what motivates a survey respondent to actually vote. In swing states, state polling had stopped a few days before the election, excluding input from late deciders and preventing detection of a late-breaking move to Trump.

Many polling models overstated minority turnout and understated white (suburban, rural) turnout, creating a bias toward Clinton.[33] Moreover, some voters did not honestly reveal their preferences to pollsters, a phenomenon known as the "shadow Trump" vote. Feeling demonized by negative media coverage of him, some supporters were afraid to reveal their true preference for fear of social sneers from friends and coworkers. In addition, certain demographic groups, such as undereducated voters, are difficult for pollsters to reach,[34] thus creating a bias toward those who do respond.

Creating an aura of inevitability around a candidate alienates voters who expect a competitive, equal playing field— not a "rigged" system.

Beginning with the primary, many voters realized that establishment figures in both parties had picked favorites. Among Democratic leaders, it was Clinton; among Republicans, anybody but Trump. As a result, many alienated Sanders supporters never jumped on the Clinton bandwagon, and Trump support grew stronger the longer big GOP donors and national party leaders sat on the sidelines.

Democratic Party officials faced criticism for anointing Clinton long before the Sanders campaign ended. (He won twenty-three primaries and caucuses.) After WikiLeaks revealed that DNC officials sought to tip the scales in her favor, it became clear the rift between the party and Sanders supporters could not (and would not) be easily healed even after Sanders threw his support to Clinton. The lingering animus toward her was reflected in lower turnout among Sanders supporters, notably millennials, and in votes for third-party candidates.

On the Republican side, heavily publicized resistance to Trump among sixteen more establishment candidates (Jeb Bush topped the list) actually worked to his advantage. Trump's image as a maverick *increased* turnout among ignored voters who considered themselves forgotten—a pattern that continued into the general election. These voters were further emboldened when the press and "Never Trump" Republicans dismissed the crowds at Trump rallies as unlikely voters. Rally attendees were described as only coming out of curiosity to see a reality show celebrity in person and taking a few selfies to send to friends and family. In reality, these voters flocked to a candidate that spoke directly to them, in language they could understand, about issues they cared about.

After the election, the Clinton campaign was criticized for not scheduling enough in-person appearances in critical swing states. Surrogate appearances, including those by current and former U.S. presidents, are no substitute for an in-person visit by the nominee. In contrast, the Trump campaign was largely a campaign of one—Trump himself—"the only major star, political or otherwise, in his universe."[35] In the nine days before the election, Clinton made eighteen appearances in seven states; Trump thirty-two in thirteen states.[36]

Messaging and slogans matter!

Presidential historian Doris Kearns Goodwin has written that a well-chosen campaign slogan can be crucial: "In certain campaigns, [slogans] can be crucial if they capture a mood of the country or a quality of the candidate or a promise to the electorate. It doesn't often happen but when it does, the slogan provides a shorthand for the entire campaign."[37]

Such was true for Trump's "Make America Great Again!" The slogan, emblazoned on ball caps, resonated immediately with voters looking for someone to right America's course; some way to return the prosperity many had before the Great Recession and outsourcing of manufacturing jobs; and some assurance of safety from terrorist attacks in their own backyards. As Trump's first campaign manager acknowledged, "It was simplistic, and it didn't target any demographic. It targeted *every* demographic"[38] (emphasis added). On the campaign trail, Trump repeatedly gave voters what they wanted: "big promises, declarative sentences, and slug-you-in-the-gut slogans"[39] rather than detailed policy speeches.

The Clinton campaign struggled to select a slogan. It rejected eighty-four before narrowing the selection to two,[40] each designed to expand the Obama coalition: "I'm With Her" (women) and "Stronger Together" (minorities).

Equally crucial are messages that can turn a candidate's seemingly insignificant statement into an albatross. In 2012 and 2016, the losing candidate's statement was replayed endlessly from September to Election Day. Each alienated nearly half the electorate.

In 2012, it was Romney's elitist-sounding "47 percent" declaration:

> There are 47 percent of the people who will vote for the president no matter what. All right, there are 47 percent who are with him, who are dependent upon government, who believe that they are victims, who believe the government has a responsibility to care for them, who believe that they are entitled to health care, to food, to housing, to you-name-it. . . . These are people who pay no income tax. . . . [M]y job is not to worry about those people. I'll never convince them they should take personal responsibility and care for their lives."[41]

In 2016, it was Clinton's labeling of some Trump supporters as "deplorables"[42]:

> "You know, just to be grossly generalistic, you could put half of Trump's supporters into what I call the basket of deplorables. Right? The racist, sexist, homophobic, xenophobic, Islamaphobic—you name it."[43]

That statement weakened Clinton's ability to attract crossover votes from Republican women as Obama had in 2008 and 2012.[44] But even worse was losing support from working-class white Democrats. Among these "Trump Democrats":

> It became painfully obvious . . . over the last eight years that national Democrats no longer treat them with respect or believe they are capable of living dignified lives. They have seen their way of life under assault, whether in the form of attacks on gun ownership, the focus on climate change over growth, or implicit claims that they are bigots. For people who voted twice for President Obama, these last insinuations might have been the most offensive and damaging of all.[45]

At a post-election Harvard forum, Trump's campaign manager honed in on Clinton's allegations of bigotry, concluding that Trump won because "he promised to make the nation safe and prosperous, not because of prejudice."[46]

There is always an October surprise and an ensuing debate about the impact on the general election.

The first stunner took place on October 7 when *The Washington Post* released a 2005 video showing Trump making lewd comments about women on a hot mic with *Access Hollywood* host Billy Bush.[47] The Clinton campaign quickly tweeted: "This is horrific. We cannot allow this man to become president." Clinton herself wasted little time in releasing a video contradicting Trump's claims that it was just "locker room talk."[48] At the same time, GOP leaders and candidates at all levels hurriedly distanced themselves from Trump by making high-profile un-endorsements and suggesting he step aside as the nominee. Days later, a *Washington Post-ABC News* poll of likely voters showed nearly two-thirds said the Trump tape would not affect their vote; 40 percent agreed that Trump's remarks were locker room talk, including 56 percent of non-college-educated white women.[49]

The more impactful October surprise occurred on October 28—less than two weeks before the general election and after early voting had begun in several states. FBI Director James Comey informed several congressional committee chairs about new information that prompted the FBI to reopen its investigation of Clinton's handling of classified information. The reopening came as a shock because the FBI had closed the investigation in July with no charges of wrongdoing.[50]

A second email-related bombshell exploded just two days before Election Day. On November 6, Comey *closed* the reopened investigation. But the damage had been done. In post-election comments, Clinton staffers identified Comey's two letters as the top reason for her loss. From the campaign's perspective, Comey's actions allowed Trump to re-energize wavering Republicans and stopped Clinton's progress in solidifying support from Democrats and gaining undecided voters. Trump supporters interpreted Comey's first letter to mean that something big had surfaced proving Clinton's guilt. His second letter coming so close to Election Day seemed to validate Trump's claims that the system was rigged against him.

Legal challenges to the voting process (recounts) and calls to abolish the Electoral College have become predictable post-election responses for the defeated party.

Since the 2000 election (Bush vs. Gore), losing candidates have turned to the courts to challenge the fairness of various elements of the voting process— registration, voter IDs, eligibility checks, equipment failures, along with charges of voter intimidation and vote suppression. In 2016, fears of foreign and domestic hackers altering the transmission of election results and registration and voter history data bases were added to the list. Unexpected results in some Rust Belt states (Michigan, Wisconsin, and Pennsylvania) prompted Green Party candidate Jill Stein to push for recounts there to discern possible inequities in vote casting or counting—an effort later joined by the Clinton campaign. While some Democrats worried about the image of a sore loser, others argued for a true count and the need to identify any voter irregularities that could subvert our democracy.

Calls to abolish the Electoral College have grown louder after the 2016 election because it is the second time in the five most recent presidential elections that the winner of the popular vote lost the Electoral College vote. Both times, a Republican (George W. Bush, 2000; Trump, 2016) was elected and a Democrat defeated (Al Gore; Clinton). Abolishing the Electoral College would require that three-fourths of the states agree to electing a president via the popular vote—an uphill climb, given that much of Clinton's victory margin came from two states (California and New York) and that she reached out disproportionately to urban, rather than suburban or rural, voters.

LOOKING AHEAD

As the curtain closes on the most unconventional, negative, and long campaign in recent memory, analysts are already trying to determine the lasting effect that Trump's landmark election will have on American politics. As *The Atlantic's* Ron Brownstein writes, "[in] an election that became virtually a cultural civil war between two Americas, Trump's side proved much more enthusiastic and united than Clinton's. And it has now propelled America into an unexpected, and perhaps, unprecedented, experiment."[51] The enduring results of that experiment, like so many other great changes in our nation's history, are anything but certain.

The dynamics of the 2016 election raise several important questions. First, will the two-party system still dominate American politics in light of a growing number of independent voters, especially millennials? Second, what impact will changing communication technologies and an increasingly diverse electorate have on voter mobilization and messaging? Third, how will voters be educated about the truth in campaign rhetoric?

Worries about truth have surfaced because the traditional role of the press as fact checkers has been weakened by perceived bias. So, too, has the use of public opinion polls designed to yield *representative* views of citizen opinions on key issues. The growing tendency of voters to turn to social media, with little or no concern about what is true, presents serious ethical challenges to campaign strategists and candidates. While "the truth shall set you free," the looming question is Who will tell voters the truth?

NOTES

1. Michelle Cottle, "Hate Him or Love Him, Trump Is What the Democratic Process Produced," *The Atlantic*, November 22, 2016, http://www.theatlantic.com/politics/archive/2016/11/hate-him-or-love-him-trump-is-what-the-democratic-process-produced/508454/.

2. Stuart Rothenberg, "Was the 2012 Republican Autopsy Wrong?" *Washington Post*, November 22, 2016, https://www.washingtonpost.com/news/powerpost/wp/2016/11/22/was-the-2012-republican-autopsy-wrong/.

3. "Trump and the Democrats," *Wall Street Journal*, November 11, 2016, http://www.wsj.com/articles/trump-and-the-democrats-1478823996.

4. Michael Tesler, "Views about Race Mattered More in Electing Trump than in Electing Obama," *Washington Post*, November 22, 2016, https://www.washingtonpost.com/news/monkey-cage/wp/2016/11/22/peoples-views-about-race-mattered-more-in-electing-trump-than-in-electing-obama/.

5. Ibid.

6. Tamara Keith, "Bitterness Overwhelms as Trump and Clinton Campaign Staffers Face Off at Harvard," NPR, December 2, 2016, http://www.npr.org/sections/thetwo-way/2016/12/02/504093288/bitterness-overwhelms-as-trump-and-clinton-campaign-staffers-face-off-at-harvard.

7. Karen Tumulty and Philip Rucker, "Shouting Match Erupts between Clinton and Trump Aides," *The Washington Post*, December 1, 2016, https://www.washingtonpost.com/politics/shouting-match-erupts-between-clinton-and-trump-aides/2016/12/01/7ac4398e-b7ea-11e6-b8df-600bd9d38a02_story.html?.

8. Republican National Committee, *Republican Growth and Opportunity Project*, published online, 2013, http://goproject.gop.com/RNC_Growth_Opportunity_Book_2013.pdf.

9. Janet Adamy, "One Factor in Hillary Clinton's Defeat: Lack of Support from Some Women Voters," *Wall Street Journal*, November 11, 2016, http://www.wsj.com/articles/one-factor-in-hillary-clintons-defeat-lack-of-support-from-some-women-voters-1478865602.

10. Sarah Jones, "Hillary Clinton's Celebrity Feminism Was a Failure," *New Republic*, November 10, 2016, https://newrepublic.com/article/138624/hillary-clintons-celebrity-feminism-failure.

11. Jocelyne Zablit, "Trump Fared Well with Women Voters Despite Sex Assault Claims," *Agence France-Presse* (via *Yahoo! News*), November 10, 2016, https://www.yahoo.com/news/trump-fared-well-women-voters-despite-sex-assault-050433269.html.

12. Omri Ben-Shahar, "The Non-Voters Who Decided the Election: Trump Won Because of Lower Democratic Turnout," *Forbes*, November 17, 2016, http://www.forbes.com/sites/omribenshahar/2016/11/17/the-non-voters-who-decided-the-election-trump-won-because-of-lower-democratic-turnout/.

13. Brennan Center for Justice, "New Voting Restrictions in Place for 2016 Presidential Election," last updated September 12, 2016, http://www.brennancenter.org/voting-restrictions-first-time-2016.

14. Jack Brewer, "Why Hillary Clinton Couldn't Rally the Black Vote," CNBC.com, November 11, 2016, http://www.cnbc.com/2016/11/11/why-hillary-clinton-couldnt-rally-the-black-vote-commentary.html.

15. Laura Bonilla Cal with Leila Macor, "Record Latino Vote Turnout Not Enough to Give Hillary a Win," *Agence France-Presse* (via *Yahoo! News*), November 10, 2016, https://www.yahoo.com/news/record-latino-vote-turnout-not-enough-hillary-win-08270 4479.html.

16. Roberto Suro, "Here's What Happened with the Latino Vote," *New York Times*, November 9, 2016, http://www.nytimes.com/interactive/projects/cp/opinion/election -night-2016/heres-what-happened-with-the-latino-vote.

17. Ruben Navarrette, Jr., "Why the Latino Vote Didn't Save America," *The Daily Beast*, November 9, 2016, http://www.thedailybeast.com/articles/2016/11/09/why-the -latino-vote-didn-t-save-america.html.

18. Ronald Brownstein, "Millennial Voters May Cost Hillary Clinton the Election," *The Atlantic*, September 19, 2016, http://www.theatlantic.com/politics/archive/2016/09/ hillary-clinton-Millennials-philadelphia/500540/.

19. Steve McQuilkin, "White Evangelicals Just Elected a Thrice-Married Blasphemer: What That Means for the Religious Right," *USA Today*, November 10, 2016, http://www .usatoday.com/story/news/politics/elections/2016/11/10/conservative-christians-boorish -trump/93572474/.

20. Amanda Prestigiacomo, "Watch: Dinesh D'Souza's Case for Christians to Vote Trump," *Daily Wire*, October 18, 2016, http://www.dailywire.com/news/10038/ watch-dinesh-dsouzas-case-christians-vote-trump-amanda-prestigiacomo.

21. Tamara Keith, "Bitterness Overwhelms."

22. Art Swift, "Americans' Trust in Mass Media Sinks to New Low," *Gallup*, September 14, 2016, http://www.gallup.com/poll/195542/americans-trust-mass-media-sinks -new-low.aspx.

23. "Voters Don't Trust Media Fact-Checking," *Rasmussen Reports*, September 30, 2016, http://www.rasmussenreports.com/public_content/politics/general_politics/septem ber_2016/voters_don_t_trust_media_fact_checking.

24. Karen Tumulty and Philip Rucker, "Shouting Match."

25. Aaron Zitner, "Hillary Clinton's Campaign Team Accuses Trump Strategists of Appealing to White Supremacists," *Wall Street Journal*, December 1, 2016, http://www .wsj.com/articles/hillary-clintons-campaign-team-accuses-trump-strategists-of-appealing -to-white-supremacists-1480643742.

26. Karen Tumulty and Philip Rucker, "Shouting Match."

27. Sorin Adam Matei, "Did Social Media Elect Donald Trump?" *I Think*, November 14, 2016, http://matei.org/ithink/2016/11/14/did-social-media-elect-donald-trump/.

28. Julia Love and Kristina Cooke, "Google, Facebook Move to Restrict Ads on Fake News Sites," *Reuters*, November 15, 2016, http://www.reuters.com/article/us-alphabet -advertising-idUSKBN1392MM.

29. Sue Shellenbarger, "Most Students Don't Know When News is Fake, Stanford Study Finds," *Wall Street Journal*, November 21, 2016, http://www.wsj.com/articles/ most-students-dont-know-when-news-is-fake-stanford-study-finds-1479752576.

30. David Ignatius, "In Today's World, the Truth Is Losing," *Washington Post*, November 29, 2016, https://www.washingtonpost.com/opinions/global-opinions/in-todays-world -the-truth-is-losing/2016/11/29/3f685cd2-b680-11e6-b8df-600bd9d38a02_story.html.

31. "Sparks Fly as Teams Clinton, Trump Review Bruising Campaign," FoxNews.com, December 2, 2016, http://www.foxnews.com/politics/2016/12/02/clinton-campaign-team

-says-trump-gave-platform-to-white-supremacists-blames-fbis-comey-and-wikileaks-for
-her-defeat.html.

32. Tamara Keith, "Bitterness Overwhelms."

33. David Catanese, "Top Takeaways from Donald Trump's Triumph," *US News*, November 9, 2016, http://www.usnews.com/news/politics/articles/2016-11-09/top-take aways-from-donald-trumps-triumph.

34. Andrew Mercer, Claudia Deane, and Kyley McGeeney, "Why 2016 Election Polls Missed Their Mark," *Pew Research Center*, November 9, 2016, http://www.pewresearch .org/fact-tank/2016/11/09/why-2016-election-polls-missed-their-mark/.

35. Tom McCarthy, "The Last-Minute Map: How to Read Each Presidential Candi- date's Final Stops," *The Guardian*, November 7, 2016, https://www.theguardian.com/us -news/2016/nov/07/clinton-trump-final-campaign-stops-election-what-it-means.

36. Ibid.

37. Doris Kearns Goodwin quoted in Al Tompkins, "How Important Are Campaign Slogans?" *Poynter*, July 27, 2004, http://www.poynter.org/2004/how-important-are-cam paign-slogans/24436/.

38. Aaron Zitner, "Clinton's Campaign Team."

39. Michelle Cottle, "Hate Him or Love Him."

40. Gregory Krieg, "Hillary Clinton's Would-Be Campaign Slogans, Ranked," CNN .com, October 19, 2016, http://www.cnn.com/2016/10/19/politics/wikileaks-hillary -clinton-campaign-slogans-ranked/.

41. Lucy Madison, "Fact-Checking Romney's '47 Percent' Comment," *CBS News*, September 25, 2012, http://www.cbsnews.com/news/fact-checking-romneys-47-percent -comment/.

42. Dan Merica and Sophie Tatum, "Clinton Expresses Regret for Saying 'Half' of Trump Supporters are 'Deplorables,'" CNN.com, September 12, 2016, http://www .cnn.com/2016/09/09/politics/hillary-clinton-donald-trump-basket-of-deplorables/.

43. Chas Danner, "Hillary Clinton Says Half of Trump Supporters Are 'Deplorable,'" *New York Magazine*, September 11, 2016; http://nymag.com/daily/intelligencer/2016/09/ clinton-says-half-of-trump-supporters-are-deplorable.html.

44. "Sparks Fly as Teams Clinton, Trump Review Bruising Campaign."

45. Henry Olsen, "Can the Republican Party Keep Trump Democrats?" *National Review*, November 21, 2016, http://www.nationalreview.com/article/442347/donald -trump-election-win-white-democratic-voters-republican-party.

46. Aaron Zitner, "Clinton's Campaign Team."

47. David A. Fahrenthold, "Trump Recorded Having Extremely Lewd Conversation about Women in 2005," *Washington Post*, October 8, 2016, https://www.washingtonpost .com/politics/trump-recorded-having-extremely-lewd-conversation-about-women-in-2005 /2016/10/07/3b9ce776-8cb4-11e6-bf8a-3d26847eeed4_story.html.

48. April Siese, "Clinton Campaign Releases Highlight Reel of Trump's Lewd Com- ments," *The Daily Dot*, October 7, 2016, http://www.dailydot.com/layer8/hillary-clinton -trump-lewd-comments-video/.

49. Chas Danner, "Clinton Maintains Lead in Two New Polls, but Trump Tape Impact Is Mixed," *New York Magazine*, October 16, 2016, http://nymag.com/daily/intelligencer/ 2016/10/clinton-holds-lead-in-new-polls-but-trump-tape-impact-mixed.html.

50. Adam Goldman and Alan Rappeport, "Emails in Anthony Weiner Inquiry Jolt Hillary Clinton's Campaign," *New York Times*, October 28, 2016, http://www.nytimes.com/2016/10/29/us/politics/fbi-hillary-clinton-email.html.

51. Ronald Brownstein, "How Trump Won," *The Atlantic*, November 9, 2016, http://www.theatlantic.com/politics/archive/2016/11/how-trump-won/507053/.

Index

243

About the Contributors

Alan I. Abramowitz is the Alben W. Barkley Professor of Political Science at Emory University and a senior columnist for *Sabato's Crystal Ball*. His most recent book is *The Polarized Public: Why American Government Is So Dysfunctional*.

Matt A. Barreto is cofounder and managing partner of the polling and research firm Latino Decisions. He has a Ph.D. in Political Science from the University of California, Irvine, and is currently Professor of Political Science and Chicana/o Studies at UCLA.

David Byler is an elections analyst for *RealClearPolitics*. David joined *RealClearPolitics* after graduating from Princeton University with a degree in Operations Research and Financial Engineering.

Anthony A. Cilluffo received his bachelor's degrees in economics and political science from the University of South Florida after spending his junior year at the London School of Economics and Political Science. He is currently a research assistant at the Pew Research Center.

Rhodes Cook was a political reporter for *Congressional Quarterly* for more than two decades and is a senior columnist at *Sabato's Crystal Ball*.

Robert Costa is a national political reporter for the *Washington Post* and a political analyst for *NBC News* and MSNBC. He covers President Donald J. Trump and Congress, and frequently appears on *Meet the Press*, *Morning Joe*, and PBS's *Charlie Rose*.

Ariel Edwards-Levy is the polling director and a staff reporter for the *The Huffington Post*, where she covers politics and public opinion and cowrites the *HuffPost Pollster* newsletter.

Natalie Jackson is senior polling editor at *The Huffington Post*. She has a doctorate in political science from the University of Oklahoma, with heavy emphasis on statistics, survey methodology, and American politics.

Kyle Kondik is managing editor of *Sabato's Crystal Ball*, the University of Virginia Center for Politics' nonpartisan newsletter on American campaigns and elections. He is the author of *The Bellwether: Why Ohio Picks the President*.

Susan A. MacManus is the Distinguished University Professor in the Department of Government & International Affairs at the University of South Florida, Tampa Campus. She has been a longtime political analyst for a number of Florida media outlets, including in 2016 for the Tampa Bay ABC affiliate, ABC Action News, and sayfiereview.com (a well-known Florida political news aggregation site).

Diana Owen is associate professor of political science at Georgetown University and teaches in the Communication, Culture, and Technology graduate program, and has served as director of the American Studies Program. She is the author of *Media Messages in American Presidential Elections*, *New Media and American Politics* (with Richard Davis), and *American Government and Politics in the Information Age* (with David Paletz and Timothy Cook).

Ronald B. Rapoport is the John Marshall professor of government at the College of William and Mary.

Larry J. Sabato is the Robert Kent Gooch Professor of Politics at the University of Virginia and director of its Center for Politics. He is the author or editor of more than twenty books on American politics and elections.

Greg Sargent is the author of *The Plum Line*, a blog of reported opinion from a liberal perspective, for the *Washington Post*.

Thomas F. Schaller is political director at Latino Decisions. He has a Ph.D. in Political Science from the University of North Carolina and is currently professor and chair of the Political Science Department at the University of Maryland, Baltimore County.

Gary M. Segura is co-founder and senior partner of the polling and research firm Latino Decisions. He has a Ph.D. in Political Science from the University of Illinois and is currently Dean of the Luskin School of Public Affairs at UCLA.

Geoffrey Skelley is associate editor of *Sabato's Crystal Ball*, the University of Virginia Center for Politics' nonpartisan newsletter on American campaigns and elections.

Walter J. Stone is a professor of political science at the University of California, Davis. Rapoport and Walter Stone are the authors of *Three's a Crowd: The Dynamic of Third Parties, Ross Perot, and Republican Resurgence.*

Michael E. Toner is former chairman of the Federal Election Commission (FEC) and is cochair of the Election Law and Government Ethics Practice Group at Wiley Rein LLP in Washington, DC.

Karen E. Trainer served in the FEC's Reports Analysis Division and is a senior reporting specialist at Wiley Rein LLP.

Sean Trende is the Senior Elections Analyst for *RealClearPolitics*. He is the author of *The Lost Majority: Why the Future of Government Is Up for Grabs and Who Will Take It*, and he coauthored the *Almanac of American Politics 2014.*

Janie Velencia, formerly the associate polling editor at *The Huffington Post*, coordinated the poll aggregation on *HuffPost Pollster*. She's also written on the 2016 election, public opinion, and the state of the polling industry. She is a graduate of the University of Michigan.